A HAND IN THE WATER

A HAND IN THE WATER

The Many Lies of Albert Walker

Bill Schiller

HarperCollins*Publishers*Ltd

http://www.harpercollins.com/canada

HarperCollins books may be purchased for educational, business, or sales promotional
use. For information please write: Special Markets Department, HarperCollins Canada,
55 Avenue Road, Suite 2900, Toronto, Ontario M5R 3L2.

First edition

Canadian Cataloguing in Publication Data

Schiller, Bill, 1951–
A hand in the water : the many lies of Albert Walker

ISBN 0-00-255751-7

1. Walker, Albert, 1944– .   2. Platt, Ronald J., d. 1996.   3. Murder — England.
4. Criminals — Ontario —Paris — Biography.   I. Title.

HV6535.E53W66 1998   634.15'23'092   C98-931401-4

98 99 00 01 02 03 WEB 10 9 8 7 6 5 4 3 2 1

Printed and bound in Canada at Webcom

For
M

Always

Desire is nothing personal: it is an affliction that was lying in wait for us from the outset, a perversion in which we get involuntarily swept up, a refractory medium into which we are plunged at birth. For Freud, what makes us human subjects is this foreign body lodged inside us, which invades our flesh like a lethal virus and yet, like the Almighty for Thomas Aquinas, is closer to us than we are to ourselves.

Terry Eagleton
writing in *London Review of Books*

Contents

Acknowledgements

First and foremost I wish to thank my great and good friend, Mary Kirley, without whose calm enthusiasm, patience and friendship, the reporting and writing of this book would never have been contemplated. Her careful first readings of the original chapters were invaluable, and her many, many thoughtful suggestions proved to be a kind of compass as I moved through this project for more than a year.

Additionally, I am privileged to have her beautiful and haunting photograph grace the cover of this book.

Many English murder mysteries begin with a conversation on a train. So did this one. To my professional colleagues Helen Branswell of Canadian Press and Aileen McCabe of Southam News, my thanks for a conversation in early 1997, and their generous insistence that I embark on this project.

I owe a debt of gratitude to my kind and gifted British agent, Andrew Hewson, not only for the professional advice while in Britain, but for steering me to his indefatigable and brilliant Canadian colleague, Jan Whitford. It was these two talented people who first saw the exciting possibilities for this book.

My thanks to Iris Tupholme, vice-president and editor-in-chief of HarperCollins Canada Ltd., whose sustained enthusiasm, constant encouragement and belief in this project kept me finely focussed and confident throughout. Her editing, together with that of Jocelyn Laurence, taught me so much and, of course, made this manuscript into a far better book. To them I owe a deep debt of gratitude.

Additionally, I owe thanks to several people at *The Toronto Star*: to weekend editor Joe Hall, for generously reading the manuscript and making countless useful suggestions; to publisher John Honderich, for his unqualified support and a very timely tip about chapter headings which focussed my efforts early on; to my foreign editor, Peter Goodspeed, for generosity, encouragement and helpful contact during many long months.

Outside the publishing and newspaper business, I was the beneficiary of uncommon kindness from some very special people: James J. and Peggy Feehely and their family of Tottenham, Ontario, for friendship, work space and a home; Margaret and Barney Rogers of Hampstead, for support, supplies and comfort during several months in London; and to my own family and that of my spouse, the Kirleys, for acts of understanding and generosity.

For expert legal advice and more, I thank Bert Bruser of the Toronto firm Blake, Cassels & Graydon.

For personal references I wish to thank stalwart lawyers Edward W. Ducharme and Harvey T. Strosberg of the firm Gignac Sutts, Dame Helen Suzman of Johannesburg, South Africa, and Lou Clancy, former managing editor of *The Toronto Star*.

For additional legal advice, not related to the manuscript, I thank my friend and brother Thomas D. Schiller of the firm Schiller, Coutts, Weiler and Gibson.

Many other friends and colleagues also contributed to this book in different ways. My thanks to Guelph-based journalist Mark Bellis, for coralling important legal documents; the Berlin-based journalist Alexandre Pajevic, for important calls to Switzerland and for translation; *The Toronto Stars*'s Brian McAndrew for the unsolicited supply of Ontario contacts; Erin Combs, photo editor, and Tony Bock, photographer, of *The Toronto Star*; and to my friend Peter Cheney of *The Globe and Mail* for undinting support.

I wish to thank the legendary switchboard of *The Toronto Star*, whose ability to track down anyone, anywhere, at any time—with grace and aplomb—makes them one of the finest assets any media outlet could ever hope to have.

I wish to thank everyone at HarperCollins Canada, especially Nicole Langlois, Judy Brunsek and Valerie Applebee, and everyone who had a hand in the complicated and demanding task of bringing this book into print in such a professional and timely fashion. They are an extraordinary team and it has been a pleasure to work with all of them.

Finally, there are others I would wish to thank publicly, but cannot. I have promises to keep. My gratitude is nonetheless genuine.

Bill Schiller
Exeter, England
July 1998

A Note to the Reader

This book was written with the benefit of a series of pre-trial contact visits with Albert Johnson Walker at Her Majesty's Prison, Exeter, in the summer and fall of 1997. No lawyers were present; guards were in the general area, but the visits were not monitored.

Extensive research was conducted throughout England, in London, Essex, Harrogate and Devon; in Switzerland, in Geneva and Basel; and in Canada, particularly in the central Ontario towns where Mr. Walker worked and lived and in Toronto.

Available material on the public record was voluminous. But other material had to be gathered from sources on a confidential basis.

I was gathering facts. But I tried never to lose sight of my primary task: to tell a story, in essence, to be a storyteller of fact. This is what I have set out to do.

PART I

1

A HAND IN THE WATER

THE ENGLISH SOUTH COAST

The promise the Rolex Watch Company made to the young Ron Platt when he purchased his Oyster Perpetual model in Osnabrück, Germany, in 1967, was to deliver time in precise, scientifically measured units, in an elegant fashion for as long as the bearer was proud to wear it. For Ron Platt, a soldier in the British Army's Signal Corps, that would be a lifetime.

In the spring of '67, Ron had just turned 22, and everything lay before him: education, career, opportunity, life itself, with all its myriad and enticing possibilities. He saw himself as a bit of an adventurer, because by the time he joined the British Army at 19, he had already seen some of the wider world. His formative years were spent moving about the hinterlands of Canada, from the Saskatchewan prairies, with their billiard table-like landscapes, to the forested foothills of the Rockies and beyond.

His father was a teacher from Wallasey, near Liverpool, his mother a homemaker with infinite patience for a husband whose fascination for Canada kept him moving back and forth across the Atlantic. Consequently, as a boy of 10 until he was 18, Ron had trudged through the worst of Saskatchewan's bitter snowstorms and hiked the lower reaches of the Rockies. He felt this experience had bestowed upon him not only a knowledge of the majesty of mountains but the wisdom of silence.

But this seeming self-assurance was little more than a façade, for underneath that silence, Ron was a shy and fragile individual who kept mainly to himself. He avoided pursuits like sports, parties and social gatherings that might bring him into regular contact with others, preferring instead the solitary sanctums of hiking and nature photography. In time, Ron Platt became a loner.

In the 1960s, the Rolex Watch Company of Geneva, Switzerland, began an international advertising campaign targeting the rugged individualists who are now the company's enduring market: sportsmen, outdoorsmen and achievers from exciting walks of life who saw themselves as different from the majority of men, cut from different and precious cloth, people ready for adventure but who, at the same time, felt they maintained a kind of elegance throughout. Today, a Rolex communicates style and success.

Its wearers make up a kind of exclusive club, and Ron Platt, a young Englishman fresh from Canada, believed, in his own quiet English way, that he belonged to it.

A Rolex, of course, also "told" time with legendary Swiss

chronometric accuracy, although what few people knew, and Ron did, was that the Rolex Watch Company was actually founded in England by an orphaned German entrepreneur by the name of Hans Wilsdorf. His partner was a London financier, Alfred J. Davis, a somewhat shadowy figure of whom very little is known to this day. In the aftermath of WWI, Wilsdorf relocated the company to Geneva, home to the world's finest watchmakers since the 17th century. Long before banking became the mainstay of the Swiss economy, these same skilled craftsmen had already made their timeless mark on the Swiss national heritage.

Wilsdorf never gave up his London connections, and when he wanted his first and biggest splash of publicity for the world's first truly waterproof watch—which the former pearl trader dubbed the "Rolex Oyster"—he chose the English Channel to do it. To prove that his watch was waterproof as advertised, he had it attached to the wrist of a 26-year-old English typist by the name of Mercedes Gleitze, who was making her eighth attempt at becoming the first British woman to swim the English Channel. All previous attempts had failed, but in October 1927, after swimming 15 hours through steel-grey water and thick fog, she touched shore at Dover and collapsed unconscious.

The Rolex continued without a hitch.

From that historic moment, the Rolex Oyster became a symbol of survival, and the association of Rolex with outstanding achievement was well and truly launched.

It was in the hope of cleaving to some of that good luck and distinction that Ron Platt, while on leave from the Signal Corps, strode into the jewellers Carl of Osnabrück and bought his own, and only, Rolex Oyster.

He dutifully filled out the one-year guarantee papers, carefully noting the watch's customer-specific serial number—154402, his number now—and signed on to a lifetime of adventure, achievement and undying elegance.

Or so he believed. Decades later, on the afternoon of Sunday, July 28, 1996, more than 60 feet beneath the waters of the English Channel once successfully plied by Mercedes Gleitze, Ron Platt's body lay still on the sea floor.

It had been there for six or seven days, stretched out among a field of sunken cobblestones as big as fists. From that field of fists, Ron's open right hand emerged like some sunken piece of coral or floral adornment. On it was the Rolex watch, still attached and, like its owner, utterly motionless.

On the immense channel floor, far, far below the sea's mirrored and sunny surface, Platt's drowned body had lain, decomposing and building up the abdominal gases necessary to float it to the top. A heat wave, one of the hottest of the year, had swept the English south coast, calming winds, stilling the waters and driving much of the fishing trade into the local pubs, because in weather such as this, the fishing goes off. The fish abandon their normal haunts and seek pockets of cooler, deeper water.

Drowning is among the most terrible types of death. In those "purple depths," as seafaring people refer to them—those submerged canyons measured in the hundreds and thousands of feet—the pressure alone can crush a body, and orifices and cavities containing air will rapidly rupture. As putrefaction—the actual decomposition of the flesh—finally sets in, the fish will feed ravenously on whatever is left, stripping flesh from the bone.

The sea is somewhat kinder at 60 feet. One imagines that Ron Platt, stretched out along the seabed, motionless except for the gentlest of currents coursing through his greying brown hair, may have almost looked peaceful. He was dressed in a blue and white chequered long-sleeved shirt, buttoned down at the wrists, green corduroy slacks with a "Made in Canada" patch on them, a brown leather belt looped from his left to right, blue woollen socks and brown Hobos lace-up shoes. The shoes were almost brand-new.

The "goose flesh," which comes to the dead three to five hours after death, would have been long gone by July 28. Rigor mortis, which begins with the stiffening of the eyelids and works its way down to the toes, would have lingered as long as four days in the water, but that too had passed. By now, Ron Platt's musculature would have been relaxed and at ease among the passing fish on the bottom, and his five-foot nine-inch frame would have appeared flexible, if a tad bloated. His lungs, after all, were filled with seawater. Normally it is this added weight that helps to keep a drowned body down until the build-up of gases tilts the balance and brings the body, Lazarus-like, to the surface.

That usually happens some six to ten days after drowning, and consequently, on July 28, seven or eight days after Platt hit the water, those gases may have already lifted him just a nick off the bottom, maybe more.

The mechanics of drowning are as horrific as any in forensic science. As the post-mortem examination would later confirm, Platt—had he been conscious—would likely have submerged and wildly struggled amid a choking, ever-building froth. As the air in his lungs was replaced with water, he would have been dragged slowly downward in a nightmare from which there would be no waking—from which no shout or earthly scream could summon aid.

After a subsequent period of calmly descending into the depths, Platt's body would likely have been overcome by a climactic convulsion, not unlike the thrashing of a fish in that last desperate moment before it is swept up in a predator's net. On his way down during that final frenzy, had there been anything to clutch or cling to, Platt would have desperately grabbed it and held it in his dying moment in what pathologists call Cadaverie Spasm. But there was nothing in Platt's hands now. They were open, empty.

The final convulsion and exhalation would have sent crazed plumes of jewelled-like spicules rising through the deep to the surface of the water as Platt's final post-mortem gesture on this earth.

Examination would later show that Platt's trachea and bronchi were filled with foam; his stomach contained seawater; his inner ear had haemorrhaged; and his skin had the wrinkled quality of a man who had been in the bath for too long, a quality which, in pathology, is called "washerwoman's hands."

Fish had quickly made their mark on Platt, and given sufficient time, they could even have devoured him, stripping his body clean and leaving nothing behind but his skeleton, his clothes and a watch on the immense sea floor.

But that wasn't what happened.

"Every Rolex Tells a Story," the Swiss-based company boasts. Indeed they do. In fact, the company invites its customers to write the company's head office to tell their tales of derring-do and survival.

"We always look forward to hearing what our watches and their owners have been doing," a little brochure produced by Rolex modestly says before introducing a series of stories so stunning in their originality, it proves the old adage that truth often is stranger than fiction. Here are tales from the depths of the sea floor to the heights of Everest; from the Sahara desert to snow-capped Alpine slopes; from English adventurers in the heart of Africa to American pilots who crashed to earth in Vietnam. They are rich and varied—and true. And they burnish and brighten Rolex's reputation in a way that Madison Avenue advertising could never hope to do.

A Rolex, as the company claims, "is no ordinary watch," and it follows that its wearers are by no means ordinary people. An English gentleman once wrote the company from western Uganda to tell how, while travelling with a group of Bakonjo tribesmen at least four days from the nearest telegraph, he had slipped and fallen and had almost plunged into a ravine, but for a "thin but very strong vine" and the precious watch upon which it had snagged. Afterward, throughout the treacherous journey back, the watch by which he had clung to life continued to give accurate service, a talisman to accompany its owner through some of Africa's most difficult terrain.

A former U.S. airforce pilot recounted how, after his aircraft had been strafed by enemy gunfire over North Vietnam, he was forced to eject and was rocketed through the craft's canopy. In that nanosecond of ejection, bursting through glass, his helmet shattered, his gloves were lost, and his skin was violently peeled from the upper parts of his body. Rescued deep inside enemy territory by a U.S. combat helicopter, he was flown to a medical field unit, where military doctors noted that despite the hellish ordeal, the Rolex watch was still working. In fact, it had survived in far finer condition than had the patient: it was utterly unscathed.

From Canada, only a few years before Ron bought his own watch, a deep-sea fisherman told a tale of the loss of his boat, *The Haida Girl*, which sank in 35 fathoms of water. Inside the boat, his Rolex lay on the galley floor for 22 days submerged in mud and muck. When the boat was finally raised, he found the watch, and with a quick snap of the wrist, it instantly recommenced active service as though the two, owner and watch, had never parted.

So it was no miracle that Ron Platt's watch had also survived. Strapped to Ron's wrist, lying there on the sea floor, the light that glinted off its scratchless synthetic crystal lent it a kind of submarine phosphorescence. It was entirely intact, for Hans Wilsdorf's Oyster patent promised nothing less. The watch's hermetic seal ensured oyster-like waterproofing to a depth of 300 feet, and Platt's body lay only 60 feet down.

True, time had stopped on the watch, but that was in keeping with the Oyster Perpetual's specifications. The watch was inextricably bound to its master, for its mechanical movement depended upon human motion. As long as the owner was alive and moving, the watch would remain active. If, however, he put the watch down and left it for 40 hours, or should he cease moving for the same period while wearing it—that is to say, if he were to die—then the watch, too, would stop.

Inside, Ron's Oyster Perpetual was as clean and dry and ready to be efficient as it had been the day the year-long process of its manufacture was complete.

It needed only to be wakened.

On a day in 1967 in Rolex's dust-free factory in Bienne, Switzerland, watchmakers put the finishing touches on this magnificent piece of engineering. Sealed inside its stainless-steel case were 500 component parts, a world of pinions and pawls, bridges and bars and balance cocks. Before the watch was shipped to the company's headquarters at 18 rue du Marche in Geneva, from where it would eventually be transported to Germany, a battery of tests would ensure that the product was perfect in every respect.

On July 28, 1996, that intricate inner world remained unchanged, even 60 feet down and six miles out from the nearest point of land.

For there is no such thing as a Rolex "second." Rejects are destroyed.

Ron Platt knew this too. Throughout his life, a life which turned out to be not at all as successful as he would have liked, his watch became the one thing from which he would never ultimately part. In a quiet and understated way, he felt it communicated that he knew something about quality and the finer things in life.

It also became something more for him: a symbol of his youth, a time when so much lay ahead.

There are rewards for such unflagging brand loyalty, and time would prove that in Platt's case, it even extended beyond the grave.

Along with the Rolex on Ron's wrist, there was another detail, invisible to the human eye but obvious to the small fishes foraging about Platt's body. Beneath that thick hair gently coursing in the water, across the left crown area of Ron Platt's head, was an impressive crack through which blood had seeped into the scalp and mixed with seawater. The gash was about four inches long and could only have been delivered with extreme violence.

Clearly the blow could have been dealt by another person, but it just as easily could have been caused by a boat propeller or some other nautical object.

One detail, however, was highly interesting and suggestive: the pockets of Platt's corduroy pants, as he lay there on the seabed, were clearly turned out. It is unlikely, given the gentle movement of the sea at that level and in that place, that they could have been turned inside out by the currents. More likely, one might deduce, they had been yanked out by some person.

That detail begs the question: If these pockets were yanked out, was Ron Platt the target of an attack, perhaps a robbery? Was he murdered and then his body dumped here?

Was there, then, someone on the water that day, someone up top who may have witnessed that final frenetic gesture, the bubbles roughly surfacing to the top, signalling Ron's last frantic struggle?

From the evidence on the sea floor, lying in the subdued half-light of an intermittently sunny day, it was difficult to say. Ron Platt could have taken his own life, drowning himself, his head then knocking up against a sharp rock, the propeller or rudder or bow of a passing ship. Perhaps he pulled his own pockets out before doing himself in, intent on leaving no clues, hiding his last desperate act from his family and friends. Embarrassed for them.

It was at least symbolic, for at the time of his death, Ron Platt was out of pocket yet again. His real pockets were empty, his hands empty and his heart full of the frustration of a life that had failed. He was a desperate man in dire straights, too proud, too stubborn, too silent to speak up or call for help. He had become hermetic. A loner.

Who could say definitively that he had drowned or was murdered? His presence at sea—or indeed in the town of Dartmouth, where he had spent the last night of his life—was unknown to his family, unknown to friends, unknown to anyone, apparently.

His contacts with his family were always sporadic and unpredictable, and in recent months he had all but lost touch with them. He was divorced from his wife, gave up a son for adoption in Yorkshire, split from a longtime girlfriend in Harrogate and had not spoken to his elderly mother in High Wycombe for weeks. Hence, by the time his body was down seven or eight days, no one had filed a missing person's report. No one knew Ron Platt was missing.

But all that was about to change. As Platt's body lay on the channel floor, a massive cloud of muck was being raised by something mysterious and unseen, approaching from the north, sending the fish into an absolute frenzy: nets. Suddenly Platt's body was wrenched up off the bottom, swept into a long, hemp-hewn pocket of webbing and pulled with speed up through 10 fathoms until, finally, it broke the surface of the channel's coastal waters, where a swarm of birds screamed overhead.

Had Platt's watch been working, it would have shown the time to be just approaching 3 p.m. on July 28. But the watch had stopped. Ron Platt had died an untimely death.

2

A DISCUSSION ON THE ROUGHS

It was a balmy night in the pine-scented coastal town of Torquay, and Andy Woffinden strode into his local pub, The Kents, and ordered a pint of lager. It was high summer, July 1996, and Andy had just turned 20.

He would be dead in just a few hours.

He was looking forward to six more weeks of school-free days in Torquay, the pleasant, whitewashed holiday resort three hours west of London by train. In fall, he planned to return to the local Devon College and continue his studies. Tonight, however, Andy had arranged to meet a group of friends for an evening of drinking and banter.

Torquay grew into a fashionable destination during Victorian times, when the British Empire was at its height and wealthy English families spent their summers here relaxing in elegant seaside hotels. At the turn of the century, the city's most famous daughter, the young Agatha Christie, used to play here with her dog

Scotty along these broad boardwalks lined with imported palms.

Today Torquay still retains a kind of dreamy, if faded, Victorian elegance about it, and its oldest and biggest hotel, The Imperial, maintains a special mystique, being the fictional haunt of Hercule Poirot and other Christie characters.

Andy's friends soon arrived at the upscale pub in the Torquay neighbourhood of Wellswood, and among them was Tom Jennings, who had just flown in that day from a Mediterranean holiday in Ibiza. Sunday nights were always busy at The Kents, with teams of patrons competing in the pub's popular general knowledge quiz, a contest not unlike Trivial Pursuit.

The competition, as usual, was intense, and at 10 p.m., a team from a nearby table was awarded the top prize of a chilled bottle of fine champagne. A bell clanged last call, and the patrons of The Kents drank up, spilled out into the street and began peeling off for home.

But for Andy and Tom, the night was not over. A friend gave them a lift to Meadfoot Beach, a meandering mile down below, and in the animated conversation along the way, the two decided they'd free up one of the pedal boats stored along the beach—pedaloes, as they're called—and take a moonlit tour of Tor Bay. Andy had done it only the previous week, he said, and it had been brilliant.

High on a cliff overlooking Tor Bay, a few lights still shone in the luxury Kilmorie Flats, shimmering like stars in the soft sea air.

Andy and Tom freed one of the pedal boats and were soon churning their way into darkened waters, suppressing their laughter for fear of being spotted by passersby and reported to police. The beer had made them giddy, and, in no time at all, they had pushed farther out into the harbour than Andy had expected.

"I'm not a very good swimmer," he shouted above the noise of the cranking pedals.

"Ah, c'mon," Tom laughed. "I'm sure you're better than me."
But Tom was wrong.

About 400 feet out, the boat began leaking, and within moments it was sinking. The two pumped furiously at the pedals, but the pedalo wouldn't budge. They screamed for help, but the harbour's flashing yellow caution light was the only reply. Quickly they scrambled out of the pedalo and leapt into the bay's darkened waters.

Andy went down, disappeared and came shooting back up, flailing.

"I'm not going to make it!" he screamed, choking on water.

"Swim back to the pedalo!" Tom shouted. *"Swim back!"*

As Tom himself swam back and clung to the boat, he turned and saw Andy for the last time. Andy was thrashing around in the water, choking, coughing, fighting. Then he disappeared.

It was sometime after that, an inquest later learned, that Tom's panicked screams caught the attention of a night watchman patrolling the harbour in a boat. He rushed out into the bay and hauled Tom aboard. He was in shock. It was a schoolboy prank gone horribly wrong.

For the next two and a half hours, the propellers of a Royal Air Force helicopter cut through the night above Tor Bay, scouring its searchlight over every inch of water. But Andrew Woffinden was not to be found—not this night, nor the next morning.

The sea would offer up the body only when it was good and ready.

So it was not surprising that one week later, when Devon fisherman John Copik hauled in a body off the coast of nearby Teignmouth, he immediately thought he'd snagged "the pedalo lad," as Andy Woffinden had come to be known.

So did everyone else.

Brixham-born John Copik had been a fisherman for more than 30 years, from the time he was 16. But this particular weekend was the first he'd ever been to sea with his son Craig as mate. Craig had decided to delay his studies at a London college for a spell to spend some time with his father at sea.

To those who didn't know John Copik, his broad face, Prince Valiant-style hair and short, powerfully built figure suggested the cut of a plain, hard-working man. But Copik was one of the most competent seamen in the historic fishing port of Brixham and knew the sea well. He had earned his Mate's Ticket from the Merchant Navy by the time he was 21.

Should he wish, Copik was authorized to captain a ship around the world. He knew the waters of the English south coast so well that, for him, even the charts produced by the Admiralty surveyors were never good enough. He would regularly set down overlays on top of the charts and draw his own highly detailed versions.

The seabeds of Tor and Lyme bays may lie unseen in depths of as much as 150 feet, but Copik had been fishing them for years. He knew these bays as if their waters had once parted and he alone had been allowed to record it all.

He was an entertaining storyteller, too, who loved to confer nicknames on friends and colleagues.

Young Craig he called "The Bat." When people asked why, John would explain, "What else can you call a young fellow who only goes out after dark and always comes home before first light?"

It was just before first light on Sunday, July 28, that John and The Bat set out from Brixham at 5 a.m. aboard the blunt but efficient *Malkerry*. The sun rose 35 minutes later.

The weather forecasts had predicted a calm and sultry day along the coast, with intermittent sunshine and temperatures peaking at about 21 degrees Celsius, which would eventually make the *Malkerry*, with its exposed metal deck, a little like a simmering skillet.

There was a light early-morning drizzle as the Copiks steamed out into Tor Bay headed for a point called Hope's Nose. As they reached a rock behind the Nose, John and The Bat shot the gear out behind them: a long length of fishing net known as Rock Hopper gear, which came tumbling from the stern as the Copiks prepared to fish a heavily cobbled stretch of water known locally as The Roughs.

Few fishermen bother to trawl The Roughs, because the rocks there can tear up a set of nets in no time at all and the time and cost it takes to repair them makes the fishing expensive. But John knew this ground well, and he always fished it on summer weekends.

Down below the surface, the trawling net finally extended to its full length, and when John was satisfied that it had touched bottom, he set the boat's trawling speed at a steady three knots and the day's hunt began.

Rock Hopper gear is aptly named: it comes fitted with bobbins that act as wheels. These hop over the rocks along the seabed, while chains help keep the bottom line tight to the sea floor. The chains have the added advantage of stirring up everything off the bottom to form large, turbulent clouds that frighten the fish into the net. Eventually, the fish make their way into the cod end, where they become trapped.

After two and a half hours of trawling, John and The Bat hauled up the cod end, leaving the rest of the net down, but found very few fish, and those that were caught were of very little value. There were no sea bass, and that was the lucrative catch John was really after. So they shot the gear out again and headed toward Budleigh Salterton.

The day was beginning to heat up. It was a day of neap tides, when there is little difference between high and low water, and the sea was still and limpid. It seemed like a small and waveless lake, calm, harmless, its surface as smooth as glass. There had been no wind for a week now.

A few hours later at a place near Otterton Point, John and The Bat pulled the cut rope once again and hauled in the cod end to check the catch. Again, there was nothing.

Copik stared at the empty nets and glanced across at The Bat as if to say, "What a bloody lot of luck you've brought to this enterprise." He was certain they were headed for a dull day of fishing. It was about to evolve into one of the more memorable days of his life.

John had had others, of course. In fact, it was almost 28 years ago to the day when, aboard the S.S. *Gothic* and asleep on the third deck, he'd heard what he believed was the ship's faulty fire alarm and thought to himself, "Should I bother?"

When he opened his cabin door, the other side of it was ablaze.

"The *Gothic* was built in 1948 with a completely wooden interior," Copik would tell friends in the Bullers Tavern. "So with 20 years of varnish on it, that ship went up like a volcano."

They were 2,000 miles out from New Zealand. Four passengers and three crew members died on board and had to be buried at sea. The cause of fire was never determined, John said.

He knew about death at sea.

Now, growing testy after hours of fishing with nothing to show for it, John and The Bat shot the gear a third time and started heading for home a little tighter toward shore to cut the distance. The small boat continued to tug, the nets continued to jerk along the bottom, and the tension between the two lent the boat a rhythmic roll.

At a point just off the River Teign, unnoticed by either John or The Bat, the jerk of the Rock Hopper gear held for just a fraction of a second longer. It was approaching 3 p.m., and they were six miles out from shore.

Moments later, John Copik turned from the controls and called to The Bat, "Let's haul 'em in, mate!"

The Bat pulled the cut rope, and as the cod end emerged through the waters and drew close alongside, John Copik could see that their luck had changed. The net was loaded with fish, and there seemed to be an especially large one trapped inside, probably a porpoise, he thought.

As the net drew closer yet, however, this was no porpoise. A human face stared back at Copik through semi-liquefied eyes, its mouth slightly ajar. It was a dead man, fully dressed.

In all of his years of fishing, John Copik had never dragged up a body—not once—and it sent a chill through him.

"I think we got ourselves a friend here, Bat," said John, trying to sound casual.

John Copik had read about Andy Woffinden, "the pedalo lad," in the local *Herald Express*, and he was certain, at first, that this was him. John and The Bat heaved the net on board, gently manoeuvred it above the fishing pound and carefully released the cut rope. As they did, the body and the mass of fish beneath it went slithering into the pound, wet and solid.

Pushing the nets aside, the Copiks set their hands on the edge of the pound and leaned inside for a closer look. There, resting on top of a glistening bed of sea bass, squid, gurnards and crabs, was the body of a man in corduroys, brown leather shoes, woollen socks, a long-sleeved shirt and, on his right wrist, a black and silver watch with a stainless-steel band. It was a Rolex.

"Lord Almighty," said John Copik breathlessly. "What have we got here?"

"Shall we keep 'im?" The Bat asked.

John looked up from the body and stared at The Bat: that really was the question, wasn't it? They could throw him back.

Among the fishing fraternity, picking up a "floater" is a bad omen, and few fishermen will ever touch one. On a single day, so one story went, a body in Tor Bay was picked up four different times by four different fishermen, as one after the other tossed it back, until someone finally brought it ashore.

It wasn't just bad luck, of course. There were all kinds of complications John had to consider.

So for the next 30 minutes, John Copik would later tell the police, there was "a bit of a discussion" on board about what to do.

If they brought the body ashore, it meant they would ultimately lose time at sea. The Copiks would have to be questioned by the police not once but probably several times. They'd have to appear at the inquest, and should there be a trial, they would also have to attend that. Obligations like these could keep them off the sea for days.

On the ledger of losses in John Copik's mind, the figures began to mount. If the body was never identified, John, as skipper, would be obligated under nautical tradition to give the deceased a proper burial at sea, with all the time and cost that would entail. Then there were the European fishing rules to contend with:

under hygiene guidelines issued from Brussels, any fish brought in with a body had to be thrown back. That would be another cost, for they would be forced to dump the day's catch, including the sea bass.

John was completely convinced that if he kept this body, it would cause him more grief than it could ever be worth. If he brought the body in, he would lose money, real money; that much was certain.

Why not give him a burial at sea right now, John thought? Why not pull him out and throw him back into the same waters from which he'd been dredged? Someone else would pull him in and eventually sort it all out.

There were other factors to consider, John knew. What would his wife, Pauline, think if, on the first day out with the boy, he snagged a body and threw it back in? What kind of an example would that be for his son?

"Well?" asked The Bat.

"He belongs to somebody," said John. "I'd like to think that if it were me, somebody'd bring me in."

Yet the cost, John kept thinking as he paced the hot metal deck, the cost would be astronomical. The selling price of a 40-kilogram crate of sea bass was now £400—almost $900. And on Brixham's busy quays, his mates were already having a better month than he. There was real money changing hands down there, and he wasn't part of it.

Better to throw the body overboard, John thought. Better to just toss him back in and forget all about it. That, clearly, was the sensible thing to do.

The call came into the operations room of Her Majesty's Coast Guard overlooking Brixham's inner harbour on channel 16, the distress channel, at about 3:30 p.m.

Officer Kathy Cocker took it and immediately shifted it over to working channel 67, logging it onto the Coast Guard's Adas computer system as she did so.

The voice on the VHF line identified himself as John Copik on board the *Malkerry*. He'd got a body in his nets about six miles out from the mouth of the Teign, and he was coming in, he said. He thought maybe the Coast Guard should know about it.

Area supervisor Paul Aggett was in the operations room at the time and keenly interested. A dredged-up body is a rare occurrence. Six miles out made it rarer still.

Aggett was a chunky, grey-haired firecracker of a man whose bright blue eyes suggested mischief-making, an impression that was only slightly diminished by the formal white shirt of his Coast Guard uniform.

Both Cocker and Aggett glanced at the massive wall map to their right, showing the English Channel and the French and English shores in minute detail, and immediately placed Copik's coordinates on the map. Aggett himself had been a Brixham fisherman for 14 years before signing on with the Guard, and he knew Copik.

"Ask him how old it looks," Aggett instructed Cocker.

"I don't know," Copik's voice came down the line. "D'you want me to ask him?" How was he supposed to know how old the body was, John thought?

"Ask Copik what colour hair the body has," Aggett pressed Cocker.

"Dark," replied Copik. "Dark brown or black."

"Tell him not to move it," said Aggett. "Tell him not to touch it. We're coming out."

Aggett radioed one of his inflatable Sea Rider vessels out in the bay. It was in the middle of rescuing a married couple whose boat had stalled, leaving them stranded. Aggett instructed the officer in charge to moor the couple's boat to one of the bay's five-knot markers and leave them. In minutes the officer picked up Aggett, who was waiting at King's Quay, and the vessel roared off into the bay.

Half a mile off Brixham's breakwater, which points northeast out into the sea like an accusing finger, Aggett boarded the *Malkerry*. He immediately surveyed the body and noted that the pockets of the trousers were roughly turned out and it was wearing a sturdy pair of leather lace-up shoes.

"Think he's the pedalo lad?" asked Copik.

"Maybe," said Aggett. "Can't say for sure."

Aggett had participated in the hunt for Andy Woffinden, and the only thing the search-and-rescue team had retrieved was a Nike-style running shoe they thought was his. But with no body retrieved yet, they couldn't be sure.

As Aggett and an assistant leaned in to pull the body out of the pound, crabs went scuttling off in all directions. The two lifted it up and laid it down on the deck, and as they did, Aggett noticed a large gash on the back of the dead man's head, "about the size of a bullet hole," he'd later tell police.

The face was distorted and bruised, and the entire body was covered in fish scales and sand. A thin gold chain was caught up over his chin.

Aggett had brought a Coast Guard-issue, black plastic body bag with four handles, and with some help from The Bat, Aggett lifted the body and laid it inside. Then he zipped it shut and radioed ahead to issue instructions that King's Quay in Brixham's inner harbour be cleared of the public and sealed off with police tape. They were bringing a body in.

As they steamed toward the Quay, it was silent and a little awkward with the dead man lying on the deck. Copik turned around from the control panel and stared at the body bag, then he glanced over at The Bat and tried to ease the tension.

"Well, I wouldn't exactly say he's been much of a deck hand," John said.

As the *Malkerry* made its way back into port, John could see crowds of people moving quickly toward the quay. The police tape had acted as a magnet. He moored the *Malkerry* to the quay, Aggett and his assistant lugged the body bag ashore, and the crowds strained against the tape trying to catch a glimpse of the black leather case.

At first glance, the port of Brixham, just five miles south of Torquay, seems a lot like any over-touristed harbour, with its arcades and souvenir shops. But Brixham is more than this. The port has had an established fishing industry since the 13th century and today is still regarded as the mother of Britain's deep-sea industry. Copik and his colleagues are proud of that and take themselves seriously.

So when the young police constable leading the questioning on the quay suggested the dead man's pockets might have been pulled out because John had rifled through them looking for a wallet, John was angry.

"You must be taking the piss out of me," he snapped. "Take the wallet and leave the Rolex?"

"What time did you haul him in?" the constable asked.

"'Bout three," said Copik.

"Why didn't you radio in for 30 minutes?" the policeman pressed.

John Copik was already regretting that he'd brought the body in.

"I didn't think it was urgent," Copik replied. "It wasn't like the kiss o' life was suddenly going to bring him back. The Bat and I had some thinking to do out there."

The policeman bent down and examined the body more closely. There wasn't a single piece of identity on it. He was certain this was the pedalo lad. Andy Woffinden was, after all, the only person in the region who was reported missing at sea. This had to be him.

John and The Bat, however, weren't so sure now. Andy's drowning had been an accident. To them, the condition of this body, especially with the gash on the head, suggested something sinister. But how could they identify him without any papers?

"What about the Rolex?" The Bat asked. "Maybe it's got some sort of serial number on it."

"G'won," the constable chided, dismissing the suggestion with a wave of the hand. "You been watching too many Inspector Morse movies, you have. And besides," he said, "it's a fake. It's not even moving." As he'd said it, he tugged on the watch's stainless-steel band. The watch briefly began ticking.

"Oh it's a fake, is it?" John taunted, glancing over at The Bat approvingly. Chip off the old block, the boy was.

The constable was embarrassed and took a quick look at the back of the watch, but there was no number to be found anywhere.

The detectives from the Criminal Investigation Division stationed at nearby Paignton arrived, including Detective Constable Ian Clenahan, followed by the medical examiner, Dr. Fisher. As they did, tourists and locals continued to jostle each other behind the tape, craning their necks to catch a view of the body or a snippet of conversation. Clenahan, a young detective who had just been posted to the region from mid-Devon, bent over to have a look at the body. He searched the pockets and found nothing, examined the watch and noticed that it had stopped at 11:35—whether a.m. or p.m. was not clear. The date window displayed the number 22.

The police seemed in agreement: based on the best evidence available, the body was likely that of Andy Woffinden. The bruised face, the turned-out pockets, the gash in the head were probably nothing more than the result of having been shaken and stirred at sea, then dragged along the seabed in Copik's nets.

Aggett, however, remained troubled about the crack on the head.

The crack on the head, police explained, could have been dealt by a propeller or the prow of a passing ship.

"Well, he certainly couldn't have been conscious when he went over," Aggett persisted. "If he had been, he'd have struggled to get his shoes off so he could swim."

Maybe, someone offered. But he could have been drunk when

he went in and unable to take off his shoes. Or it could have been suicide, someone else offered, in which case he wouldn't have wanted to take them off.

Dr. Fisher declined to speculate on the cause of death, nor would he make any pronouncement aside from declaring the body dead. He did, however, offer a cautious statement on how long the body might have been under: certainly more than 24 hours, he said, but probably not more than seven days.

By now, the young police constable was anxious to make amends with Copik for his earlier suggestion of theft.

"Do you think you'll be wanting any counselling?"

"We most definitely would," Copik said. "How 'bout the nearest pub?"

With that, he and The Bat walked back to the *Malkerry*, climbed aboard and churned their way across the inner harbour to their mooring. There, they scrubbed down the deck and got the boat ready for its owner, who would be taking it out that evening. They had dumped their catch, but they still had to sort through the nets to check for damage.

They weren't tied up long when another fisherman, the short, blond-haired Derek Meredith, came along and spotted an anchor tangled up in Copik's nets that lay on the deck in the early-evening light.

"Do you want it?" Meredith shouted down, gesturing toward the nets.

Copik interrupted his hosing down of the deck and glanced up, then down at the anchor and back again.

"Why? D'you want it?" asked John.

"Yeah," Meredith said. "I think I can use it for my speedboat."

"You're welcome to it."

Derek Meredith climbed aboard, pulled the anchor from the nets, climbed back out again and sauntered off. Under his arm was the anchor that, until 3 p.m. that afternoon, had held the body scooped up in John Copik's nets tight to the sea floor.

No one thought anything at all about the anchor that day. Murder wasn't on anyone's mind.

3

AN UNEXPECTED CALL

The big blue doors of Torbay Hospital's mortuary flew open, and the stretcher bearing the black body bag was wheeled in and moved swiftly into the refrigeration area. The white door to compartment B was opened, the lower stainless-steel shelf pulled out, and the body bag was lifted from the gurney and placed on the shelf. The shelf slid back and the door slammed shut. Russ Brooking, a big, broad-shouldered technician in his early 30s, adjusted the temperature to 5 degrees Celsius. The body lay there until the next morning, when Robin Little, the coroner's officer for Torbay, comprising the municipalities of Torquay, Paignton and Brixham, arrived for work at 7 a.m. It was Monday, July 29.

The folder containing the paperwork left by the young constable was labelled "Unidentified Male" and in it was a brief police report filled out on a standard coroner's form, a statement from John Copik and Copik's telephone number.

Little grabbed a coffee, started leafing through the report and quickly decided it was thin and inconclusive. He phoned Paignton to register his concern with the inspector in charge, Keith Wayte.

"I don't like it," Little told Wayte. "I'm not happy with this report at all."

A handsome, square-jawed, white-haired man, Little was in perennial good humour, but he could be blunt whenever he sensed a case wasn't being investigated properly.

"What seems to be the problem, Robin?" asked Wayte.

"The body your chaps brought in here last night," said Little. "It says here this man was found six miles out at sea, pulled up in a fisherman's nets. He's fully clothed—even has his shoes on and laced up—and yet your men don't think there's anything suspicious about it."

Little was entirely comfortable with Wayte. They had known each other for years, and Little had been harshly critical of the local detectives before, saying they were never interested in a body "unless it has a knife stuck in its back and the investigation is going to be easy." Robin Little had been a police officer for nearly 30 years before coming to work for the coroner's office permanently. He dealt with death on a daily basis, from the banal to the bizarre. His office in the basement of Torbay Hospital, high on a hill above Torquay, was right next door to the mortuary itself and was routinely invaded by the smell of ammonia spirits.

Wayte was defensive. "You know the only missing person in the region is this pedalo lad, Robin. We've been on the lookout for him for a week."

"I know that, Keith. But this man's got a gash on his head, he's dressed up like he's going out for dinner, and he's found six miles out. And your man seems to assume it was probably nothing more than an accident."

"Well it could well be," Wayte replied evenly.

"Of course it could be. I'm just saying your men ought to take a closer look at this one. Six miles out? He didn't just swim there."

Wayte wasn't convinced there was anything truly suspicious about Copik's find. After all, the body had probably been in the water for days before it was gathered up in the fisherman's nets and dragged along the bottom. He'd be surprised if the head hadn't been bashed about. For the moment there wasn't much to go on, he told Little. According to the young constable's report, there was no identification on the body and no clue to help the police identify it. They would have to put a notice in the local press to see whether they could raise some information.

"By the time that comes around, Robin, it'll be up to the new man. Up to Sincock."

"When's he due?" Little asked.

"Officially, Thursday. But he's not arriving till the week of the twelfth. Apparently he's got some tidying up to do up there."

"Up there" was Barnstaple, North Devon, where Chief Inspector Phil Sincock was earning a reputation as one of the best detectives in Britain. He had just won a special commendation from the chief constable for a conviction in a high-profile murder case. For only the third time in British judicial history, police had convinced prosecutors to charge a man with murder before they had even found a body. Sincock had been that sure. Days later, the body did turn up, and the accused, a man named Bob Field, got life in prison.

Sincock first came to national attention in 1990, when he took a Devon murder case that had lain unsolved for 10 years and conclusively pinned it on a criminal named Keith Rose. Rose was already doing 15 years for kidnapping. The investigation, which relied heavily on forensics, had been stunning. Sincock and Superintendent Mike Walsh had retrieved Rose's gun, which had been dropped in battery acid and rendered unfireable, and discovered a way—with the help of the F.B.I.—to make it work. A tiny mark on the casings from the bullets now fired from Rose's gun matched perfectly those from the bullets that had killed the victim. Sincock and Walsh won commendations for their work and death threats from Rose. He, too, got life.

It was exceptional detective work, especially for a young man who had never had the benefit of any specialist training or university degrees. Sincock had been born in Penzance, Cornwall, the son of a man who had worked hard all his life only to be swindled by an unscrupulous business partner. When Phil's father fell on hard times, the young Sincock quit school and got a job in a local tin mine to help out. Later, when his father became a civilian worker for the Devon and Cornwall police, Phil followed, becoming a uniformed constable at the age of 19, and later, a detective.

Now Sincock had been appointed Detective Chief Inspector for South Devon, "F" Division. He was moving up quickly.

Little told Wayte that he'd phone back the moment the autopsy results were in, and at close to 2 p.m. that day, Dr. Clive Hay, a senior pathologist at the hospital, took the elevator down to the morgue. Hay and Little donned white smocks and rubber boots, and with the assistance of technician Brooking, they pulled the body out of the refrigerator and wheeled it into the autopsy theatre, a little enclosed world of gleaming stainless-steel, blue rubber hoses and running water. As Little undressed the chilled corpse, which was still covered in sand, fish scales and debris, Hay began his physical examination, uttering his observations to Little, who recorded them onto a pad of legal-size notepaper:

"Male. Age 35 to 45.
Height: 5 feet 9 inches.
Build: slim.
Weight: 63 kilograms.
Hair: brown, slight greying and receding.
Early decomposition.
Estimated time in water: at most 7 days.
Large laceration to back of head; bruising on left hip."

There was a tattoo on the body's right hand, but it was difficult to make out. Little took the dead man's hand in his own and rubbed his thumb over the markings.

"Looks like stars to me," Hay said. "But it's difficult to tell."

"Tattoo back of right hand, appears to be stars (5) joined together."

The faded stars did seem to be linked together, almost like a constellation, and above the stars was the Rolex watch. Little turned back to his legal pad.

"Watch time and date: 11:35 hours, the 22nd.

Watch is automatic and self-winding."

The two men carefully examined every piece of clothing, and Little noted any significant details in his notepad before placing each item in a separate plastic bag: the brown leather Hobos lace-up shoes, "with good tread pattern"; the green corduroy trousers with a tag that read "Made in Canada"; the navy-blue, jockey-style underpants with a "Made in USA" label; and finally the blue and white chequered shirt, long-sleeved and buttoned down.

"He didn't seem to like sunshine much," Robin Little observed, reaching for his notes again.

"Always wears long-sleeved shirts buttoned down
to the wrist. Tan on back of hands only."

The face had a few days' growth of beard and moustache. Hay then began examining the crack on the back of the dead man's skull.

"What exactly do we know about the circumstances of this man's death?" he asked, peering into the wound.

"Nothing," Little replied. "Absolutely nothing."

"Let's see the police report."

Little set the file down on a stainless-steel counter, and Hay quickly read through it. As a pathologist for the district of Torbay, Hay examined many of the bodies that passed through this mortuary. Most were run-of-the-mill. But if suspicions of foul play arose, he was obliged to call in the Home Office pathologist.

Hay was troubled.

"All things considered, I'm not satisfied," he told Little. "I should think we'd better get the Home Office involved. I can't make a determination of cause of death based on this. You'd better call Dr. Fernando."

A set of dental impressions were taken in the hope that dental records in the national registry in Eastbourne might help identify the body. Once these were taken, the post mortem was suspended.

The following afternoon at 3 p.m., Dr. Gyan Fernando, the Home Office pathologist for Devon and Cornwall arrived at the hospital mortuary, and the meticulous process of examining the body began again in earnest. Fernando, a small, dark-haired, bespectacled man of Sri Lankan origin, had a reputation as a quiet, unassuming perfectionist. Every major organ was methodically removed, weighed, cut open and examined: heart, 294 grams and apparently healthy; lungs, left 1079 grams and right 766 grams, voluminous and waterlogged; liver, 1543 grams and unremarkable; brain, also 1543 grams, with no evidence of disease or injury.

The kidneys, however, carried a strange piece of forensic foreboding. Fernando found a small, two-centimetre renal carcinoma on the left kidney that was malignant.

"It's doubtful he knew anything about it," Fernando said.

The injuries on the body were all duly noted: a well-defined but unexplainable five-centimetre bruise on the left hip; a three-centimetre crack on the back of the skull, which might have occurred before or after death—Fernando couldn't be sure—and some minor lacerations about the chest and back that must have been caused by being dragged along the sea floor over sand and gravel. None of these injuries, however, could have killed the man, Fernando determined. The blow to the head had caused no brain damage, and there was no underlying fracture. It was the condition of the lungs, laden with water and "consistent with drowning," and the fact that the body had been found at sea that led Fernando to make his final pronouncement: death by drowning.

He added one speculative observation. Although the blow to the head could not have caused death, he noted, "it could have caused loss of consciousness," and "if this was a deliberately inflicted ante-mortem injury, and if the deceased lost consciousness, then it is quite possible that he had been subsequently thrown in the water to drown."

That was one possibility: murder. But Fernando also added, somewhat cautiously, "The injury could have been sustained accidentally, with the deceased falling into the water and drowning."

The body was then stitched back up and returned to refrigeration compartment B. As the door slammed this time, Brooking adjusted the temperature to minus 25 degrees Celsius. They'd freeze it, just in case. It might have to be looked at again.

News about the mortuary's "unidentified male" spread quickly throughout the region's police forces. The next day, Robin Little received a phone call from a friend who had heard about the case. Every Rolex comes with a customer-specific serial number, he said. Perhaps the Rolex company itself might be able to help identify the body?

Little dialled Rolex in Bexley, Kent, and explained the circumstances of the case to a Mrs. Hyland. His friend's information was indeed correct. Ever since 1955, Mrs. Hyland explained, every Rolex was made with a serial number clearly inscribed on its casing. In this way, a record of every repair and servicing to a customer's watch at any Rolex service centre in the world could be kept in Rolex's central registry as part of the company's pledge to quality control. Little slipped the watch out of its plastic bag as he listened and flipped it over in his hand for the umpteenth time, knowing full well that there wasn't any number on the back. He had looked there many times and there was nothing. The watch, he concluded, must be a fake.

"The number isn't self-evident, of course," Mrs. Hyland added. "It's on the shoulder of the casing, hidden beneath the bracelet, just where the bracelet joins the case. You can't see it without taking the pins out and removing the strap. Have a look and ring me back if you find anything."

Little replaced the receiver and looked up. "Russell," he said, addressing Brooking, who was seated in the office, "have you got anything to push these pins out and get the bracelet off?"

Brooking returned from the mortuary with a small, strong needle, and the two of them hunched over Little's desk as Little nudged one and then the other pin out and carefully removed the bracelet from the casing. There, inscribed on the side of the watch was the number: 154402. Thirty years of police work, Little thought, and none of it had been lost. He still knew how to do it.

He rang Mrs. Hyland straightaway and gave her the news. "Excellent," she said. "I'll make some inquiries." The next morning, Thursday, August 1, she rang back to tell Little that the watch had been manufactured in Bienne, Switzerland, in 1967 and shipped to Carl of Osnabrück, a jeweller's shop in Germany. Unfortunately, she noted, Carl had closed his doors more than 10 years ago, but that didn't really matter. The records were centralized. If Little would be kind enough to dispatch the watch to her offices in Kent, she said, she'd be pleased to assemble more information for him. He needn't ship it to her directly. He could bring the watch to a Rolex dealer in Exeter, and they would ship it on. That afternoon, Little took the watch to the jeweller, a 20-minute drive, where the manager had the watch packaged and couriered.

Little telephoned Inspector Wayte about the developments, then dialled his own superior, Hamish Turner, Her Majesty's Coroner for the county of Devon, whose offices overlook the water on Torquay's Marine Parade.

"A bit of luck?" said Turner gazing out his second-floor window toward the bay. "What sort of luck?"

Hamish Turner was a well-known local personality, a tall and elegantly dressed, ageing bachelor with flaming red hair who lived in a rambling pink house called Woodah, with spacious gardens and several greenhouses on Torquay's Babbacombe Road. A lawyer by training, Turner had taken an active interest in the case in the five days since the body was discovered. In his 17 years as deputy and 15 years as coroner, this was the first time his office had ever examined a body that had been pulled from the deep in a fisherman's nets. Occasionally, bodies that had floated to the surface were brought in, as were others that had washed up on shore. But nothing had ever come up in a net—and from so far out at sea. He found it fascinating.

"The Rolex had an identification number on it," Little said.

"How extraordinary," Turner replied. "Can the company help identify the body?"

"Not yet," Little said. "But they will."

"Good detective work, Robin! Well done!"

The next day, Friday, August 2, Little reported another development to Turner: the dead body of Andy Woffinden had been plucked from the sea that morning by the skipper of a local boat. The pedalo lad had been down 12 days.

The following Tuesday, Mrs. Hyland telephoned back to tell Little that the company's records showed the watch in question had been repaired twice in the 1980s, but for the moment, she could offer nothing more. Then on Wednesday, August 7, she called again.

"We have two addresses in Harrogate where the owner of this watch once lived," Hyland noted, "the most recent being in 1986."

"Do you have the name of the owner?" Little quickened.

"Of course," Mrs. Hyland said. "Platt. Ronald Joseph Platt."

Little picked up the phone and dialled the police. Dental records were summoned in due course and the dead man's identity was soon confirmed.

The following Monday, August 12, Phil Sincock arrived at the Paignton police station, and he was briefed on all current cases, including the once "unidentified male" who police now knew to be Ronald Joseph Platt.

"Is that the Rolex chap?" Sincock asked.

"That's right, boss," said Ian Clenahan, the detective constable in charge of the file.

"Do we know anything about this fellow yet?"

"Not yet," Clenahan replied. "We're still checking."

That week, using national health registries, council tax receipts and other state records, Clenahan tracked Platt from Harrogate to an address in Chelmsford, Essex, 100 Beardsley Drive. Clenahan then telephoned police in Chelmsford and spoke to Sergeant Peter Redman. Could he make a few routine inquiries about Platt on behalf of Devon and Cornwall, Clenahan asked?

On August 20, Redman learned from the landlord of the Beardsley Drive address that Platt had lived there as recently as June 21, when he moved house. The landlord had no idea where Platt had gone, he said. The only piece of information he had was the name of the reference Platt had provided six months earlier, when he'd moved in.

The reference was a David W. Davis, and his mobile telephone number was 0589-972726. Redman hung up and dialled it.

Not far from Chelmsford, in a plain-looking, two-storey, white stucco home in a quiet cul-de-sac in a sleepy Essex village, the phone was picked up and answered by a man.

"Hello?"

"Is that David Davis?"

"Yes, it is."

"Is that David Davis who acted as a reference for a man named Ronald Platt, who leased a flat in Chelmsford recently?"

"Yes? Who is this?"

"It's Sergeant Peter Redman, Mr. Davis, phoning from the Chelmsford police station. I'm not quite sure how to tell you this, but—there's been an accident at sea and a body has been found."

"Oh my God," Mr. Davis said.

"We believe it may be the body of your friend, Mr. Platt."

"Oh my God."

PART II

4

THE BABY, THE COUNT
AND THE BRIDEGROOM

CANADA

The cloud built and billowed seemingly without end, with a kind of magical internal combustion, creating clouds within clouds that constantly overtook each other—huge, white monstrosities they were, endlessly billowing and ever rising.

Then came the sound of laughter, slight at first, then growing, wave upon crashing wave. When the clouds began to clear, there behind them stood the unsmiling visage of 23-year-old Albert Johnson Walker.

It was the evening of October 25, 1968, his wedding day.

Pranksters had put a smoke bomb beneath the shiny hood of his big, boat-like American car, producing not only this harmless but dramatic display of simulated steam but much amusement among the guests, who had spilled out onto the lawn laughing. The bridegroom, however, smartly dressed in his rented tuxedo, found it funny not in the least.

Albert Walker did not like laughter at his expense.

Nevertheless, the evening's celebration had gone well. Albert and his new bride, Barbara, were married in the university chapel in Waterloo, Ontario, in a ceremony attended by their families and friends. Then they had returned to the quaint town of Ayr, where Albert's new parents-in-law, Jack and Hilda McDonald, had carefully and conservatively raised their three children: son Ken, their first, and the twins, Barbie and Bob, in their home on Hall Street, in the shadow of Knox United Church.

To the Hall Steet reception came uncles and aunts and old friends of the McDonalds, and young couples with screaming, running children, to wish the newlyweds their best on their exciting journey together into a new world. Albert and Barbara were excited too: their marriage was sure to be an exhilarating adventure.

Ayr was not unlike many southwestern Ontario towns in those days, with a sturdy, purpose-built town hall, library and bank. Its name, like that of the River Nith and the surrounding Dumfries Township, harkened back to Scotland, from where many of its earliest settlers had come in search of new-world prosperity. Their descendants had found it, as the entrance to the town's northern reaches bore witness: prosperous bungalows standing amid sheltering poplars, with freshly paved driveways reaching out to the road and mail boxes with neatly stencilled names.

Down in the city, it was the profligate '60s, the land of television, big cars, borrowed money and eternal optimism. Out here in the conservative countryside, though, it was quieter and more reserved, more dignified.

Out where the Canadian-Pacific Railway crosses Northumberland Street, stood the two landmarks of the Ayr community: to the left, the grain elevator of the Ayr Feed and Supply Company; to the right, the local farmer's Co-op, with its farm implements and garden supplies, which in springtime featured boxes of brightly coloured petunias and other potted plants heralding the arrival of warm weather after another long winter.

Ayr looked for all the world like the homey Ontario town it was, a well-ordered, rural oasis conveniently located just off the main 401 Highway that seemed a picture-perfect place in which to settle down and raise a family. And Jack McDonald, who looked after maintenance in the nearby Shirley, Dietrich and Atkins plant, where saws for retailers like Canadian Tire and even the big lumber mills were made, had done just that. Now, he hoped, so would his daughter and her new husband, Albert Walker.

Jack had his concerns, however, for things had moved perhaps a little more rapidly than he was accustomed to. One moment, it seemed, Barbie was a bright and lively red-headed girl who liked Highland dancing, did well in school and became class valedictorian. She had high marks in math, moved confidently on to university and seemed destined to make her life in business or teaching or one of the professions. Then, suddenly, she had come home from university one summer day, bringing a man, a mere boy he must have seemed to Jack, who announced that they intended to marry. This certainly wasn't the way he had done it when he had gone down to Roseville to ask Mr. Rohr for Hilda's hand.

On top of it all, this boy-man, this Albert, was openly and even flamboyantly affectionate with her, with Barbie that is, his only daughter—in public—indeed in his and Hilda's presence. Old friends would say it grated on Jack and made him feel uncomfortable.

For Jack was a conservative man. Every afternoon, he came back from work in nearby Galt to home and family. He read the evening paper, watered his lawn on summer evenings, went to the United Church on Sundays and was well respected within his community. If a neighbour needed a helping hand, he was there to lend it. His wife belonged to the Women's Institute, played bridge with a circle of ladies and kept a tidy, orderly home.

Only yesterday, it seemed, Barbie and her twin brother Bob were bombing around town in their little red Volkswagen, "Norbert," neighbours remember them calling it, laughing, calling each other by their mutual nickname, "Biz"—what it meant, Jack never did understand—and the very idea of marriage seemed safely distant. Now here he was, at his own daughter's wedding reception, having married her off to a man he barely knew, whose father was a truck driver and whose circumstances seemed, frankly, not as prosperous as his own. Although as a Christian, Jack never put on airs, he found it odd that Albert's father couldn't make it to the wedding because he was "on the road." Barb had only met Albert August 9, Albert's birthday, and now, scarcely 90 days later, they were married. Everything had just happened so quickly, Jack felt. He was uneasy about it and hoped he'd done the right thing by giving his blessing.

But it was what Barbie had wanted, at least what she had said she wanted, and who was Jack to deny his only daughter, just turned 22, wishing to "have and to hold . . . till death do us part"?

She was smitten with Albert. Only 23, he was already worldly and romantic in a way that she had only dreamt of. He said he had crossed the Atlantic and lived in Italy, working with the Red Cross aiding victims of the massive floods in the mid '60s, the ones *National Geographic* had documented so well, which clearly proved his Christian credentials. Then there was his knowledge of banking and finance, which he seemed to speak of so persuasively and convincingly that one would almost think he ran the trust company where he worked, Canada Permanent, a company that sounded more like a hair-do than a financial institution, even though he was only a trainee.

Then there was his physical presence: he was six foot one, dark-haired and handsome. He had an oval face with a strong chin and shining brown eyes and carried himself with an air of confidence and poise. Barbara's petite figure and beautiful red hair seemed to set his dashing figure off even more. Some thought Albert's short footsteps for such a tall man were a bit feminine, but Barb didn't see it that way. He seemed able to out-talk anyone on just about any topic, and Barb liked the fact that he was always throwing his big arms around her publicly and cuddling her in a way that no other boyfriend had ever dared. He was just so—so different. Barb also liked his dreamy talk about Europe and how they'd save and go there before having children, how they'd "do their thing," as people put it. It just seemed that, with Al, a world was about to open up to her in a way she'd never thought possible—not until retirement, anyway. Al wanted to travel now and work and retire later. He turned all the conservative conventions upside down: If they wanted something and wanted it now, why shouldn't they have it? Who said they had to do it the way their parents' generation had? His thinking seemed positively impulsive, and there was something to be said for that. It was liberating and filled with possibilities.

Behind that romantic talk, though, was a hint of something murky and hidden, the hint of a possibly troublesome past, a past to which Albert Walker would rarely refer. For despite the fact that he'd been born and raised in the very same region, his upbringing was a world apart from Ayr's quiet, sunny prosperity.

Albert would tell acquaintances that he had grown up in an "affectionate," "encouraging" and "stable" environment. But to confidantes, he told another story. There had been rough patches, he confided. His family was poor, his father often absent, the mother a strict disciplinarian—of necessity, perhaps—but with a hand as firm as that of any man. Which version was true in Albert Walker's mind? In time, he would disown his family and bury his past. But he wouldn't bury it deeply enough.

August 1945 and Bill Walker, a truck driver and now father of five, was driving his wife, Jean, and newborn son, Albert, back home from hospital, where Albert had been born on the ninth day of the month. About 12 miles northwest of the city of Hamilton, that busy industrial complex synonymous with Big Steel, he turned left onto Regional Road 597 heading west and, a half-mile down, pulled in right and climbed the little dirt lane to a lilac-covered hill and their humble new home. Across the threshold they carried their newborn, Albert.

Only the year before, Bill and Jean had decided this modest insulbrick house on the outskirts of tiny Freelton would be a better place to raise the kids than the family's cramped quarters down in Hamilton's Market Street. He and Jean, a strong, broadly built, churchgoing woman who could lift 100-pound bales of hay as well as any man—and did—packed up the kids and moved out to the country. They brought their belongings with them, including an upright cherrywood piano that Jean used to teach classical music to local schoolchildren. In the early years, the house was filled with music, as Jean put her pupils through their paces.

Music aside, though, the home was hard: there was no electricity and, hence, no lights. There was no modern refrigeration, no central heating, no indoor plumbing. Instead, there were coal-oil lamps, a wood stove in the kitchen and an oil-powered stove in the living room. When the icebox needed chilling, Bill fetched a block of ice. This was Albert Walker's home for the first six years of his life.

He was a quiet and shy boy growing up. So quiet that his primary school teachers put him in the back of the classroom, where Albert always behaved, daydreamed and failed. As a child, he was soft and sentimental. He was also particular about his clothes and appearance. Even as a little boy, he'd take an hour to get ready for school. When the Walkers moved down the road to a farming property at Harpers Corners and the family dog broke into Albert's rabbit pen and killed five, brutally snapping their necks one by one, Albert was devastated. His mother tried to console him, but she had seven children and a household to organize. That night, Albert went to sleep with his older brother Bill—they slept in the same bed until Albert was 14—whimpering. Albert cried for three days.

With a young family to provide for, Bill Walker was almost always on the road, hauling Niagara produce to Florida or Texas, steel to Vancouver and Halifax. Expenses were high, and whenever an opportunity arose to "tag on" another run and earn a bit more, Bill seized it with both hands. As a result, he couldn't always show up when he said he would.

When he did, however, Albert remembered. After a hard week's driving, there would be his father, standing behind Jean at the kitchen sink, the sound of tap water running, and he'd watch his old man's hand sweeping around her from behind as she washed up and he'd hear his mother whisper, "Bill, not now—not in front of the kids."

"And why not?" his father smiled, pulling her tightly.

Albert looked up and watched in silence and wonder.

His mother was master of the house. On this, there was no debate. If his father came home to carp or complain, a simple, stern "Bill!" ended it. There was silence.

By the time Albert arrived at high school, he'd failed twice, and the educators of the day decided he should enter what was euphemistically called "the opportunity class." It was a pleasant way of saying a student's opportunities were limited; those that existed should be grasped immediately. The student was to leave after completing grade 10 and get a job.

When Albert reached that grade at Hamilton's Westdale High, he dropped out. He was nearly 18. But by then, he had already honed his survival skills into a complex set of manipulative tools. Albert had always known, even from an early age, that he'd live not by the sweat of his brow or any knowledge school might bring but by his wits and cunning. One summer season of driving trucks for his father's firm reinforced that belief.

"I'll never get my hands dirty the way Dad does," he vowed to his mother. Albert always thought he was a cut above his family. Sometimes he joked and said he was adopted.

In 1963, after attending a local clerical college, Albert got a job in a candy factory and, on Saturdays, worked in a local men's shop. In Hamilton's north end, his teenage friends were wearing jeans and leather jackets and combing their hair in ducktails. But Albert was wearing $200 suits with a conservative cut, London Fog raincoats and Boston shoes. It was why he'd taken the Saturday job in the first place. He managed to coax the owner to let him have the clothing off the mannequins at a discounted price. He loved to dress and loved to sell. The latter was easy, because he was always selling himself. He believed in Albert Walker, even if few others did.

With his smart, affected clothing and his ever-present black umbrella, his friends took to calling him "The Count." But it was more than just the clothing. It was Albert's superior air. As a consequence, The Count had few real friends. When he went to Europe in 1966, after two years of saving, he went alone. He returned penniless, with holes in his shoes as big as silver dollars, but boasting of his womanizing. He had seen some of the world, he said, and he decided he wanted more of it.

An adult training course soon earned him his high school diploma. And then Albert fell in love.

Engaged to be married, only months before the wedding, his fiancée broke it off. Crushed and angry, Albert turned inward. He was down on women, a lady who knew him at the time would recall.

A few months later, he met Barbara Anna McDonald of Ayr. She was pretty, red-headed and smart, and came from a family that seemed to represent most of what he wanted: stability, security and small-town respectability. By now, after having lived at a half-dozen addresses over his 23 years, he was hungry for a home.

As for the wedding guests that night at the home on Hall Street, few people really knew him. Some might say that that included Barbara Walker.

Over time, Albert had developed the gift of greeting someone for the very first time as though he had known them well for years, or wanted to. The big smile, the firm but soft handshake, were completely unthreatening and open—or so it seemed. For behind those smiling eyes, always, there were busy calculations being done, a summing up of all the pluses and minuses about the interaction, the drafting of a kind of ledger of possibilities, if you will. Behind the sparkling eyes and the warm, inviting smile, there was always more, and sometimes less, than many bargained for.

On the day they were married, Barbara brought $2,000 in savings to the union. To her surprise, the bridegroom brought debt. The big car was quickly sold and "Norbert" the Volkswagen was appropriated. Barbara was determined to put Albert on the path, financially speaking, of the straight and narrow.

Albert Walker was clever. But wisdom, true wisdom, would always elude him.

On the one hand, as a young man, he was fascinated by travel and possessed a burning curiosity, a lust, really, for the finer things in life. Yet he lacked the patience and self-discipline needed to study and understand worldly things, and he always envied those who did. He wanted the status of a university degree, but, as Barbara observed, he was never prepared—as she was—to work for it.

Despite his months-long stay in Italy, for example, he never learned even a smidgen of Italian. In later years, even as an adult student of French, he could never distinguish between *il* and *elle*; and while he professed himself to be a serious lover of classical opera, the narrative lines he could recount were few.

"Oh, I just love to be swept up by the romance of it all," Albert explained years later, throwing his hands over his heart with a dramatic flourish.

Drama, he did learn. By 1968, when he met and married Barbara, he had developed a calculating flair for it. He could summon tears with an actor's skill at almost any moment, and, properly applied, he could convince people, Barbara in particular, to forgive his most outrageous transgressions, including marital infidelity. Sometimes, though, the method was so badly misplaced as to resemble farce. There would come a time, in 1997 when Tony Blair was elected as Britain's prime minister, that he would puddle up explaining what Blair's election meant to him.

"I've always been a socialist," Albert would say.

Yet over the course of a lifetime, many would be taken in. Barbara Walker was certainly not the first, nor would she be the last.

The year after the Walkers were married, psychologist Theodore Millon created a stir in psychology circles with a study on psychopathology that focused in part on a Canadian ne'er-do-well, Roger, who was involved in financial mismanagement.

"Handsome, well-educated and suave in manner, he had always been skilful in charming others, especially women. Faced with economic adversity, Roger allied himself with a group of stock promoters involved in selling essentially worthless shares of 'sure-bet' Canadian mining stock. This led to other 'shady deals'; and in time, Roger became a full-fledged 'love swindler' who intrigued, lived off and 'borrowed' thousands of dollars from a succession of wealthy and 'lonely' mistresses."

In many respects, Roger could be the psychological prototype for Albert Walker. Roger's charm, practical intelligence and driving love of money inherently constituted the basic model. But in time Albert could be said to have become a new, improved version, equipped with a cunning that would make Roger's virtually pale by comparison.

Albert, too, was handsome and well educated—the latter, in his own manipulative way—and possessed an amazing ability to convince others, especially women, to do things they would never normally do. In time, Albert also would turn to selling worthless shares to kind, unsuspecting couples and spinsters. But that would come later.

The American Psychiatric Association uses the term "sociopath" to describe a person exhibiting certain patterns of behaviour with antisocial personality disorder. These are people whose behaviour falls somewhere in that grey area between "mad" and "bad," and who are almost always dangerous to know. Sociopaths, as any introductory psychology text will explain, are people who tend to lack genuine feeling and are incapable of either love or loyalty. They act on impulse and are driven by desires for their own immediate gratification. In seeking to satisfy these desires, they have no real sense of guilt or anxiety; all codes of conduct are simply shunted aside. Indeed, experts say, sociopaths care little about the past and not at all about the future; in other words, the consequences of their actions mean nothing to them.

Albert possessed these latter qualities to a T. He could dismiss with ease worries that would have given other people ulcers.

Yet despite science's ability to describe sociopathology, the debate continues as to whether it constitutes a classifiable disorder. The causes of such behaviour are similarly debated. Some professionals believe it may be genetic, while others insist the behaviour is learned. Either way, there is one aspect about sociopathic behaviour about which there is no debate: therapy is useless. In essence, there is no cure.

In 1970, after two years of scrimping while Albert worked at a trust company and later a department store, the Walkers left for Scotland. They lived in Garscube Terrace in Edinburgh, where Albert sold insurance for the Combine Insurance Company of America and took a creative-writing course through a local school board held at the university at night. Albert had always dreamt of living and working in Europe, and since he and Barbara both had Scottish roots, Scotland seemed ideal.

The young couple who lived above them, Tom and Ann Chadwick, were impressed by the young Canadians. Albert was utterly irrepressible and forever upbeat. Everything was possible, he'd say. Success was just around the corner. They'd never seen such enthusiasm for life. But in February 1971, Jack McDonald suffered a fatal heart attack, and the young couple's European adventure was brought to a sudden end.

Arriving back in Ayr, some would recall, Albert seemed preoccupied with the untimely nature of Jack's death, breathlessly recounting how it was "all he could do" to pack up and get him and Barbara back in time for the funeral. Of course he professed sadness at his father-in-law's passing and paid his respects to Hilda and her children, but in the eyes of some, he seemed curiously detached.

He and Barbara briefly moved into the Hall Street home with Mrs. McDonald before getting their own place nearby. Soon they became part of Ayr's community life and stalwarts in the local United Church. Albert sang in the choir and eventually became a church elder.

By now, Albert had become a dyed-in-the-wool Anglophile. He took to tweeds, secured employment at the university library and communicated a kind of wise and worldly demeanour which obscured the fact that he had been a high school dropout. He was now a lofty librarian; what matter if he only supervised the stacking of books on shelves?

In his spare time, he took to researching his family's European ancestry and developed a lifelong love for English thrillers, especially those involving espionage, dual identities and murder, works by Frederick Forsyth, John Le Carré and others. He loved that world in which plausible characters, applying ingenious tactics, always achieved the impossible—and commanded the reader's grudging respect along the way, regardless of the characters' amoral ends. It was a special world.

At the weekly Sunday dinners at the McDonald house, which Albert and Barbara always attended, occasional guests recalled how he lorded his experience over the rest of the family now, how he held himself higher up and was frankly uninterested in anything anyone else had to say. He had developed an annoying egocentricity, and people in town knew that it made Barbara's twin brother Bob bristle. For Albert, every human encounter was a dramatic opportunity to demonstrate his superiority; every conversation was a kind of combat.

Despite his arrogant ways, Albert still managed to make himself a favourite of his mother-in-law, fawning over Hilda at just the right time and frequently showing her unaccustomed physical affection in public.

Albert always said that Hilda's rigid German upbringing had discouraged physical affection, and his sudden, unrestrained attention won him a special place in her heart.

In 1972, Barbara and Albert had their first child, a girl, Jill, and in 1975, another, Sheena. By now Albert was searching for more lucrative means by which to support a growing family. He even turned to market gardening, raising crops on a secondary property cursed with poor, light loam entirely unsuitable for farming, trying desperately to inch ahead by selling the produce in local markets. In the heat of high summer, Hilda would come out to lend a hand to her only son-in-law and daughter, carrying buckets of water to try to salvage the Walkers' withering fortunes.

Albert tried a number of jobs: he worked at Ayr Feed and Supply; he worked as a herdsman; he continued to try his hand at insurance sales. In the end, it was Barbara, always clever with figures, who developed what would eventually become their best chance for success. Primarily a young mother, she still carried a local reputation for being bright with numbers, and as early as 1973, she had begun handling income tax for neighbours. On late winter evenings, she would be hunched over the kitchen table poring over other people's assets and liabilities in search of a modest tax refund.

Albert was transfixed by how casually friends and acquaintances, and even complete strangers, would reveal their personal assets to Barbara, pulling back the veil on what he considered to be their most guarded secret: their money. Gazing down at these papers heaped upon the kitchen table in front of Barbara one evening, Albert saw the future.

Until that moment Albert Walker had metamorphosed into something new nearly every year since they were married, moving through eight different jobs in a decade. Now, all of that restless, desperate casting about would end.

In 1978, he and Barbara incorporated Walker Financial Services, and later they would buy out Oxford Bookkeeping in neighbouring Woodstock, bringing the owner, Al Boggs, on board to smooth the transition and help with expansion.

With Barbara busy raising their two little girls, the couple decided that Albert, whose latest job was as an insurance salesman with Mutual Life, would run the company and be the smiling, confident front who would convince customers to entrust Walker Financial with their every financial need. He envisioned a string of offices throughout the region offering a range of services for farmers, families and friends: Barb's tax advice and accounting, his life insurance packages and, eventually, maybe even general investment counsel.

At about the same time as the incorporation, Albert determined they needed a bigger house which would allow Barbara to raise the children and allow him to adopt the country-squire pose he coveted, in keeping with his new station in life. That year, 1978, only a week before their tenth wedding anniversary, the Walkers entered a bid on a handsome 75-acre piece of Brant County property on the outskirts of Paris, Ontario, just down the road from Ayr and only a few miles from the historic Paris Plains Church. With its windows pointing toward heaven, the church had been built in the early part of the last century by the free labour of its own pioneer congregation. This was fitting, for Albert fashioned himself as a kind of modern-day pioneer: restless, risk-taking and always in search of new frontiers.

Not far to the west of the church, the Walker's property was an L-shaped parcel just off County Road 15, on a concession known locally as Watts Pond Road, named after a malarial, pike-infested bog that straddled the biway just east of their property. Their plot was smaller than the surrounding farms, where locals held an average 200 acres or more, but the south-facing two-storey century stone house that came with the property had history and character, and Albert and Barbara believed it also held potential as an investment. It had a natural stone fireplace, sturdy plaster walls and ceilings and smooth pine floors, as well as four large bedrooms upstairs, where Albert and Barbara could sleep and, at the same time, watch over their young children.

Al and Barb Walker paid $145,000 for the house and took out a mortgage with the Victoria and Grey Trust Company. When they closed the deal on October 30, 1978, in a lawyer's office in downtown Cambridge, they signed a standardized affidavit to their age and spousal status that seemed to hold within it, in its precise legal language, the seeds of a future that would soon be past.

"When we executed the attached instrument," the affidavit read, "we were each at least eighteen years old. And within the meaning of section 1 (f) of The Family Law Reform Act, 1978, we were spouses of one another."

That October, Alan and Isobel Barron, the farmers who owned the property, signed an indenture promising "quiet possession" of the said 75 acres. If only the Barrons could have guaranteed it. These 75 acres with the stone house would be the scene of the Walkers' own war. Quiet possession there would not be. In fact, in time, the house would become a battleground; its walls would resonate with mounting anger and almost unspeakable accusations and become the backdrop for the bitter conflict that would mark the final dissolution of the Walker union.

In the fall of 1978, though, all of that was almost a decade distant. The Walkers still felt themselves to be pioneers in life, love and business, excited and optimistic about the territory ahead. County Road 15, they thought, would lead to prosperity—and it would. But beyond that, it would also lead to ruin.

5

I WILL BE YOUR LORD

For Albert Walker, the 1980s were years of charm and appetite. For a decade at least, money led Albert Walker into those lofty realms where people are permitted to make up their own morality, improvising as they go along. In a certain sense, society lets them, because the vast majority of people often confuse money with other things, like intelligence and sound judgement, propriety and moral rectitude. Albert himself was one of these people. Money didn't just change the rules, he knew; it actually conferred upon the bearer the power to make them. That was the wonder and magic of money, and Albert Walker desperately wanted to be touched by that magic.

Beginning in the late 1970s, Albert assumed greater control of the Walker business and became the sole architect of his and Barbara's future. With Barbara increasingly tied down to the home with two new children—Duncan was born in June 1979 and Heather Jane in 1982, making it four in 10 years—he didn't actually have to wrest control away from her; it was simply, fatefully, there for the taking.

During this decade of dream and accomplishment, Albert Walker not only distanced himself from his family but actually reinvented himself. He achieved levels of respectability and security which had always been beyond his grasp, and later still, he would transcend the furrowed fields of Brant County and, in a manner of speaking, soar off into the horizon like a legend.

Albert Walker would become famous.

Back in 1978, all of that seemed unthinkable. Once the company was incorporated, Albert Walker set off across five counties, from one country kitchen to the next, currying favour with local farmers, taking in their income tax forms, getting a sense of how much frontage they had, then pitching directly to their needs, and not just income tax advice and preparation, but life insurance policies, financial planning, whatever he could. In no time at all, Albert had a very good sense of who owned what in the neighbourhood. Ever since witnessing the reading of his father-in-law's will in 1971, Albert never ceased to be amazed by how much money these farmers and small-town working men were able to quietly accumulate. They paid their taxes too, almost blindly, as Albert was to discover. This almost always served as his strategic point of entry in any discussion, the space into which he could insert himself and his company to pry open the door to those secret savings.

"Do you realize your tax liabilities here?" Albert would ask, elbows on another unfamiliar table, sipping another country wife's cup of coffee. Well, no, in fact they hadn't. They just thought everyone paid tax; it was their duty, a moral obligation, a lot like voting or attending Sunday services. Didn't everyone feel the same?

"And are you deducting your wife as an employee?" he'd ask, sitting back now, legs and arms crossed, almost like a knowing father.

"Well, no," the farmer countered. "Can I?"

"Not exactly," Albert smiled, unfolding himself, leaning forward now, elbows back on the table, arms outstretched, getting ready to sermonize. Spouses weren't actually eligible to be deducted as paid employees under current tax law, he explained, but if the farmer could make an arrangement with, say, his brother-in-law over on the next concession, they could "swap" wives, so to speak—strictly in terms of tax, of course—where each wife could be listed as working on the other man's farm. And when the tax refunds came in, the two farmers could just exchange cheques.

"Is it legal?" the farmer asked.

"Of course it's legal," Albert assured them. "Everybody does it. Revenue Canada knows too. That's what the loophole is there for."

Such a clever, friendly and helpful man, they thought. A real professional and an established churchgoer too.

During these years, Albert realized the value of churchgoing to an aspiring businessman. Every Sunday, dressed in a freshly pressed white shirt and a carefully selected suit and tie, Albert Walker would pull up into the parking lot of Knox United Church, at the foot of Hall Street where his mother-in-law Hilda still lived, and march his family in through the church's front doors.

Here he sang in the choir, assisted Barbara in the local Sunday school, helped with a church youth group and, eventually—much to Hilda's delight—became an elected church elder. When he transferred his membership to St. Paul's down the road in Paris, Ontario, he did much the same.

Compared with membership in any of the local service clubs, the church, Albert knew, was the most important club going. You couldn't build a business in these parts without it. Albert professed to be a true believer, of course, but he was also a pragmatist: being a Christian, a public and even prominent one, communicated that he had a binding sense of moral good.

He knew the Liturgy of the Faith well, but he also knew that a small-town businessman could bank on Christian principles.

To underline his commitment to Christianity, Albert Walker would be heard to say from time to time, "You know, I often thought of entering the ministry myself." It was true that he had taken English literature and religious studies courses as a part-time student at university, and there were many who thought he probably would have made a good minister. He was so helpful, so concerned and had such a gentle touch. There was even a rumour that when he was younger, he'd gone to Oxford or some other prestigious university in England. He seemed almost tailor-made for the ministry, and if you half-closed your eyes, it didn't really take much to imagine him in a priestly collar, dutifully ministering to those in need.

In some respects, it was not unlike what he was doing now. Making his rounds, Albert told clients that his personal business philosophy was simple: business was really not so much about profit but about "helping people out." If you were helpful, prof-its would follow. Business was, in a way, not unlike the ministry—but a ministry of the here and now, of opportunity.

There was certainly nothing wrong with success.

After Sunday services, Albert always stayed for the coffee hour, and it never went unnoticed that he mixed with the most impor-tant people in the community, the pastor, other church elders, the most prominent people at Knox United, the "elect," if you will. If he seemed to count himself among them, that was as it should have been.

When Bob and Betty Staley, long-established members of Knox United, first met Albert in the 1970s, they thought Barbara lucky to have found such a fine, upstanding fellow. He sang in the church choir with them and had a lovely voice. When the Staleys needed tax advice, they, too, eventually turned to the younger couple. After all, who could possibly be more trust-worthy? Albert Walker was a pillar of the Ayr community, a family man, a Christian, a respectable, well-spoken, small "c" conservative, in many ways the very embodiment of those qual-ities which distinguished sunny Ayr itself. Moreover, the Walker company had been incorporated in the village. For a time, Albert and Barbara even set up shop in the Bank of Commerce build-ing on Northumberland, right across from old John Watson's pioneering foundry, the farm-equipment factory that had helped build Ayr's prosperity.

Albert Walker may have come from someplace else, but he was part of Ayr now—perhaps not born there, like Barbara, but most definitely bred.

Over the years, even when the Staleys moved away to tiny Van Dorf, north of Toronto, the couples still kept in touch, played bridge and even vacationed together. The Staleys were proud to call the Walkers their friends. When their daughter married a young lawyer by the name of David Penhorwood, little Sheena was the flower girl. The families were close.

But no one was prouder of Albert Walker than his mother-in-law, Hilda. The tradition of Sunday dinners continued on Hall Street, where Albert could hold forth, but now, occasionally, the Sunday get-togethers would move to Albert and Barbara's home on Watts Pond Road, which meant Hilda would have to make the 10-minute drive. At the end of these dinners, a half-hour or so before Hilda left for home, her only son-in-law stepped briskly out the side door and turned the car around so that it pointed outward and she could pull out safely into Watts Pond Road without strain or risk of accident. Albert was so thoughtful, she believed, even with the small things. Before his mother-in-law got into her car, Albert would give her a wide-armed hug and kiss. Years later, Albert would tell an acquaintance that Hilda would always confide to him in a whispering voice, "You know, Albert, you're the only one who does that."

In her eyes, Albert was a model businessman: hardworking and successful, but one who also had time to be considerate and affectionate. Perhaps more important to Hilda than any of these attributes was his unquestionable relationship with God. Every Sunday, Albert Walker could be relied upon to be standing tall in his pew at Knox United, either gripping a choral book or *The Book of Common Prayer*.

With thundering organ accompaniment, he sang his praise of

God to heaven. Albert Walker believed in God, and because he did, Hilda McDonald believed in Albert Walker.

On weekdays, he'd drive to his office in nearby Woodstock, a 30- to 40-minute route down old Highway 2, through fields of soybeans, wheat and corn, past Princeton, across Horner Creek, down through Creditville and finally past the garish strip mall of fast-food restaurants, gasoline stations and car dealerships that stretches along Woodstock's northeast end, testament to the region's growing middle-class wealth.

Money was getting a little easier now, and bankers friendlier. The surrounding automotive economy was bouncing back, and in 1980, a boom cycle was under way.

"C'mon over to my table later," local banker Al Birt told David Davis, one of his clients, as he bumped into him at a local lunch spot one afternoon. "I've got someone I want you to meet."

That's how easy it had become for Walker by then: even the bankers were promoting him. A few minutes later, the British-born Davis, a tall, strapping man at six foot four, dressed in coveralls, came lumbering over to Birt's table to shake hands with a man the banker introduced as Al Walker, who was dressed in a dark, pin-striped suit and tie and had not a hair out of place. He seemed, to Davis, to exude big-city success, yet he was local.

Davis operated a local feed service out in the county and mentioned he'd been having trouble with his current bookkeepers.

"Bring your books along to us," Walker assured him. "We'll look after you." That week, Davis brought his books along to Walker Financial Services, then operating out of modest basement offices on Huron Street in Woodstock, and handed them over. Shortly after, Walker helped Davis put together a successful loan application to get his business affairs in order. Walker asked him to fill out a few forms and hand over his birth certificate, and in no time at all, he called Davis back to say that the loan had been approved. Albert had a way with bankers.

Eventually Walker was able to move from his basement location to the more spacious main and upper-floor offices of an old three-storey brick building on Riddell Street, steps from Woodstock's main banks and trust companies. From the porch, he could see the tower of Woodstock's city hall and the spire of a United Church. And he saw that it was good, and he would become a permanent part of Woodstock now.

In September 1982, after Albert and Barbara flew to the Cayman Islands, Walker announced that his continued pursuit of new and innovative ways to legally avoid tax for his clients had led to the creation of a new division of his company in the Carribean tax haven: United Canvest Corporation (Cayman) Ltd. This, he explained, would allow clients to shift funds out of Guaranteed Investment Certificates and other fixed deposits—which he always offered at just a margin of a per cent better than the banks—into equally secure investment units down in the Caymans.

The advantage, Al explained to clients, was that they could report half the earned interest as a tax-free capital gain, rather than straight income, if they decided to report it at all. It was their call.

Months later, reading *The Financial Post*, Walker read of attempts by a large and prestigious Canadian trust company to create a similar offshore, tax-free investment vehicle not unlike his own.

"Five months ahead of the big boys on Bay Street," Albert boasted to Al Boggs, whose bookkeeping firm he'd bought and whom he'd kept on as an employee. "Not bad at all."

"I don't know how you do it, Al," Boggs said. "You always seem to be able to take an idea from here, an idea from there, put them together and create something entirely different."

Albert Walker, banker-innovator. He liked the sound of it, and he liked being a step ahead of the educated elite of the nation's financial institutions. He had always envied professionals for their education, despised them, really. His had been humble origins, but he had dreamt and charmed and worked his way up. Albert Walker began to believe that he was one of those rare individuals who had been blessed from birth with special gifts—the kind that formal education cannot buy. Success and the faith of others was an intoxicating elixir. He was an important person now with important appointments.

On a Wednesday in April 1983, at about 2 p.m., he got an unexpected call from his only brother, Bill.

"You've got to come quickly. Mom's dying."

Jean Walker was 67. She had suffered a series of heart attacks and didn't have long.

"I've got a business meeting," Albert said. "I can't make it."

Jean Walker died that day. Albert arrived later, at about 10 that evening. That Friday he attended the funeral, and, for almost everyone in the family, that was the last time they saw him.

Albert was pointed toward the future, not the past. He dreamt of making the *Forbes* magazine list of the world's richest business personalities, and he told friends that the innovative Chrysler Chairman, Lee Iacocca, was his hero and role model. To Albert Walker, it seemed that he could do just about anything he wanted.

In the late 1980s, when Marjorie Richardson, a churchgoing woman in her 70s, wanted to sell a large parcel of land north of Toronto and share the proceeds with her daughter Betty Staley and son-in-law Bob, she and the Staleys turned to Albert Walker for advice.

The Toronto real estate market had been steadily heating up since the early '80s, and late in the decade, it was positively on the boil. Her land, near the Highway 404 extension north of the city, was prime for development, and as the market peaked, Marjorie, Bob and Betty sold it and became millionaires overnight. Walker had engineered the deal, guiding them through negotiations like a good shepherd. Ten months later, Marjorie's son Bill Richardson, who had looked on during the Staley sale, wanted to do the same with a parcel of land he had inherited. He, too, turned to Walker, who then orchestrated a magnificent bidding war. In total, the two deals netted almost $10 million.

The Staleys and the Richardsons were thrilled at their success and asked Walker to take some of the proceeds and invest them in the Caymans and deal with much of the rest as Walker, in his wisdom, saw fit. Bob and Betty presented their old choral colleague from Knox United with a set of spool candleholders as a memento of their thanks. Bill and his wife, Sheila, gave him a cherished antique mantel clock.

The Staley-Richardson investment was the single biggest vote of confidence in Albert Walker's young financial career. When the Richardson's finished with a few disbursements, they sent Walker a cheque for $5,125,000 to be invested. Walker had a photocopy of it framed and mounted on his office wall as a timeless testament to his genius. He was trusted, talented and well on his way. Indeed, he seemed almost invincible.

Beyond all this apparent success, however, there remained inside Albert Walker a deeper craving. Emotionally, secretly—to no one but Barbara—he was one of those boy-men who never seem to surpass adolescence, who can never be loved enough, never be praised enough, never be satisfied. He had an insatiable appetite for attention, a craving that was breathtaking. It was as though he was cursed by some kind of emotional tapeworm that devoured every single gesture of affection as if it had never occurred at all. Men of this kind are always wanting, their partners always exhausted, and the techniques they use to sate these appetites know no emotional bounds.

Years later, Albert would reveal to an acquaintance that, as he slipped into bed one night in the middle years of his marriage, he drew his wife close, kissed her tenderly and whispered, "I love you, Barbara."

Above the silence that night, out of the mustiness of bedcloth-
ing and sheets, there seemed to be an air of comfort and satisfaction.

"Do you like that?" Albert asked. "Do you like it when I do
that?"

"Yes," Barbara said.

Then abruptly, "Well I like it too," Albert said, pulling back.
"And I'd like it if you did it to me more often."

Duped. Played with. Barbara burned.

"I suppose it was a dirty trick," Albert mused afterward. "She
got angry—really angry. But I'd made my point."

The bed as battleground—the discomfort of trying to fall to
sleep in a confined space with someone with whom you are angry.
Then it's separate beds in separate rooms and sleep comes, and
increasingly it comes more easily, and then those emotional ties,
once so intimate, ease and stretch and eventually dissolve. There
is no snap to it, no dramatic moment when you hear it breaking
and you can rush to make one last effort to repair or stop it.
There's just the knowing, after a time, that it has been lifted
away. Gone. Afterward, it's difficult to imagine it ever really
existed.

"But you see," Albert recalled later, "my wife just couldn't do
that. Could not."

What? Express affection? Show love? Give?

"No. I mean the words," Albert said. "The words. She could
not say: 'I love you.'"

An extraordinary claim, like so many he would later make, but
one delivered with conviction. Albert was always very good at
drama. He claimed "the problem" lay with Barbara's rigorous
Scottish-German upbringing. He insisted that displays of affection had not simply been frowned upon but unknown in her
family. It was a barrier, he insisted. It was a problem—her problem, not his.

He'd made his point that night in bed, he said, and that seemed
to transcend everything. For Albert, making his point was always
most important.

Based on this belief that he was somehow being short-changed on the ledger of love and affection, Albert believed he had both emotional and moral grounds to look elsewhere. He didn't need to look far.

Albert always promoted himself as a modern man. In fact, he boasted he was actually "a feminist." He always believed in giving young, single mothers who had been separated or divorced a chance to pull their lives together, to earn a living and learn about finance. It became one of his trademarks to hire women in need, ostensibly to do them a favour, as a kindred spirit, "a feminist" and as a Christian.

Of course, they didn't have to be separated or divorced. He hired married women as well, as long as they were young and attractive, it seemed. No one paid much attention at the time, but in retrospect, years later, it was obvious.

To outward appearances, during Albert Walker's decade of dream building, the Walker family fortunes seemed to be faring well: both business and family were growing, income was increasing, and Albert's reputation as a Christian businessman remained rock solid. There were major vacations to Europe and the U.S., skiing in Vermont with a new church minister, and eventually, Albert even bought a small sailboat and had an in-ground swimming pool installed, the latter a possession the locals regarded as the ultimate sign of success. Prominently displayed on his desk in his office was the smiling portrait of his family. No one suspected that there were problems brewing at home. But there were—and they were serious.

It began with noises spiralling and spilling down from the upper floor, down the creaking and carpeted staircase, all the way down to the main floor of the Watts Pond Road home. Barbara was stunned, almost ill. They were coming from the bedroom, her bedroom, and Jill was—what?—maybe 14 at the time, and just starting to look attractive in a young-girl-becoming-a-woman way. Barbara had been noticing—or was it her imagination?—that Albert had been paying more attention to Jill lately in ways that made Barbara feel uncomfortable. But she wondered whether it wasn't just Albert's bizarre way of being mean, of getting back at her for some slight, real or imagined. He might only be trying to annoy her in his own nasty way. At first she had refused to read anything more into the excessive attention he paid to Jill, but then Albert had started embracing and cuddling her more and more frequently, in a manner that seemed too adult, too muscular, too much. In a way, these displays of affection seemed calculated to communicate desire—to Barbara. Albert was often and openly urging Jill to "hop into bed" with him, but always, of course, in a joking fashion. Yet there was an edge to these invitations, and Barbara didn't like it. In time, she came to think the unthinkable: there could be an incestuous relationship under way. The very thought of it placed her on the border of shock.

Now the noises kept coming and coming and spiralling down, and Barbara decided she had to act, to move swiftly, stealthfully and silently up the staircase to confront whatever truth lay there. At the top of the stairs, she marched straight into the bedroom and found Albert and Jill in bed.

"Jill, you're too old to be in bed with Daddy! Get back to your room!"

It wasn't the only time it happened. Then, Barbara had no proof that sexual intercourse between father and daughter had occurred. She had clearly disturbed them, but she didn't know whether she had caught Albert in the act. Sick with worry, she decided to have a talk with Jill to warn her about "older men," in a general way, to see if she might illicit some accusation about Albert. She didn't want to confront Jill directly on the issue of her father; she didn't want to make an issue of something she wasn't sure of or make an accusation she couldn't prove. Most of all, she didn't want to provoke in her young daughter's mind the spectre of an evil so terrible, only to discover that it might not have occurred at all. But she wanted to act as a responsible mother.

Jill was quiet during the conversation, one during which Albert's name never came up. Barbara hoped that if Albert had been molesting their daughter, Jill would say so and they would deal with it. But Jill didn't speak his name. Instead she mentioned the name of the husband of a friend of the Walkers, who, she told her mother, had tried to kiss her on the lips. This might be cause for concern, Barbara thought, but at least it wasn't the worst.

Still, Albert's jokes and urgings to Jill continued until she was 16 or 17, ending suddenly when Jill got a boyfriend. Barbara was never really certain what was going on. The suggestion of incest remained an ugly, unsettling possibility, one that crept into the upper floor of the Walker home and stayed there, resting uneasily like some rough beast.

About the same time, Albert starting having what men euphemistically call "sex problems," and he couldn't perform. Barbara put it down to his being "sexually insecure," and Albert promised he'd take it up with the family doctor in Kitchener.

Outwardly, there were no signs of any pernicious evil gnawing at the pillars of the Walker home. On Sundays, the Walker family went to church, and Albert continued to perform his duties as a church elder. Each week, he religiously took *The Book of Common Prayer* in his hands and solemnly read from the Liturgy of the Word. And there on page 630, the last page of the little red book, is A Table of Kindred and Affinity, "wherein whosoever are related are forbidden by The Church of England to marry together." The list of the 25 people that a man and a woman are forbidden to marry or have sex with one another begins:

"A man may not marry his: Mother, daughter . . ."

The private lives of the Walkers were complicated now. Albert Walker had made them so, first privately and soon publicly.

The first public warning of Albert's proclivities arose within the hallowed confines of the church itself. Albert and Cathy Newman, the wife of a young assistant minister at St. Paul's United, in Paris, Ontario, created a stir by openly flirting with one another. At first it seemed innocent and people tried to dismiss it. But Albert became more brazen about his intentions, and when the minister and his wife's wedding anniversary came up, Albert bought and delivered two blue five-speed bicycles for the couple. Renegades, the bicycles were called, and they cost Albert more than $400, half of what he was putting into the collection plate each year.

It soon became clear that there was more than flirting going on. Confronted, Albert later insisted he had actually been motivated by a deep desire to help a woman in need. To hear him tell it, it was almost a Christian deed on his part. He certainly saw nothing wrong with his involvement: he was already experiencing marital difficulties. He and Barbara were drifting, in fact had drifted far apart. By May 1988, when Barbara finally woke up to Albert's affair, she refused to sleep with him anymore—"cut me off," Albert complained.

Later, the marriage of the assistant minister and his spouse fell apart, and Albert Walker eventually washed his hands of the affair and moved on. He needed some "space," he told the minister's wife. He cut back on his official church duties as well: the congregants of St. Paul's United in Paris took a dim view of such brazenness and slowly began to shut him out.

He and Barbara underwent marriage counselling, and in October 1989, there was a kind of reconciliation: Barbara had forgiven him, and they were sleeping together again. But it was a short-lived truce. Soon he was acting as recklessly as ever—and strangely.

It was about that time that Albert first detailed to Sheena, when she was only 13 or 14, an account of his original sexual experience as a young boy with a young girl. She was puzzled, for this seemed to be far more than just a "facts of life" lecture. Why, she asked a friend, would her own father be telling her such details?

Albert had always been publicly affectionate to his daughters, particularly Jill, whom he'd sometimes take on business trips. Increasingly, though, his attention was turning toward Sheena, the second oldest, whom he now openly called "Daddy's girl," as in, "Sheena is Daddy's girl, aren't you, Sheena?" Then he would tell her, in front of others, including Barbara, that if Sheena ever had a problem, she should come to him and not her mother. He would always, always look after her. For those outside the family who witnessed these exchanges, it was always a bit uncomfortable. Albert would lay on a hug and a kiss and inject an element of humour to his words, but they seemed slightly dark and spiteful toward Barbara. By now Albert had become a master of the nasty art of building himself up by putting other people down, and it was not uncommon for him to publicly humiliate Barbara in subtle and not so subtle ways. In Albert's game playing, the children were often pawns, because Albert knew that winning their affection was the best way of getting at Barb.

Money, too, was a good basis for humiliation. "I wouldn't even bother getting out of bed if I made as little as that," Albert would say to Barbara, whenever she dared to mention her contribution to the household income.

As for the company, it had become "his" now. The fact that Barbara had built it from their kitchen table was only useful insomuch as it helped to contribute to company lore. The way Albert saw it, if it hadn't been for him, the business would still be at that kitchen table. Instead, he had built it, by 1988, into five offices with 18 employees directing $12 million of other people's funds. That was *his* doing, he'd say.

Albert had also grown more impatient with Barbara's idiosyncrasies—her tendency to be late for things, for example—and his temper manifested itself in mean-spirited ways. On a vacation in Ireland once, he drove around the Ring of Kerry at high speeds to punish her for her lateness having held him up. More bizarrely, he would occasionally suggest some secret life he had that she knew nothing about, alluding to "mafia connections." He was growing stranger, more aggressive, more distant.

Those arms that had once romantically swept Barbara up and away now seemed, at worst, positively threatening. At best, slung casually around the slim waists of younger women, they hurt and humiliated. Albert Walker had become a bully, a calculating, hurtful and brutal bully.

Adding grievous insult to real injury, he would confide in Sheena about his girlfriends, introducing her to one and trying to build an alliance with Sheena by telling her later, "Don't tell your mother."

Sheena felt uncomfortable with the situation, even though her relationship with her mother was, like that of many teenage daughters, rocky, to say the least. But Albert was her father, some-one she looked up to—as others did—as a successful businessman and generous father. He could do no wrong.

Throughout the family turbulence, Sheena managed to maintain a steadiness in her own life that was admirable for her years. She was a boisterous 14- soon to be 15-year-old girl who was popular at school, fun to be with and still managed to balance a blossoming social life with good marks in school.

During this period, her father suddenly began to buy her leather jackets, cashmere sweaters, perfumes, things she hadn't really been interested in as a tall, athletic pre-teen growing up and having pool parties at home with friends. Poised to become a young woman, her father lavished her with gifts. His gestures might have been perceived as intrusive, but Sheena chose to see them as fatherly affection.

This lavishness had become typical of the Walker style. Outside the home, too, Albert had developed a tendency to buy expensive gifts for people he barely knew, especially women. These demonstrated his wealth and power as well as his sentiments. Wealth and power opened doors, sometimes even bedroom doors.

Someone to whom he turned such attentions around 1989 was a young married woman who worked in his office, Genevieve Vlemmix. She was, like many of the women who worked at Walker Financial, attractive and trusting, although a little more so than most on both counts. This was the love affair that set destructive passions alight between Albert and Barbara, triggering an intense and explosive anger. Things were about to get ugly now, and inventive. In the end, Albert's well of power and inventiveness would prove bottomless.

Genevieve had first come into Walker's office in 1987 with her husband, Harry, an ambulance driver who wanted to invest in a Registered Retirement Savings Plan. Genevieve's mother and grandmother were long-standing clients of Walker Financial, and collectively, they would ultimately invest about $500,000 in Albert's Caymans division. Consequently, Al was the first person the 29-year-old Genevieve and Harry thought to turn to when they decided to invest their savings. Albert was grateful. Genevieve was beautiful.

In the months following that first meeting, Al made repeated offers of part-time employment to Genevieve, in front of Harry, and eventually in late 1989, she came on board to sell investments from the Woodstock office. Genevieve confided to Albert that she and Harry were having marital difficulty, and Albert commiserated, saying he and Barbara had gone through difficult times too, in fact *were* going through a difficult time. Barbara and he hadn't slept together since May 1988 and were currently keeping separate bedrooms, he said.

In May 1990, Albert took Genevieve with him on a business trip to Switzerland as his "executive assistant." Her presence, he explained to her, would give him "greater credibility," and she would act as interpreter, since she was fluently bilingual in English and French and he couldn't speak French at all. In Switzerland, they stayed at the historic and refined Three Kings on the Rhine in Basel.

Albert's earnest search for Swiss venture capital came up empty-handed in interviews with potential Swiss investors, but his relationship with Genevieve deepened. In Basel, and during four days in Geneva, where they stayed at the Hotel L'Arbalette, saw the sights and enjoyed some romantic dinners, Albert and Genevieve decided their futures should intertwine.

By now, Albert was living in another world. Business had been good for him in the 1980s. In 1986, he had bought a shell company listed on the Alberta Stock Exchange and became—as he was so proud to tell anyone—the CEO of a publicly traded corporation: Walker Capital Corp. It would essentially become the parent company of Walker Financial Services. Never mind that the stock was worth as little as 10 cents per share: presentation, as Albert Walker knew so well, meant much in business, as well as in life.

Walker had brought a young lawyer, young church minister and an experienced financial consultant on board as directors and in one swoop corralled the church, the law and the world of finance. He seemed to be constantly jetting back and forth from Toronto to Calgary, the Caymans and Switzerland, looking, he said, for that essential venture capital, talking up the tiny company's grandiose plans to make new, profitable acquisitions in England, the U.S. and Canada.

He had used the company to raise $1 million on the issuance of preferred shares in 1988, and by 1990, he was telling journalists he planned to raise another $12 million and take control of a Canadian trust company by year-end.

"He won't provide names . . . " a *Calgary Herald* report read ominously, noting that "the English literature graduate" who had "studied accounting" felt indebted to Calgary for the "opportunity" it had afforded him and his young company.

By this time, Albert was laying down his lines like a character out of one of his beloved Forsyth novels. He had never graduated from any university, and in the only accounting course he had ever taken he had earned a D. But he was a corporate citizen above suspicion now, and he knew it.

Albert Walker was finally starring in his own life, produced and directed by Albert Walker, the screenplay written in his own hand, with a musical score that would no doubt include some of his favourite arias, for opera, too, had become an apparent passion.

Walker Capital Corporation, Albert pronounced, had the potential to become "one of the best small publicly held companies in Canada." More and more clients were encouraged to invest more and more of their savings with Albert. He was taking in deposits and issuing promissory notes, guaranteeing a healthy fixed rate of return, usually for a term of three years. Albert had the knack, too, of convincing clients whose investments came due not to cash them in but to roll them over into another three-year term.

"Make interest on your interest," he'd say, and the clients complied and were issued new promissory notes.

To Genevieve, he must have seemed like some prince or lord who had suddenly landed in her lap. Articulate and handsome, wealthy and apparently worldly, Albert seemed to be offering her a second, better, more romantic chance at life.

At least that's what he wrote to her in a love poem penned in his own hand. Everything they touched was holy, he said. Everything was possible.

> My Dearest Genevieve,
> We are halfway there
> And we <u>will</u> succeed
> God and all his power
> Is with us
> Our love is stronger
> Than all the Universe
> You must understand
> by now that what we
> touch becomes good
> We have the power
> Feel it
> Acknowledge it
> And know that it is good
> We are the chosen ones

Our love for each other
Amplifies the power
We will use it for good
And to strengthen ourselves
Be my lady and
I will be your Lord.

                                        A.

To Genevieve, Albert seemed to know just the right thing to say to a person who didn't feel good about herself. Now he was taking that talent to another level, mixing religious symbolism and poetry with a brand of Svengali-like power. Genevieve was swept away. They were discussing marriage now.

By the time Genevieve and Albert returned to Canada from their Swiss adventure, spring was well under way. The crates of petunias were set out in front of the farmers' Co-op across from the Ayr Feed and Supply Company, and the gently warming air was pregnant with the promise of another intense summer. Meteorologists were predicting it would be a scorcher, possibly the hottest on record.

In the Walker household, it would be the summer from hell.

6

VEERING OUT OF CONTROL

Still spring 1990, and the lights of Albert Walker's 1984 Oldsmobile 88 hug the wide curves of a darkened country highway, the tires peeling white noise off the asphalt like skin, shooting sound off into a starry night.

Inside the car's confined inner space, illuminated only by the dimly lit dashboard and the occasional flash of passing headlights, Albert Walker is at the wheel, bringing his daughter Sheena and a friend, Jenna Olender, back from a dance at Paris District High School.

There is girlish giddiness inside this car, talk of boys and teenage teasing and laughter and then a lull, followed by silence and then a deeper silence that holds.

"Jenna," Albert asks, his eyes glazed on the road, "what do you think of drugs?"

Mr. Walker—always engaging, always probing, treating you almost like an equal. He makes it feel as if he's one of us. How many adults take the time to ask 14-year-olds anything? It sort of props you up, puts you in the position of expert, really, someone worth consulting, someone worth listening to.

There was a time when Mr. Walker said to Jenna that no matter what happened to her friendship with Sheena, he hoped that "their friendship"—Jenna's and his—would continue and that she would always feel comfortable enough to meet with him and talk.

"*Their* friendship," he had said. It struck Jenna oddly at the time. What friendship was he talking about? He was Sheena's father, right? Like, was there anything else? What had he really meant? The thing was, he hadn't really said it as though he were Sheena's father. The tone was, well—different, suggestive of something else. Jenna began wondering if she had maybe missed something, overlooked a moment or a conversation when this "friendship" with Mr. Walker had actually taken some bigger, wider curve? It was weird.

Until now, she had sat at the Walker dinner table and listened to Mr. Walker lecture her and Sheena and the other kids on study habits and try to push his love of *Phantom of the Opera* on them, blaring it from the stereo. The tales of Mr. Walker's studiousness as a young man became part of kitchen-table banter—dinner and after-dinner talk.

It sounded so impressive. The picture he painted made sense and made them feel that good marks really were attainable, provided you set out a course of study and stuck to it.

There was the young Mr. Walker as a schoolboy, years before he was to become the president of a company listed on the stock exchange, taking down notes during classes, coming home, rigorously rereading them before reading the next day's material. Then the next night: rereading both previous day's notes before reading the following chapter, and so on and so on and so on. By the end of the week, by the end of the year, he knew it all, he'd say. Every bit of it. He barely needed to study for final exams, so imbedded was that knowledge then. It had actually become part of his permanent database, part of who he was.

That, he would say, was the difference between knowledge and wisdom. Time, concentration, self-discipline and reward. It sounded so convincing.

"The other students used to call me Professor Albert," Mr. Walker would proudly say.

Upstairs in Sheena's room, with the ballet slippers hanging from the wall, Jenna and Sheena shared the secrets of young girls growing up with a kind of candour that boys would never really risk. Boys were always so busy in groups, on baseball diamonds, on hockey rinks, it was always a "team" thing, a "pack" thing, activities done in the safety of numbers, hanging out. Girls got close, revealed emotion, confided, cried, compared. Sometimes they could be mean; but they always made up.

Sleepovers at Sheena's were part of growing up. They were special in winter, because you got to play Ouija Board in front of the Walkers' beautiful fireplace: Ouija by firelight, while the snow outside blanketed everything. It was great. In the heat of summer, there was the pool. Sheena was the only one in their group who had a swimming pool. Plunging into the cool blue of the deep end, the submerged sound of bubbles curling up past your ears as you touched bottom, then shooting to the top and breaking surface in a fit of wild, spitting laughter and gasping and more laughter.

"Drugs," Mr. Walker had said. At first it seemed sort of cool for him to ask, and he wouldn't ask if he didn't want to know— or didn't already know.

"Well, Mr. Walker, you know—I mean, you know what it's like in high school nowadays."

"Hunh-hunh."

"I mean, I don't think there's anything really wrong with mari-juana or hashish, you know? I don't think they really do anything bad to people."

"Hunh-hunh."

"But I mean, I'm not telling you I'm a regular user or anything like that. I'm no druggie, if that's what you mean."

"Hunh-hunh."

"But heroine and cocaine—that's really dangerous, and I think that's, like, really wrong because they can do damage."

Silence.

"Jenna," Mr. Walker said, "do you think love is the drug?"

It jolted her and cut the conversation in her throat. It wasn't just the word, it was the tone, the way he said "love," stretching it out like a long piece of elastic, his voice going a little deeper, giving it a kind of honeyed tone. Love is the drug. It was a line from Brian Ferry's Roxy Music, and it sent a rising chill moving through her body like liquid. Not fear so much as uneasiness, a numbing, slow, low-sounding, low-pulsing alarm. Something was wrong.

At 14, Jenna never really had much use for the word "inappropriate," but she knew now: this was it. That question, that tone, that word—they were "inappropriate."

What Jenna didn't know then and couldn't have known was that she wasn't the only one Mr. Walker was hitting on. But no one was talking then. It was only later, much later, that the truth would emerge.

Albert Walker was veering out of control.

Weeks after his conversation with Jenna, Albert Walker walked into the Bank of Commerce in Woodstock, Ontario, in June 1990 and presented the manager with an application bearing his and Barbara's signatures for a $90,000 second mortgage in the name of Walker Financial Services against their matrimonial home.

Albert had been more upbeat lately and talked to Barbara about buying a sailboat, a new computer, maybe even "a little sports car" for her. So when he brought her the application for the mortgage, making a vague reference about needing to "tidy up" with the lawyer, Barb simply signed. At the time, Albert had more than $150,000 in three separate accounts at his and the companies' disposal. The loan was approved and payments arranged to be made once every six months. The first payment was due in December 1990.

Later in June, the walls of that same matrimonial home resonated with the sound of screaming that had by now become all too familiar. The Walkers were doing battle. For Albert, for whom there had never been any rules in either love or war, this argument would mark a strategic break.

He threw his affair with Genevieve, hidden until now, directly into Barbara's face like a bowl of cold, dripping water. The ruthlessness of it all left her enraged and nearly breathless, and she demanded he leave the home immediately and take his clothes with him.

Albert countered, thundering his demand that she should be the one to leave, taking the two youngest with her to make room for Genevieve and her child, who would move in as soon as Barbara was gone.

"You'd better do as I say, or you'll get nothing from this marriage!" Albert raged. "If you mess with me, I'll blow you away. I'm warning you! Blow you away!"

Albert felt himself to be firmly, utterly in control, but what transpired at 953 Watts Pond Road that day wasn't brinkmanship. There would be no last-minute pulling back, or even any intention of doing so, for Albert Walker was now moving progressively forward with the stealth of a master chess player.

Though badly burned, Barbara was determined to show Albert she could not be trampled on, and weeks later, on one of those typically hot southwestern Ontario summer nights when Albert Walker was away, Barbara decided to take revenge. Early one morning, she bundled Albert's clothing together, his tailored Baumler and Warren K. Cook suits—size 42 tall—the endless supply of high-quality shirts, his fancy ties, even his underwear, stuffed it in the car like so much loot and drove it at dawn to Genevieve's house and flung it in the driveway.

Albert was livid. He countered by descending on the farm in a frenzy, ripping Barbara's clothing out of the closet and throwing it down the stairs, shouting at Sheena to throw it into the trunk of his car. Barbara fought to retrieve it, but the confrontation spilled out of the house and into the yard, and she feared Albert would literally slam the trunk on her hands if he had the chance. Albert pushed past her, slammed it, gunned the engine and was gone, furious.

It was a stormy and unsettled time, made worse by Albert's constant scheming, aimed at keeping Barb continually off balance. He even vowed at one point that he would never see Genevieve again: he would transfer her out of his Woodstock office to another location and the relationship would be over and done with, he said. The office staff were loyal to Barb and had turned against the younger woman, blaming her for the Walkers' marital troubles.

By the end of June, Barbara had had enough, and she fired the first of what would be many legal volleys in the War of the Walkers. Summoning the assistance of an established firm of lawyers in the Ontario city of Cambridge, she had them dispatch a "Dear Sir" letter to Albert at work, citing Genevieve as his "paramour"—the legal language, even at the height of battle, pulling a bit of French lace out of the air—and seeking a separation and "reasonable" settlement.

In Walker's Woodstock office and even in Paris, the town where Alexander Graham Bell received the world's first long-distance phone call in 1876, people were burning up the wires with talk of the Walker schism. Amid the angle-parked cars on main street, from the I.D.A. pharmacy to the I.G.A. supermarket and in that air space where the residents of the Penmarvian Retirement Home gaze warily out their windows to the lawns of the Wm. Kipp funeral parlour across the street, the Walker split was the whispered talk of the town.

Hilda was stunned and confused. For the life of her, she couldn't understand why her daughter would want to separate from Albert, who, in her eye, had always seemed like such a sensitive son-in-law.

His pride pricked—how dare Barb be the one to get the

lawyers involved?—Albert decided he'd find a new and inventive way to take the intensity of the conflict higher.

On July 28, 1990, while apparently on business in London, England, Albert penned Barbara what appeared to be a heartfelt letter.

> Dear Barb,
>
> It's 3 a.m. and I have not slept at all tonight. My wake-up call is for 4:30 a.m. because I have to leave by 5:30—I might as well stay awake now and sleep on the plane. I've been doing a lot of thinking tonight, about you and I and the children—and I know in my heart and in my mind that the course of action that is taking place is leading us down the path of destruction.
>
> What I did was wrong and it hurt you. I'm really very sorry and hope that some day you will forgive me. I love you, Barbara, and never want to leave you. But you still want me to leave because—why? because I hurt you so—because all of our friends know and because you know that they know your pride won't allow you to let me stay?
>
> If I go, I will never return, and if I go, it will almost surely destroy Duncan and Heather Jane. I know that if you go, the family will never survive and the effects of the marriage will go on and on until the day that we no longer exist. The children, especially Duncan and Heather, will be unstable for years and years. They will do drugs and will seek out affection in relationships that will fail. They will have difficulty in school, and that in turn will affect their careers and on and on.
>
> You say that you still love me. If that is true, and I still love you (and I do), that fact alone tells me that we can keep this marriage together. We have

had tough times before and survived, and if we did it before, we can do it again. And if you love your children, and I know that you do, you will not choose to see them hurt.

I made a terrible mistake, and you were able to show me that I was making a terrible mistake. You showed how much you wanted me to stay and pleaded with me to stay for the children's sake. I am now pleading with you to let me stay for those very same reasons. Please, Barb, don't let your hurting and your pride destroy this marriage, this family and our children. Please don't do this. I love you and I love my children. I cannot bear to see it all destroyed. If you choose to carry on on this path of destruction, do so with the knowledge that it is your decision, not mine, and that the children will know this. They will know that you made the final decision to break up the family, the home—causing them to lose that home, their older sisters and their daddy.

If you love me, if you love your children, please don't destroy us all.

We (you and I and the children) can make it work. Our love for each other and for our kids will help us through. Be brave, don't do what your mother or brothers or friends think you should do. Do what's best for us—you, I and our children.

I love you sweetheart.

Al

Barbara was by now well versed in what she called Albert's "excellent line of bullshit." She was highly skeptical, with good cause. No sooner did Albert arrive back in Canada than he quietly began organizing a secondary home, a brand-new, yellow-brick, three-bedroom backsplit on Viscount Road in a new development on the outskirts of nearby Brantford. Then he surprised everyone by announcing that on his birthday, August 9, he would fly the whole family for a week's holiday to Europe.

There was, of course, a *pro forma* invitation extended to Barbara to join them on the trip, which he knew he'd have to make so as not to make an issue of the journey which might prevent it. He could count on Barbara not wanting to come.

Barb braced for what she sensed was a subterfuge, the precise details of which she couldn't possibly imagine, though she suspected he might be trying to move money out of the country in advance of a divorce. She was overwrought with anger and worry.

On the surface, Albert's move was a master stroke, meant to communicate how carefree and unconcerned he was in the heat of conflict, but one that also dripped with money and power. Only he was in a position to demonstrate such generosity to the children, of course, for he controlled the money. Over the years, Albert Walker had come to know the intimate financial details of just about everyone with whom he had ever come into contact, but cleverly—like the precise details of his difficult early years—he had always hidden his. His accounts were always kept separate from those of Barbara. If knowledge was power, Albert knew, financial knowledge was power squared. He had always managed to guard his own financial knowledge with a dexterity that never drew attention to himself. He carried that secrecy over into business too: no one, for example, ever dealt with the United Canvest Caymans portfolio except Albert, and Albert kept those documents in his own filing cabinets under lock and key.

Predictably, Barbara turned down the European trip, and she couldn't interfere with Albert's taking the children. She and Albert had yet to formally separate, and the issue of the children's custody had only just been raised. On August 9, on Daddy's birthday, Sheena, Duncan and Heather boarded the plane with Daddy in Toronto bound for Britain.

The children knew nothing about the real reason for their

father's trip. To Duncan, now 11, and Heather Jane, only 8, it simply seemed Daddy's wonderful way of being close and loving with them by taking them on an exotic and exciting adventure. It was exotic and exciting—and they were indeed taken, but they knew none of it. In reality, this vacation was an elaborately contrived cover, an extraordinary piece of choreography mapped out, step by step, by a cunning and shrewd master who had been dancing a dance for years. Albert Walker was, much like the hymn he had sometimes sung in his very own parish church, the Lord of the Dance.

The truth was that Albert Walker needed a place to launder money—money he was even then stealing and hoarding. The British holiday would allow him to make preparations and mule some money across to an account he kept in central London. Albert was getting ready to run.

Without telling anyone, Albert Walker had long been using investors' money as if it were his own, to play with as he saw fit. He had lost a little in the '87 crash. But mostly he'd just blown it, using it to run his companies, pay for travel, fine dining, his children's dental work, anything really. Everything was fine provided he had enough money to continue to enjoy his lifestlye and pay his investors' returns at the same time. Now his company had a substantial amount of clients' promissory notes coming due, and he *didn't* have the money to pay them. He had already tried investing even more of his clients' money in outrageously risky second and third mortgages. But that hadn't worked either. He was desperate. Soon he'd be gone.

It had always seemed wrong to pry into the affairs of so righteous a man as Albert Walker—even his board of directors treated him with a deference that communicated the confidence they had in him. Board meetings were conducted with a smiling casualness; directors never really seemed to get all the information they needed ahead of time, and their repeated requests were met with polite assurances that never really delivered. It always seemed more like incompetence than calculation. Albert was, people believed, a concept person, not a detail man, and that was part of what had made him a success. It was not uncommon, for example, for meetings to be conducted by conference call, because Albert had scheduled trips to Switzerland or Calgary or the Caymans. No one could ever see at the time that Albert was actually robbing people blind. Albert was cagey, so cagey, in fact, that no one seems to remember precisely when he first fixed on the Victorian spa town of Harrogate and walked fatefully through the doors of Henry Spencer and Sons Fine Art Auctioneers. Was it one of those sunny days during his family holiday in Britain, while Sheena looked after the younger children at a hotel? Or was it some other time?

He was drawn, he told Spencer's receptionist, Elaine Boyes, by the announcement in the window of the sale of *Ben Voirlich*, by the British artist of Polish descent, Alfred de Breanski. It had sold for £21,000.

Elaine Boyes was 31 years old, and when he walked through the door, she was busy on the phone. She had never met anyone like Albert Walker before.

"Hello. How are you today?" Walker smiled charmingly. "I'm David Davis."

Albert Walker had in his possession the birth certificate of his long-standing client, the one-time feed dealer introduced to him a decade ago, who was now selling cars in Woodstock.

"And how can I help you, Mr. Davis?"

"I'm interested in seeing other paintings by de Breanski, the artist whose—"

The phone rang.

"Excuse me, Mr. Davis," then, brightly into the receiver, "Henry Spencer and Sons."

Albert Walker took a seat in the auctioneer's tiny reception area and watched Elaine Boyes with the same appraising gaze with which he watched everyone on first meeting. She seemed helpful, especially helpful, and—was it her essential nature or was it simply the job of receptionist?—she seemed subservient to the every need of others. While Albert sat, she answered phone calls, dealt in a polite and open manner with regular clients and tradesmen who came through the door; handled queries from other colleagues and referred telephone calls to still others, now and then giving a nodding smile to "Mr. Davis" to assure him that she'd quickly be back to him just as soon as she could. She seemed genial and trusting and a bit tweedy in a North Yorkshire way. She had dark hair, glasses and wore a conservative suit that made her look older than she was.

"Now, Mr. Davis, how can I help you?"

Blessed with an acute sense for personalities prime for exploitation, Albert Walker had a hunch. Even he would be awestruck, however, by the serendipitous opportunity which was about to present itself.

"I'm interested in seeing more paintings by de Breanski," Albert said. "But I've been watching you here while I've been waiting, and you really do have a talent with people. Are you always so helpful?"

Elaine Boyes blushed. She was shy and a little uncomfortable being complimented so directly by a man who had just arrived at Henry Spencer's for the first time. But this was probably just the American way, she thought. The Americans were a bit like that.

"Mr. Davis, I'm really just doing my job. It's all part of being the first—"

"No, no, no," Albert interrupted. "This is different. You've got people traipsing through here, the telephone's ringing, I'm waiting, your colleagues are coming through the office, and you treat everyone so well, individually, make them feel special. You know I—I could use someone like you."

"I beg your pardon?" Elaine said wide-eyed.

"I could really use someone like you. I'm planning on starting up a little fine arts and antiques company myself. I'm over here quite a bit now, and I'll be moving permanently from America soon and—well I know it sounds surprising, but I'm really quite a good judge of character, and I know we could work together. It would be a pleasant experience. I'd pay you well, you could travel, we could even take some instruction together down in London, at Sotheby's—one of those courses where they teach you the basics of buying and selling antiques. But of course *you* must know a lot about that already, working here."

"Not as much as I'd like," Boyes said, still flustered.

"Well I could teach you all about business and money, and we could do the Sotheby's course together, learn the ropes, you know. We could work together. I'm sure of it."

Elaine could scarcely believe what she was hearing. A man walks in the door from the States, wants to see some paintings and then offers her a job.

"Mr. Davis, you don't even know me," she smiled. "You don't even know my name."

"David Davis," Albert said, standing up to extend his soft, unwrinkled right hand, bowing slightly and smiling as he did.

"Elaine Boyes," she said, shaking hands. "Crikey, Mr. Davis, this is ridiculous. I don't know you, you don't know me. You walk through the door, offer me a job. I can't even think about changing jobs right now. I've promised my boyfriend we'll move to Canada together. That's all he thinks about is Canada. He grew up there as a young boy, and all he ever talks about is going back. It's his dream.

"Even if I were silly enough to take you up on this offer," she continued, "I couldn't work for you for more than a year, because Ron will want to go by then."

"Well—you can't blame a man for chasing a dream, can you?" Albert encouraged, almost fatherly now. "Was he born there?" he asked.

"No, no. Ron's father was a teacher in Canada. They crossed over from Liverpool when Ron was about 10. He came back in '63, when he was 18, and joined the army later—that's where he learned about electronics—but we're planning on heading off as soon as we have the money."

"Elaine," said Albert, his voice dropping to a confidential hush, "I could offer you enough money so that within a year's time, you could both just fly off."

Albert was in his element now. The wheels in his mind were clicking over with all the silent precision of a Swiss watch. There was opportunity here, he felt. He could sense it. If Ron was 18 in '63, then he and Ron were the same age. Ron could be his key to an entirely new life, a new identity, a new home, everything he wanted. He would have to be patient, though; he would have to meet Ron and get to know him. The David Davis cover Albert planned to use—was using now—was limited: he had Davis's birth certificate but nothing else. Sooner or later, Davis might need that document. He might remember and tell police he'd given it to Walker: by then a missing man. The police would come looking for him under David Davis's name.

Ron's eventual departure for Canada, however, if handled properly, could afford Walker the complete cover—a cover the police would never discover, never know about. In time, if he played his cards right, Albert could have it all: bank accounts, credit cards, a driver's licence, maybe even a British passport— and that would open the world to him. The only passport he had now was his own: Albert Johnson Walker DOB 9 Aug. 1945.

Within 30 minutes, Albert knew as much about Elaine Boyes and her boyfriend Ron—Platt turned out to be his surname—as he needed. Albert was superb during the conversation, at the very top of his game.

While Elaine would not be persuaded to take him up on his offer that day, they both agreed "to think about it." At a later date, Albert knew, both she and Ron would agree that Elaine would join "Mr. Davis" in a company he'd create, under terms she and Ron would consider generous, because Albert Walker would make them so. He would make them irresistible if he had to.

She would become the secretary and a director of the company he would control, Cavendish Corporation, be paid £1,250 per month, tax-free; she would be flown throughout Europe and indulge her hobby of photography by taking pictures of properties and antiques that Mr. Davis might be interested in buying. While there, she would do a little banking and run errands for him having to do with accounts set up on the continent. But all of that would unfold in due course. Elaine hadn't the slightest inkling of it then.

Now, he said, perhaps they both needed a little time for reflection.

"There's no pressure," he assured her, shaking hands, and he walked out the door and onto the streets of Harrogate and disappeared.

7

FINGERPRINTS

Albert should have dreaded the descent into Canada. Instead, he relished it. From all appearances, he was in the middle of a messy marital break-up, but in reality, everything was running according to plan. He returned from Britain in August 1990, with the three children in tow, looking forward to the days ahead. Albert loved being clever. It was the ultimate demonstration of his peerless superiority. It was very much as though he were starring in his own drama set to music, only he was the only person holding a copy of the score.

Barbara Walker's resilience and readiness to do battle, however, were not to be discounted. For while Albert was away, Barbara, too, had been busy. As soon as he had left for his "holiday," she revisited her lawyers and drafted a detailed affidavit seeking custody of all four children as well as the house. She had had enough. She also raised the alarm about her suspicions concerning Albert's trip, warning her lawyer that Albert was very likely trying to hive assets out of the country. It wasn't that long ago, she reminded the lawyer, that she had found the birth certificate of a Terry Hemsworth in Albert's own pants pockets. She was sure he was up to something, what precisely, she was not sure.

Barbara attached to her affidavit bank statements from three accounts Albert controlled at the Commerce Bank in Woodstock, showing liquid assets now in excess of $270,000. By virtue of the fact that he earned $120,000 per year and she but $28,000, she argued the court should order Albert to pay her tuition: she was heading back to university to get her Masters degree in Business Administration. She was steeled and ready, not just to survive but to prosper.

Barbara Walker was gallantly playing by the rules. She couldn't possibly have known what she was up against. Her husband would quickly reveal himself to be as ruthless a combatant as had ever engaged in the brutal art of divorce. It would be months before anyone would really know the enormity of his plans, and when they did, it would blow not just Barbara but everyone away.

Scarcely 24 hours back on the ground after having given the children a whirlwind tour of Britain, Albert Walker sat down on August 19 to what was surely the ugliest Sunday dinner in Walker family history. There, in the presence of Barbara, he told his 8-year-old daughter and 11-year-old son that they would now have to make a choice: your mother or me. The two older children, Jill, who was 18, and 15-year-old Sheena, had already aligned themselves with their father, and in less than two weeks' time an Ontario court judge would actually deliver them directly into Albert Walker's waiting hands.

Despite the tender ages of the two youngest, Albert had no qualms whatsoever about the moral probity of his Sunday dinner ultimatum. They didn't have to make a decision right then and there, he explained. They should think about it and let him know. That night, he spent his first night in his new secondary home on Viscount Road in Brantford.

Frightened and confused, fresh from a lovely trip to Britain with Albert and seeing their two older sisters siding with Daddy, first Heather Jane and then Duncan, in a few days' time, said they wanted to be with their father. That Friday, while Barb was away from the matrimonial home in Paris, Ontario, Albert descended on it and swept all the children into the car, disconnected the phone—imagining the latter to be yet another tidy slap in the face for Barbara—and led everyone over to his new home in Brantford. There he sat Heather Jane and Duncan down to compose—or was this dictation under pressure?—short and cutting letters to their mother in their own careful, innocent little hands.

They almost resembled school assignments, with the quality of crayon scrawled on paper. But the warmth of the medium clashed with the chill of the message.

> "Aug. Fri. 24 1990
>   Dear Mom,
>   I have decided to live with Duncan Sheena
>   Jill and dad. I hope to visit you.
>
> > > Love
> > > Heather"

When Barbara arrived on the doorstep of the Brantford backsplit that same evening, accompanied by their church minister, Mark Aitchison, she was furious. Albert promptly ordered her off the property and then, with an air of dismissive disdain, handed over the letters from the two youngest.

"They wrote these under duress," Barbara charged.

"I only told them to put down their decision in their own words," Albert said.

It was a brutal moment. Albert was in command and control, more so than Barbara knew.

Before the month was out, Albert submitted his own affidavit to the court and attached two more letters from his two oldest daughters. Sheena's was restrained, though blunt: she wrote of how she and Barbara would disagree and "often end up in a real fight," and how she didn't feel her mother showed her enough "affection." But mainly, it was the "freedom" her father offered her that seemed to win her loyalty.

"I feel that it would be better for everyone if I stayed with my father," she wrote diplomatically.

By contrast, Jill's letter was devastating. She, too, castigated Barbara as insufficiently affectionate, but she went further, painting a cruel portrait of an argumentative, scolding, penny-pinching, messy individual who was always late for everything and paid too little attention to either her own personal hygiene or that of the two youngest.

In each of the letter's 50 lines—written, it appeared, with little prompting, for it was executed in an even hand—anger was writ large.

She said her mother rarely showed any understanding of teenage problems and she accused Barbara of calling her an "ingrate, twit, bitch."

Jill's letter burned.

Albert Walker had always fanned the flames of the feud between "the two redheads," as he sometimes referred to his daughter and wife. Now it was paying dividends.

What was common about the two daughterly testimonials, however, and perhaps troubling in retrospect, was the praise for Daddy's affection. "My father shows me a lot of affection . . . and we are very close," Sheena wrote.

Jill, too, criticized Barbara for not giving her a "hug" when she needed one. "Dad . . . usually realizes that I have a problem and comforts me no matter what it is."

It sounded innocent enough. Albert Walker read these letters over carefully and brought them to his lawyer. Albert was well satisfied.

By early fall, with the heat of summer receding, the court's bitter harvest had been handed down: the Walker family was to be rent in two parts with Solomon-like dispassion. Barbara got little Heather and Duncan and, for the moment, the matrimonial home. Albert was awarded Jill and Sheena. He immediately ensconced himself in his Brantford house and appeared to begin living the life of a bachelor-father.

His planning, however, continued apace. Albert Walker had no intention of living out his days as a single parent on the outskirts of a provincial Canadian city. He was plotting his getaway. Whether intentional or not, the continuing court battle had the effect of good cover. Inquiring investors seeking a personal appointment with Mr. Walker were assured that their investments were safe in the sunny Caymans. But they understood that Mr. Walker was, well, naturally a little preoccupied, given the state of his family affairs, coupled with all the travelling he was still doing in search of venture capital.

On weekends when he wasn't away on business in Europe, he sometimes entertained the two youngest children at the Brantford home. It was part of the arrangement he and Barbara had agreed to. On one of these occasions, Albert Walker came home with some videos for them, and everyone stretched out to watch *Once Upon A Time in America*, a violent mobster movie with lots of sex, blood and murder. The film features a particularly vicious and protracted rape of a young girl.

Jenna was there with Sheena. She thought it weird that Mr. Walker would bring this kind of movie home, especially with the younger children present, let alone watch it with such passionate intensity. She was feeling a little uncomfortable again, not unlike that time in the car. With the advent of fall, she had developed a slight cough, aggravated by the silence that hung in the air—especially during the sex scenes. The atmosphere was clammy, strange.

Jenna's coughing was distracting and upsetting Mr. Walker. Impatient, annoyed and teetering on the brink of anger, Mr. Walker told her that if she didn't drink some brandy, she'd have to leave.

It was creepy. Another threatening moment with Mr. Walker. Jenna didn't want to leave and certainly didn't want to lose

Sheena's friendship by making a scene. Mr. Walker was an adult too, a parent, not someone to be challenged.

Fine, Jenna said.

Albert Walker got up, not to look for a throat lozenge or a package of medicinal cough drops in the medicine cabinet but to go to the liquor cabinet, where he poured Jenna, now 15, a glass of brandy, ostensibly to soothe her cough. She drank it in silence. When the movie was over, she would remember years later, she left and put that weird atmosphere in Mr. Walker's living room behind her. Mr. Walker was acting strangely again, and Jenna didn't want to be anywhere near him.

It was after that, on November 4, when Albert descended on the matrimonial home in search of some of his and the older girls' personal belongings, that he and Barbara very nearly came to blows. He tried to force his way in, while she tried to block. Barbara phoned the police, and Walker was subsequently arrested and charged with forcible entry. His fingerprints were taken by the Ontario Provincial Police in Brantford, and he was booked to appear in court. It was a humiliating experience. November was turning out to be a dreadful month. But there was more tension ahead.

Ever since the summer when Barbara told the board of directors of Walker Capital Corp. that Albert was up to something, the directors had been breathing down his neck, especially David Penhorwood and the Reverend Aitchison. They wanted detailed information about the company's financial dealings, and they sent Albert a lengthy letter setting out 15 demands with which Walker had to comply. One demand was that Walker no longer be able to write cheques for more than $3,000 without a co-signer. For a man like Albert, with significant cheque-writing plans ahead of him, it was a hurdle he had to clear.

Calling their demand a personal affront, Albert successfully engineered their removal and replacement at a November 23 Walker board meeting in Calgary. But by now the strain was showing. When he returned to Ontario and addressed a local managers' meeting, explaining that he planned to be away for "a couple of weeks" in December, people noticed he was perspiring. It was only days before liftoff and Albert Walker was feeling the heat.

On a grey and wintry December day, Walker called his old client, David Davis, and asked him to meet him for lunch at their usual spot out on the Woodstock strip, the Town and Country. Walker pulled up through a light, spitting snow in a recently acquired Jaguar, a sure sign of his intended permanence. No one could have possibly imagined that anyone who had just acquired a fancy foreign car might be planning on taking flight.

"I got a heck of a deal from a client who was going to lose it anyway," Walker explained to Davis.

Davis needed money again, about $35,000, for a business venture he was contemplating. Albert gave him a cheque, written on a Walker Financial account, and told him not to worry about a schedule of repayments just yet. He had a way to save Dave some money, he said. They'd work it all out when he got back.

"Heading off to Switzerland," Albert explained.

"Another business deal?"

"Yeah. Bit of a vaction too," he said. "Might do a little skiing in the Alps."

At any other table in the Town and Country, such talk would have sounded pretentious, but Albert Walker was like that. He could speak about the Caymans, Switzerland and England because he'd been there, and been there more and more frequently in the past year. Even though he had just opened yet another office in the fall—this one in Cambridge, Ontario—he was still doing an extraordinary amount of travel.

Outside along Highway 2, it might be one of those miserable grey days. But in the rarefied atmosphere in which Albert Walker lived, he could climb above the clouds, where the sun always shone, usually in a business-class seat, with a smiling flight attendant happy to offer him a glass of chardonnay or chablis, a newspaper or a magazine, keen to attend to his every need. It was a wonderful life. Not for him the major American hotel chains of the world, where you woke up in Europe but could just as easily be in Milwaukee or Muskegon. Albert always stayed in special little hotels with concierges and a sense of class: fluffy housecoats on the back of the bathroom door ready to be unlooped and slipped into and sumptuous dining rooms with linen tablecloths where he could take a comfortable seat, usually with an attractive younger woman across from him, and feel himself being looked at admiringly by others.

Seated in the humble dining room of the Highway 2 roadhouse, Albert Walker knew that soon, all of that would be his permanently. He would leave the Tupperware-coloured skies behind, escape the daily drudgery of middle-class life, leave the sameness, the confining monotony—that popular T-shirt had said it all: "DDSS: Different Day, Same Shit"—and blow Barbara away for good.

He'd run.

That humiliating experience arising out of the confrontation with Barbara still burned.

"You can't imagine what it feels like, Dave," he said. "Imagine being arrested for entering your own home—a home you bought and paid for and raised your kids in and poured money into—and then boom! The cops come in and take you down to the police station and book you on some ridiculous charge like you were a common criminal—a common criminal, for God's sake—for breaking into my own home."

Albert wasn't fulminating—the restaurant was fairly crowded—but he was quietly fuming. "They even took my fingerprints," he snarled. That lunch was the only time Davis had ever seen Walker truly angry. He would remember it for a long time to come. He thanked Walker for the $35,000 and wished him a good trip.

Albert had more decisions to make. His biggest and boldest was to take Sheena with him.

She had pleaded to go when he told her of his plan. Sheena told a friend at school, Leah Hay, that her father was thinking of leaving and had even given her $1,000 "just in case" he didn't come back. Albert had explained to Sheena how he and her mother could never live together again; how he feared she'd probably win everything in the courts. Barbara would probably bleed him dry of every penny he'd ever earned, fair and square, he said. He'd built the company. Now he stood to lose everything.

Sheena said she wanted to come with him, and Albert wanted her to come too. So they packed a trunk at the Viscount Road home and in it put his and her clothing, a special family picture album, the spool candleholders and the antique mantel clock from the Staleys and the Richardsons and had it all shipped.

Jill was sworn to secrecy.

On December 3, Albert used David Davis's social insurance number and, forging his signature, opened an account in Davis's name at a Brantford bank. In this way, if he needed to funnel money to Jill while he was away, or for any other reason, he could. The following day, December 4, the day before he was to leave on his business trip to Switzerland, Albert took the four children to dinner at Brantford's Old School House Restaurant, where he joked with Sheena openly that she should join him on his trip. Sheena only shrugged. He'd be back for Christmas, Albert said. But he was lying. If Albert executed his plan well, he wouldn't be back for this or any other Christmas. Neither would Sheena.

By now all of the component parts of his plan had been carefully put in place. He'd already taken $90,000 to Europe during his August vacation. For extra cash, he'd used a $10,000 overdraft on a joint account he and Barbara held, effectively leaving her with the debt. He'd used his American Express card to pay for more than $12,000 in British Airways tickets. He'd even made an $11,556 purchase of a diamond ring, brooch and earrings at Birk's in Toronto.

The truck driver's son who had been called stupid from an early age even left contemptuously placed clues aimed at leading everyone, especially the police, to believe that he intended to hide in Switzerland or France. There were scribbled notes from a telephone inquiry with the French consulate in Toronto about visa requirements for lengthy stays; notes about Canadian schools overseas for Sheena. There was an article from *Forbes* magazine about a Belgian-born American businessman who had defrauded others of millions before fleeing safely to Zug, Switzerland, where he lived happily ever after. Albert even took care to highlight the article in yellow. That would put them off the scent, he thought. So authentic.

By anyone's measure, it was a well thought-out plan, carefully conceived and about to be expertly executed. His years of reading espionage novels and thrillers had been helpful, and he was sure he was well on his way to pulling off one of the great getaways.

As he and Sheena boarded the British Airways overnight flight at Toronto's Lester B. Pearson International Airport, December 5, 1990, bound first for London, then on to Geneva, Albert Walker was calm and confident. He was shown to his seat, offered a small glass of champagne—fittingly celebratory, he thought—he fastened his seatbelt and glanced out the window, listening to the purr of the Rolls Royce engines. He smiled that boyish smile of his.

The 747 taxied out to the runway and took its place in line. Albert began to reflect on the execution of his plan with unadulterated pleasure. He could scarcely believe that all of the pieces had fallen into place. He'd kept inquiring investors at bay, held the directors back and bluffed and bullied his way past Barbara.

Out there in the darkness, he thought, a light would soon go on. Slowly but surely, it would begin to dawn on everyone precisely what had happened. A couple of million in investors' promissory notes would come due, and there'd be no money with which to pay them, and Albert Walker would be long, long gone.

As the rush of another jet's engines could be heard burning up the runway, up, up, up and away, the Boeing nudged forward and was now poised on the runway's apron. And there it paused.

Albert Walker rested his head back in his comfortable first-class seat and reflected on all the other things he'd done in the past several months that no one knew about and would probably never know about. For Albert Walker was getting away with more than just a few hundred thousand. In fact, Albert Walker was now a millionaire. The precise details of how he had pulled it off were nothing short of breathtaking.

8

TRUST IS EVERYTHING

Seated comfortably in the first-class cabin, Albert thought back to July 9, 1990, a hot and steamy day at the corner of King and Bay streets, the historic heart of Toronto's financial district. For the better part of a century, wealth had been won and lost at the old Toronto Stock Exchange on this corner, before the TSE moved its sprawling trading floor north and west a block. Now, amid the din of noonday traffic, Albert stood and gazed up at the shiny, towering structures of Commerce Court and across the street to the Bank of Montreal at First Canadian Place and knew that this was where he would amass his fortune. Right here. Right at this very intersection. Albert straightened his tie, brushed his lapels, gripped his black leather briefcase a little more tightly and headed straight for the door of the Canadian Imperial Bank of Commerce.

He had tried to keep his companies afloat, to keep the charade of his corporate empire going—to save face and maintain his lifestyle, if for nothing else—but it hadn't worked. His search for the "venture capital" he so badly needed to pay his Canadian clients the interest he owed them had been a bust. They'd be clamouring at the counter soon. The trip to Switzerland in May, in which he had invested so much hope in getting the cash he needed, had failed miserably. The Swiss financiers from whom he was seeking the capital injection had not been taken in by his bluster. He was out of his depth and out of his league. The numbers he'd shown them, representing potential return on investments in his company of four, six, eight and ten million dollars, had looked too good. Nor were they taken in when he said that he controlled $100 million in investors' assets when the real figure was $12 million. The Swiss sensed his shallow understanding of the financial markets. In the end, they were suspicious, and Walker came away empty-handed. Had he not had adjoining rooms with his executive assistant, Genevieve Vlemmix, at the Three Kings Hotel in Basel during his meetings, and four days of sightseeing with her later in Geneva, the entire trip would have been a waste. He had asked the Swiss lawyer who had booked the rooms to make sure they were adjoining, because, he explained, Genny was his "sister." The lawyer had faxed back and confirmed.

With his Swiss bail-out plan in ruins, it was clear: the absurd pretence he had been carrying on for years as a financial wizard would come to an end, and he would have to flee. He'd go to Europe. He'd always wanted to live there. But he wouldn't arrive empty-handed, he decided. He would gather up the remnants of the fortunes of others and take them with him. He would become a millionaire one way or another. To get away with it, though, would take an awful lot of work and planning.

Crossing the polished marbled threshold of one of the country's biggest banks, he was carrying with him a bank draft for $100,000 from a Walker company account in Woodstock. He took a seat at a customer-services desk beneath a vaulted ceiling on which the words "Industry" and "Integrity" were inscribed, and calmly told the young lady behind it he'd like to open a new account. It was his first real step on the road to escape.

Once the forms were filled out, he was silently escorted across the floor to a counter where a waiting teller took his deposit for

$100,000. Albert signed the deposit slip, retained his copy, said good-bye and left.

Ten days later, on July 19, he was back. He asked what the British currency was trading at and was told the British pound was selling at $2.14 Canadian. He signed a cheque for $21,400 and bought £10,000. He slid them into his briefcase, snapped it shut and spun the numbers on the case's lock. He smiled, nodded "Thank you," and was off, out of the Commerce building into the stunning sunshine and heat of Bay Street, heading north. He crossed Adelaide Street and turned left into 347 Bay, the offices of Friedberg & Co., a currency and precious-metals dealer. There, Albert Walker bought another £10,000, again placed them in his briefcase and moved out into the diffuse light of an increasingly hazy day. It was hot, humid and 31 degrees Celsius, and Albert Walker was perspiring, but he was light-footed and even a little light-headed with the adrenaline rush. He was off the launch pad now and might never come back to earth. From that day onward, Albert Walker was a very busy man, demonstrating the energy of someone half his age. He would soon turn 45.

The next day, a Friday, Walker picked up his new passport at the Canadian passport office at Dundas Street and University Avenue and flicked it open to his picture. The photograph was that of a big, beaming, if somewhat jowly man, with greying hair and a still-dark moustache, a man perhaps of 50, going on 55. The document was valid until July 20, 1995, but Albert Walker knew he wouldn't be needing it that long.

On Monday morning, after a weekend of thunderstorms that had broken the region's heat wave, Albert got back in his car at his matrimonial home in Paris, Ontario, and drove again to Toronto, this time to the Bank of Montreal at King and Bay, where he opened a safety deposit box. He paid $105 for the rental and was handed a key for No. 7277. Two days later, he visited the box a second time, and that evening, July 25, amid a light summer rain, he boarded a flight for London, England, for what he had told friends would be a four-day business trip. It was there he would meet Nigel Robinson and take him for dinner at the Ritz Hotel.

"Care for a drink first?" Albert asked.

To young Nigel Robinson and his wife, Sheila, seated at a table in the dining room of the magnificent Ritz Hotel on crowded Picadilly, Albert Walker was the epitome of the North American entrepreneurial class. He was good-looking, grey-haired and finely dressed, and his every gesture seemed to communicate elegant confidence. Clearly, he came from money. Why then, Nigel wondered, was he interested in renting their modest home in Melbourne Grove in a working-class district of southeast London?

"I run a large insurance and investment firm in Canada," Albert explained, "and I need to have a base for European operations I'm planning. Getting too big now and have to spread my wings a bit. I've always loved London. Such a great city." The dining room shone with light, white linen and crystal as waiters silently weaved their way through the tables amid the hum of a dozen discreet conversations. Mr. Walker ordered a bottle of chardonnay and, on tasting it, signalled his approval to the wine steward, and he and the Robinsons drank a toast. Nigel and Sheila had never dined at the Ritz before. They couldn't believe their luck. A job opportunity for Sheila had come up that would take her to Southampton, and she and Nigel had decided to let their London home for a year and temporarily move down there. Nigel, who worked for one of the London boroughs, would commute. It wasn't long after listing it that the real estate agent phoned saying a Canadian businessman had been to see the house, his references checked out—there was even a letter from a woman deacon from a church in Canada—and a dinner meeting was arranged with Walker at the Ritz Hotel.

"And will your wife be moving over?" Nigel asked.

Albert Walker hesitated and bowed slightly, as though someone had hit him in the chest with a sudden and unexpected blow.

He looked up, his eyes filling with tears, and started to say something but stopped. He was struggling for air.

"She died," he said. "I'm sorry," and he got up and left the table.

Nigel and Sheila were embarrassed. They had only asked out of politeness, but Mr. Walker had broken down so quickly, they were completely unable to respond. Moments later, he returned more composed, although his eyes were red with weeping.

"We didn't mean to be so insensitive," Sheila said. "We're so sorry. She must have been extraordinary."

"Oh, she was," Albert said. "But it's okay. I'm fine. Really."

As dinner progressed, Mr. Walker grew more upbeat, explaining there was a new love in his life, a woman he'd recently met in Switzerland. He told a romantic story about having bumped into her at a magazine stand in an airport and, weeks later, of spending a wonderful weekend with her in Paris at the posh Georges V Hotel. Albert reached into his wallet and showed them a photograph of a very attractive woman with dark, shoulder-length hair who appeared to be perhaps 10 or 15 years younger than he. She was beautiful, they remarked.

Walker said he was anxious to establish a home in London and bring his three daughters over to educate them here. His roots went back to this country, he noted. He had always felt more closely linked to the United Kingdom than to Canada. A London base would allow him to develop and look after his European business interests.

After dinner, Albert invited the young couple up to his sumptuous room and asked if there would be a discount on the lease if he were to pay it all right then and there. He wasn't certain when he would move in, he said, but it would likely be fall or early winter. The Robinsons were flexible and agreed that a discount of about 25 per cent seemed reasonable. Walker wrote out a cheque for £10,000 on his British account and said he'd be back in a week or two with one of his daughters, just to let her have a look at the house.

"I'm sure you can imagine how it is for a man my age with young daughters," he said. "I have to make sure they like it too."

The Robinsons deposited the cheque the next day, and it quickly cleared. Whatever else they might have thought about Mr. Walker, his money was good.

The same day, prior to boarding the plane at Heathrow to return to Canada in time for Sheena's birthday, Albert Walker carefully penned his "heartfelt" letter to Barbara, pleading with her to forgive all his past transgressions and give their marriage another chance. It was guile on a grand scale. "I love you, sweetheart," Albert signed off.

All that summer and fall, before boarding this final flight to England December 5, 1990, Albert Walker kept a hectic pace, jetting back and forth across the Atlantic, visiting banks, making deposits, transferring money, buying foreign currencies, purchasing gold, opening safety deposit boxes. Everyone in his office thought his busy cycle of overseas trips was simply part of his relentless pursuit of foreign investment. No one could have possibly imagined what he was really up to. No one could have known that he was actually stealing his clients' money, moving it to Europe and plotting his escape. For on the surface of things, Albert Walker's life seemed so extraordinarily crammed and complicated, there hardly seemed room to jam in anything else. Between his personal life, with his impending marital break-up and affair with Genevieve, and his professional life, jetting about Europe and planning yet another office opening, it was life lived to the fullest. Beneath all of that, however, secretly, stealthfully, Albert Walker's master plan of fraud moved relentlessly forward. His bankers and brokers knew that he was cashing bonds and moving money, but they believed he was dealing in good faith on behalf of clients. They were mistaken.

The summer of 1990 was a time of turbulence, nationally and internationally. Every time Walker boarded another trans-

Atlantic flight, the newspapers were full of it: Mohawk warriors in Quebec, after a confrontation with police, had barricaded themselves in at a reserve near Oka, sealing off Montreal's Mercier Bridge in the process. Native Canadians elsewhere were threatening to cut transmission lines and blockade highways in solidarity. In Newfoundland, a repentant Catholic archbishop confessed his failure to curb the widespread sexual abuse of children by priests. And in the Middle East, Saddam Hussein's tanks overran the oil-rich emirate of Kuwait, prompting George Bush to organize a multinational force to counter the invasion. On August 7, Saddam declared Kuwait annexed, promising that Iraqis would "fight to the death" to defend their claim. The world waited and watched.

No one was watching Albert Walker, though. That very day, August 7, Albert walked into Friedberg & Co. once again and bought five 10-ounce gold bars. The invasion of Kuwait had driven up the price of gold, and it cost Walker $452.40 an ounce— almost $23,000. It's convertability, however, anywhere at any time, made it invaluable insurance. He might need it down the road. Walker tucked the bars into his briefcase, moved out into the summer sunshine and headed for his safety deposit box at King and Bay. Inside the Bank of Montreal, he unlocked the box and spun the numbers of the briefcase's lock to 0-0-7, opened it up and carefully slid the gold bars inside. He hadn't read a James Bond novel in years and didn't need to. He was living one now.

The next morning, Walker rose early and went to yet another financial institution: the Credit Suisse Bank, also in the towering Commerce Court complex, only a mezzanine away from his own Bank of Commerce. He wouldn't be able to physically lug everything with him across the Atlantic. That would be too risky. Electronic bank transfers would do the job better. So Albert opened an account at the Credit Suisse in Toronto with $20,000 from his Bank of Commerce account, had it converted into Swiss francs and instructed the Credit Suisse to organize an account for him in Geneva and have the francs transferred there. It was a test run. If it worked, Walker decided, he'd move more. The bankers promised to confirm receipt of the funds in Geneva the moment they landed.

His Swiss account now open, Albert drove home to Paris, Ontario, and began packing his bags for his U.K. holiday with the children. He, Sheena, Duncan and Heather were to fly out the next day—August 9, his birthday. Barbara had decided to remain at home. But as Walker and his children sat in Toronto's international airport, waiting for their boarding announcement, Albert's blood pressure soared. Gazing down the room, he saw Barbara striding toward him in a fury. Had she learned of his plans of escape? Did she discover the safety deposit box? Had the Credit Suisse phoned home?

No. None of it. Barbara had simply wanted to wish the children an enjoyable vacation. When she'd arrived home late that afternoon and found the house empty, she sped off toward the airport, arriving just in time to say good-bye. Albert breathed easier. Barbara might have had suspicions, but she didn't know of his plans. Everything was still on track.

While in Britain, Albert took the children to visit Tom and Ann Chadwick in Edinburgh, longtime friends from the period when he and Barbara had lived there briefly in 1970. He, Sheena, Duncan and Heather stayed at the Norton House Hotel. They couldn't visit long, Albert said. He had business appointments to keep. Later, he came around to the house in East Dulwich again, just as he'd said he would, and introduced Nigel Robinson to a young woman he said was his daughter. All told, the nine days in Britain had been a whirlwind trip, but productive.

Back in Canada, Albert found the transfer of Swiss francs had gone without a hitch, and he resumed planning immediately. He informed the Credit Suisse in Toronto that he intended to start a business in Switzerland, which would necessitate the transfer of much larger sums. He'd need a good corporate lawyer. Could the bank's Geneva office recommend one? Finally, Albert advised the Geneva bankers that all future correspondence should be addressed to him at 50 Melbourne Grove, East Dulwich, London, SE22, England.

Albert Walker was ready now for the big push.

In the last weeks of September, he phoned his Ontario broker and organized the sale of $460,000 worth of bearer bonds he was holding for investors. Then he transferred $400,000 of that into his Geneva account. The following day, he beamed another $125,000 across. Those transfers of $525,000 totalled more than 600,000 Swiss francs.

Two weeks later, on Wednesday, October 10, he visited his safety deposit box at King and Bay for the last time. He locked it securely before leaving and walked away with the key.

On the surface of things, Albert was fighting and feuding with Barbara, contesting custody of the children, moving house, having affairs and jetting about in search of investment capital. Beneath the surface, in Albert's private underworld, he was acting out the drama of his life.

By the time he and Sheena boarded BA flight 092 for London, England, at Toronto's Lester B. Pearson Airport on December 5, he had stolen more than $2 million in less than six months. He had transferred close to $1 million to his Swiss account, muled out as much as $700,000 in gold, pounds and French and Swiss francs, and probably burned through the rest. He visited his safety deposit box nine times, travelled to Europe at least seven times—tonight's flight would be the eighth—and made another mysterious trip to Mexico. He told friends this trek to Puerta Vallarta was under doctor's orders. "Exhaustion," Albert said. On October 30, he presented himself at the counter of the Barclay's Bank in Grand Cayman and deposited $6,725 U.S. into his private bank account there. From July through December, Albert Walker had demonstrated an almost animal-like energy. If he wasn't exhausted, he had reason to be.

In the midst of this flurry of activity, he'd even managed to put the touch on one of the new board members, John Moran, whom he'd got to replace one of the directors he'd removed. Al assured Moran that his cheque for $45,000 would go straight into Walker company stock. Instead, it went straight into Walker's own account. As the crowning gesture of his contempt for Moran, before Albert flew abroad, he announced that John would be in charge while Albert, the CEO, was away. It was Walker's last laugh. It would be only weeks before investor panic set in and the lawyers laid siege. There, behind the counter, they'd find trusting John.

Trust. During his business years in Canada, everyone trusted Albert Walker, and trust, Albert knew, had meant everything. It was really how it all began, how he'd learned the ropes: how people, even bright and well-educated people, could casually hand over large sums of money, sometimes their life savings, to someone they didn't even know, and say, "Here. Take care of it. I trust you." That was how he had taken advantage of the Wilsons. It was his first real experience with financial trusts.

Albert had met Dr. Bob Wilson, a graduate in medicine from the University of Toronto, in the 1970s. By 1980, when Wilson and his wife, Leda, decided to set up an $80,000 trust fund for their daughter Mary to ensure her an income of $800 per month in perpetuity, they turned to 35-year-old Albert Walker to organize it. The Walkers had gained quite a reputation locally as a hardworking, churchgoing business couple. Wilson believed Albert was a man of promise and would probably make a million some day. Walker soon realized that as long as the Wilson daughter got her monthly cheque, he could pretty well do as he pleased with the Wilson money. Over time, no one asked questions or demanded original documents. They simply believed whatever statements they were sent. They trusted him. That was the whole idea.

Albert began to dream bigger dreams.

In 1982, he developed an offshore fund aimed, he said, at delaying and diverting tax for investors. He called it United Canvest Corporation (Cayman) Ltd., and he and Barbara flew down to the Caribbean to meet with lawyers and sign the incorporation papers. Soon Albert was advising clients to get in on the ground floor of UCC, his new and profitable investment vehicle. The circulars he issued explained that UCC could offer significant tax savings because it didn't declare annual dividends. All interest earned was driven back into the company, increasing the investor's per-share value. When the investor cashed out, half of the capital gain would be tax-free under Canadian tax law. The other half was technically taxable, but—given the fund's offshore status—some felt it was a personal call whether or not to declare it. Most importantly, the fund's security was rock-solid, since, according to the circular, "United invests primarily in high-quality money-market instruments."

Over the years, people gave Albert at least $2.7 million to be invested in UCC. Probably less than $100,000 of it ever made it to the Caymans. Many of the investors weren't even registered. In fact, the offshore fund didn't even meet government regulations. Albert did pretty well what he'd wanted with that money too. Years later, forensic accountants would speculate he probably wasn't stealing right from the beginning, just mismanaging it; but by early 1988, it looked a lot like outright theft. Innocent investors like Genevieve Vlemmix's own grandmother and mother, Blanche Goodyn and Odette van der Wolf, were taken for more than $500,000. They, too, trusted Albert.

During that time, it had been challenging for Walker to keep the UCC records hidden from Barbara and anyone else who might realize what he was up to. It was more challenging still, at the very end, to remove the records and destroy them. But Albert accomplished that too—just barely, as it turned out. Barbara almost laid her hands on them during a confrontation over the children at Albert's Viscount Road home in Brantford, the night the Reverend Aitchison had accompanied her, but when Albert appeared on the brink of violence, Barbara and the Reverend left. Barbara was sure she had seen some documentation, but she had no chance to get it. As a consequence, Albert knew no one would ever be able to unravel what happened to the $2.7 million. In time, even he would forget, he'd diverted so much of it into bonds, non-interest bearing accounts—where it languished until Albert could figure out what to do with it—and risky second and third mortgages. In desperation, Albert had pumped more than $1 million of his clients' money into perilous mortgages and told them nothing about it.

He had been willing to gamble more of his investors' savings in the hope of gaining back some of what he'd lost during his multiyear spending spree. To farm that million out in the form of mortgages, Albert had used a shell company he'd set up in 1986, 673575 Ontario Ltd., making sure to keep his own name off all the paperwork. He'd appointed one of the young women in his office, Renée Devereux, as sole director, and made sure she was always kept in the dark. Oh yes, Renée. More than once in the office, he'd laid his hands on her shoulders on the pretence of wanting to give her a relaxing backrub, but she'd always pulled away. Mr. Walker's roving hands were a well-known problem by then.

Before he'd set off for the airport with Sheena that morning, December 5, Albert had had an argument on the telephone with Renée.

"I want to know what it means, Mr. Walker," Renée almost shouted down the phone. "I want to know what's going on." She was more frightened than furious. A document had just arrived by registered mail, and her name was on it. It was from a company called Trans American Life, notifying her, as director of 673575 Ontario Ltd., that Trans American was about to pull the plug on a development project in St. Catharines, Ontario, pushing it into power of sale. The numbered company she headed had almost $1 million tied up in it, the letter informed her. All of that now could be wiped out.

"Renée, don't worry about it."

"What do you mean 'Don't worry about it?' My name is on the paperwork, and I don't even know a thing about it. I don't even know who these people are. I don't know anything. I want to see you now. Now, before you go."

"Renée," Walker said, his voice turning stern and staccato, "I said don't worry about it. It's none of your business. I'll talk to you about it when I get back."

Albert was getting out just in time. Who would have imagined his risky mortgage scam would be unveiled on the very day he was going to escape? Fortunately for Albert, however, Renée trusted him too, just like all the staff and all the UCC investors and, indeed, just like everyone else with whom Albert had ever had contact—the innocent and naive who succumbed to his charm, and who had then been stripped clean for whatever advantage Albert might find.

Somewhere down the line, Albert knew, the cover would come off it all, the ill-advised mortgage scheme, his cocked-up investments, the Caymans fiasco, everything. Investigators would descend on the Caymans, find the UCC account dry and discover the postal drop, where he hadn't bothered to pick up the mail since 1985. He'd never needed to. In the very end, UCC was just a front for Albert Walker.

In the Woodstock office, employees had always told clients who wished to invest in the Caymans, "UCC? Oh that's Al's baby. You'll have to speak directly with him." Now, when they wanted to speak with him—and they would soon—he'd be gone.

He'd had a great run, though, and there had been memorable high points. Nineteen eighty-nine had been a classic: a year that opened and closed with bookend land sales that Albert engineered for his old friends from his Ayr days, the Staleys and the Richardsons, giving him direct access to almost $10 million. He'd set a January closing date for the Staley's sale, and Albert was happier, perhaps, than he had ever been in his life. He invested almost $3.7 million of the $3.9 million sale for Bob Staley, his wife, Betty, and her mother, Marjorie Richardson, of which more than $500,000 went straight into United Canvest. "Offshore," he told them.

Not long afterward, Betty's brother Bill Richardson phoned up. Did Al think he could work the same sort of deal for them? Walker engineered a bidding war that earned the Richardsons

$5.8 million. About $5.1 million was handed over to Walker to invest, and $1.5 million was pumped directly into UCC. Or that's what he told them. There was no written contract. Everything had been done on a handshake. Al was good at that.

Bill and Sheila's deal closed in December 1989, capping the most extraordinary year in Albert Walker's career. He had begun the decade as a dreamer, an impoverished, self-taught entrepreneur trying to make ends meet. At the end of the decade, he was a man awash in other people's money. Awash, as well, in their trust. Everyone trusted Al. Everyone. Except, in the end, Barbara.

Gazing out the window of the Boeing 747 now, December 5, Albert ruminated over how she had almost blown it for him. It was Barbara who had undermined all the trust people had ever had in him. In the midst of his wonderful scheming, she had begun a whispering campaign, warning others that he was actually capable of bolting with their money. She was the one who had set them running after him, resulting in his almost being caught.

His November arrest and fingerprinting in the aftermath of their shoving match at the matrimonial home hadn't bothered him much. Sheena received her first-ever prescription for birth control pills, and the next day, November 28, the day he was supposed to appear in court in Brantford, Albert drove to Toronto instead to purchase two first-class tickets for him and Sheena costing $6,271 each.

What bothered Al most about the whispering campaign was that it had inspired the Staleys and the Richardsons to begin hounding him for a meeting to explain what had happened to all their money. Why hadn't they received statements showing that the interest due to them in April had been paid up, they wanted to know? That was the one meeting, Albert knew, he could never pull off. He'd sent letters and spread sheets to both couples, hoping to confuse and placate them, but neither were satisfied. They'd even found basic mathematical errors in Albert's numbers and shamed him by telling him so. It had all been so embarrassing. The Richardsons had a hunch that Albert had skimmed $165,000 off the top of their sale for himself. Aggravating matters further was the Wilsons' lawyer, Barney Lawrence, who seemed to be on a rampage, demanding a detailed accounting from Walker of every transaction he'd ever made with the Wilson money since 1980. Lawrence said he wouldn't stop until he found out where every penny had gone. He was like a Tomahawk missile homing in on a target. He'd already wrested power-of-attorney from Walker. He was getting closer by the day. All of that trouble, every last bit of it, Barbara had begat, Albert thought.

That wasn't the end of it either. Albert suspected her whispering campaign had even scotched his last-ditch attempts to sell the Walker company to an entrepreneur he knew named David Holden. Albert had confidently opened negotiations in the fall, asking Holden for $5 million. Albert was tired, he said. He wanted to retire. But Holden hesitated, couldn't decide, and with time running out, on December 3, Albert finally came to Holden cap-in-hand, saying he would accept a cash offer of $500,000 U.S. for the company, provided the money was transferred to his Swiss account within 24 hours. Holden smelled desperation and backed off. Albert was furious.

The drama with his old friends the Staleys and the Richardsons, however, was definitely the worst part. Only last February Albert had gone skiing with Bob Staley in Switzerland. Now, 10 months later, he was about to fly off with his money. As the two couples continued to politely press, Walker finally agreed to a summit with them both at the Richardson home December 5—today—the very day of his escape. The foursome had waited six hours for Walker to show, and if Albert had his way, they would wait forever. Unbeknownst to them, only the day before, he'd pillaged their accounts a final time, taking $45,000 from the Richardsons' and another $55,000 from a joint account held by Marjorie and Betty.

Albert had led them like sheep, not to the slaughter, of course, but to be fleeced. And they were fleeced, and in time, they'd feel foolish and angry. Some might say they were naive and gullible, but from their point of view, they were trusting. They believed in trust. Albert had banked on that.

Now as the revs of the Boeing's engines pitched a final time, the plane jolted and started to bolt down the runway, snowflakes streaking through the beams of the plane's lights.

In the first-class cabin, takeoffs are smooth and soundless and almost dream-like. While back in steerage, people hear the clunk and scream of every aeronautical part—the shudder of wings, the groan of the landing gear—first-class passengers are gently buffeted by an undercurrent of heavenly winds.

As far to the front as Albert Walker was seated that night, his ears were finely tuned to the whir of wheels racing through the dark across the tarmac. When the plane reared its head and its engines roared for the final thrust, Albert Walker knew the precise moment at which the Boeing's landing gear lifted and cleared the ground, for Albert Walker was now well and truly aloft and soaring.

The plane climbed and the twinkling lights fell farther and farther below, and finally, Albert Walker passed up through a layer of cloud and was gone.

9

GUILE AND DISGUISE

LONDON, ENGLAND

A hazy, winter sun peaked over the horizon at 7:50 a.m., Thursday, December 6, bleakly illuminating a London skyline shrouded in fog. When the plane finally docked, Albert and Sheena disembarked and walked down the long corridors of Heathrow's Terminal 4 to join the throngs of others awaiting customs and immigration clearance.

"And how long do you intend to stay in the United Kingdom?" the immigration officer asked, glancing at Walker's passport and swiping it through a computer.

The digital readout confirmed Albert's essential details: **Issuing country:** CANADA. **Number:** MB898646. **Surname:** Walker. **Given names:** Albert Johnson. **Date of birth:** 9 Aug. 45.

"Just overnight," Walker replied. "We're heading on to Geneva tomorrow." The official flicked open Sheena's passport, computer-scanned it, handed both documents back and waved them through.

It was exhilarating getting past the customs barrier. It was one thing to get out of a country, quite another to get into one. Now the door to Europe's premier gateway was flung open, and Albert Walker waltzed through. He and Sheena took the escalator down into the swirl and hum of the luggage carousels, and Albert began going over details of what had to be his first order of business: covering his tracks.

It was true that when Albert had stood before the customs official, he was holding two tickets for Geneva departing the next morning, but as soon as he checked into his double room at the Ritz Hotel, he telephoned British Airways, cancelled the tickets and rebooked them to depart for Geneva December 12. Albert had business to attend to in London. Once he finished up, he would fly on to Switzerland to look after his newly transferred wealth and, at the same time, make sure his trail ended there.

He didn't cancel the two first-class return tickets to Canada, however. He and Sheena were still scheduled to return to Toronto on December 14. Any cancellation now would send a distant early warning signal to any authority who might be thinking of pursuing him. Consequently, the return reservations stood.

In London, it was the dawn of a new day. The previous evening, when he and Sheena had left Toronto, it had been freezing and there were snow flurries. Here, however, it was warmer, more welcoming, with a forecasted high of 6 degrees Celsius. As the day unfolded, there were patches of brilliant sunshine.

The London Times of Thursday, December 6, trumpeted the fact on its front page that Salman Rushdie had defied Islamic death threats and given a public reading the night before, with bodyguards present, at the Waterstone's bookshop in the leafy neighbourhood of Hampstead. Inside the paper, the debate continued about the centrality of the novel in British life: Was it slipping, a commentator worried? Deeper still in the paper, columnist Clement Freud wrote a wonderfully whimsical piece on a visit he'd made to Totnes, in beautiful Devon, where he'd dined as a guest at the pub of British foodwriter and raconteur Keith Floyd.

It wasn't just the weather that was different in London. Britain was another world, and Albert Walker was determined to be enveloped by it.

For the moment, however, there was a problem that had to be addressed immediately. The plan to rent Nigel Robinson's home on Melbourne Grove in East Dulwich had had to be scrapped. Prior to Walker's leaving Canada, Robinson's agent in England had faxed the tenancy agreement—made out in Sheena's name— to one of Walker's Ontario offices. It had come through to Canada in plain view of staff. When one young woman brought it to Walker's attention, he was forced to explain it away as nonsense and confusion. The bottom line was clear: the plan had been exposed. Once he'd fled, he knew, someone would remember that fax. He had to find another place to live.

It had been an expensive experience. The rent cheque Walker had given Robinson had already been cashed, and the money gone. Walker was out £10,000, more than $20,000, and had nothing to show for it.

Meanwhile, the Robinsons moved down to Southampton as they'd said they would. They were puzzled as to why Walker didn't show up. His mail certainly was. Every six weeks or so, Nigel Robinson would look in on the property and find scads of it, lying just inside the door beneath the mail slot. There were statements from the NatWest Bank in London, from the Credit Suisse in Switzerland and other mail that looked like bank statements from Brazil or Colombia. Robinson kept it, thinking Walker would eventually show up. But weeks passed. Was Walker involved in something he shouldn't be, Nigel wondered? Arms trading or drug dealing perhaps? The entire experience of meeting Mr. Walker at the Ritz had been so peculiar, he thought. While Robinson continued collecting Walker's mail, Walker himself was in another part of the city, busily scouting new accommodation.

Walker visited a number of real estate agents shortly after his arrival and almost secured a flat in south Hampstead, near Hampstead Heath, the city's most outstanding natural park. It was complicated, though: the young couple there had just had their first child; they were flying to America for Christmas, then moving to Italy, and their dates were still up in the air.

During his first fugitive days abroad, Albert Walker maintained some telephone contact with Canada. He didn't want to raise suspicions or set off alarm bells. So he phoned the home of John Moran, whom he'd left in charge, and explained that he hadn't flown on to Geneva yet because of weather conditions. He would be soon, he said, and he'd be back in Canada in time for dinner at the Morans' on December 15. He was looking forward to it. He also dialled 519-758-0683 and spoke to Jill at the Viscount Road home in Brantford. Jill was to tell no one, but he would maintain contact with her.

Albert checked out of the Ritz December 12, paying a bill of £1,700, more than $3,400 for the six-day stay, and he and Sheena took the 75-minute flight to Geneva. He hadn't secured a flat in London before leaving, but he had some good leads. In Geneva, that spiritless city of bankers and U.N. bureaucrats on Lac Leman, he and Sheena booked into the Hotel Le Warwick on the rue du Lausanne, and the following day, the two drove to a bank where Albert visited one of his safety deposit boxes.

Despite the drabness of the city, Albert loved Switzerland, the snowcapped Alps, the neatly terraced vineyards, the gnarled and pruned chestnut trees that lined the boulevards of every major town and the fussy, formal Swiss themselves. Where else could discretion, privacy and secrecy be promoted as national assets? That was the real reason Albert had come here. The countryside's shuttered alpine cottages, with their clay-tiled roofs and neatly kept flower boxes, might be as pretty as a picture. But it was the Swiss banking secrecy laws that were the real attraction. Albert could squirrel away his newly acquired money here, move it around, and no one would ever be able to get at it or even know about it.

From his room at the Hotel Warwick, he could see all the way down to Lac Leman and the wall of buildings that lined the lakeside, topped with the towering neon signs announcing to all the world the pride, precision and discretion of Swiss commerce: Rolex, Bucherer, Blancpain, Credit Suisse, the Union Bank of Switzerland. There was comfort here, and class. Albert liked that. And there was money.

Albert picked up the phone in his hotel room and dialled the office of his Calgary lawyer. He called the south Hampstead couple with the flat in London. Then he phoned the Hong Kong Bank of Canada in downtown Toronto, located in First Canadian Place, steps from the corner of King and Bay. Later, he phoned the bank again.

The next day, he dined at the five-star Hotel Metropole, across from the English Gardens, taking care to pay with his personal Visa credit card so that when the bill eventually arrived back in Canada, it would be passed on to investigators trying to pick up his trail. By then, of course, he would have moved on.

After two nights in Geneva, on the morning of December 14— the day he and Sheena were to have returned to Canada—Albert checked out of the Warwick Hotel, and he and Sheena headed for Geneva's Cointrin airport. There, as a diversion, Albert bought two British Airways tickets, Geneva-London return, using his American Express corporate credit card. That bill, too, he knew, would find its way into the hands of the police, reinforcing the idea that he had fled to Switzerland and stayed.

He and Sheena were headed elsewhere.

Albert purchased another set of tickets, and with them, he and Sheena boarded a flight for Paris, where they stayed a single night. There, Albert posted a letter to his Ontario divorce lawyer. An envelope with a French postmark, he knew, would also sow confusion back home.

Albert Walker was entirely in his element now: he was in Europe, he was spending lavishly and—he was certain—he was making fools of others. He was delighted.

The following day, Saturday, December 15, the day he was supposed to dine at the home of Walker board member John Moran back in Canada, Albert and Sheena Walker took the train from Paris's Gare du Nord, across the storm-lashed winter landscape of northern France to Calais, crossing the English Channel by ferry, then continuing on to London by train. A rare and raging winter storm was sweeping Europe, cancelling flights and causing traffic pileups in several countries. Nature itself, it seemed, was providing Walker with the perfect cover. People back home would think he was caught up in the storm, temporarily cut off from communication, understandably out of touch. Instead, he had carried out a well thought-out plan. All clues to his whereabouts led to Switzerland. Once there, he and Sheena embarked on a long and circuitous route back to England, leaving no tracks across the snow-covered terrain. He had used cash when necessary; he had travelled by land, air and sea; and soon, he would evaporate into the thin, frigid air of Europe's worst winter. By rights, Albert Walker had every reason to believe he would never be found. Ever.

"I want to speak to Sheena," Barbara said. "Put her on."

"I told you she's not here," said Jill. "She's at the mall."

"She's always at the mall," Barbara fumed, frustrated. "Ask her to call me when she gets in."

"I will," said Jill and hung up.

It had been going on like this for days back in Canada. It was still mid-December 1990, and Barbara didn't have the slightest inkling where her second oldest daughter was, let alone that she'd left the country.

Ever since the Walkers' marital breakdown, Sheena and 18-year-old Jill had been living with their father at his secondary home on Viscount Road, in nearby Brantford. Now, unbeknownst to Barbara, Jill was covering for her father and Sheena, who had left the country. Before departure, Albert had lectured the children on loyalty. "Never rat on family," he'd said. Jill's loyalty was firm. Albert had never spared any expense on her. In the months leading up to his final flight, he had organized the purchase of a $7,500 Chevrolet Cavalier for her, left her the keys for his plush, red Jaguar and paid for some expensive dental work. Later, in court documents, Barbara would swear she was certain Albert had even paid for breast implants for Jill as early as December 1988. Jill was only 16 at the time.

As December 1990 wore on and there was still no contact with Sheena, Barbara began to suspect something was definitely wrong. It wasn't like Sheena not to return calls. It wasn't like her to freeze Barbara and the family out. Sheena had never liked the idea of her parents' separation and had always had difficulty coping with it.

Finally, a week before Christmas, Heather and Duncan returned from a visit to Jill's to tell Barbara they had spoken to their father and Sheena on the phone. Barbara confronted Jill. Yes, it was true. Sheena was out of the country. But it was no big deal, Jill explained. The two had simply gone on a ski and business trip to Switzerland. They'd be back December 19.

Coincidentally, on December 19, while driving her father's Jaguar in nearby Cambridge, Jill had an accident. She escaped with a dozen stitches, but the car was destroyed. Nothing was said that day about Albert and Sheena returning, nor did they return. Nor did they return the next day. Or the next. Something was seriously wrong.

When Christmas came and passed and there was no call from Albert and Sheena, Barbara called the police. It was December 27.

In the quiet post-Christmas period at the local Brantford police station, the young constable who took Barbara's call acted swiftly. After a detailed interview with Mrs. Walker, he called the RCMP at Lester B. Pearson International Airport in Toronto. They confirmed with British Airways that Walker and daughter held first-class tickets Toronto-London-Geneva return, purchased with an American Express card. They had landed in London December 6 and travelled on to Geneva December 12. Then the trail went dead.

"Apparently the return portion of the ticket hasn't been used yet," the RCMP officer told Brantford. "They're full-fare, first-class tickets. Basically open-ended. Mr. Walker and his daughter could use the return tickets any time, I guess. Or even change them."

The American Express people were as helpful as they could be, given the law.

"Constable, the rules are that I'm not supposed to give you anything without a warrant," the Amex manager said over the phone. "I could get into serious trouble for this. But if you just hang on a second, I'll see what I can do."

A few taps on the keyboard, and Albert Walker's Amex account flashed up on the screen. Yes, there were some charges in Switzerland, he said. There was a car rental in Glattbrugg, a stay at the Hôtel le Chandelier in Geneva and what looked like a dinner at the Café du Théâtre, also in Geneva.

"I can't give you dates," he said. "I'm not even supposed to give you this. I hope you understand."

The young constable sent a detailed brief to Interpol's Canadian offices in Ottawa, and they, in turn, dispatched a complete report to both the RCMP's attaché at the Canadian embassy in Bern, Switzerland, as well as to Interpol's Swiss office. Sheena was now officially a missing person. Albert would soon be listed as a wanted man. Within 48 hours of Barbara Walker's call to the Brantford police, Interpol Switzerland had good, clear photographs of father and daughter, a very good physical description of both and a short list of places where Walker was known to have used his credit card.

The Canadian police were now only two weeks behind Albert Walker. The date was December 29, 1990. That very day, Albert and Sheena Walker were moving into their new home in London.

When the train from snowbound Paris had first arrived at London's Charing Cross station December 15, Albert and Sheena took a taxi to an unpretentious, short-lease flat in Rosary Gardens, South Kensington, and Albert signed in as David Davis. He had found the flats, as he had found almost everything in life: through reading. They were listed in Frommer's guide book. Here, he and Sheena agreed that henceforth, she would be known as Noël Davis, his daughter. No one should ever be taken into their confidence and told the truth, Albert explained. The secret to their success was secrecy itself.

During that first week in London, Albert found a firm that specialized in setting up small companies, and he bought one off the shelf, as it were, called Cavendish Corporation, the company he'd need to launder all the money he'd moved out of Canada and transferred to Switzerland. Albert knew he couldn't launder his kind of sums as an individual. He needed a corporate cover. Cavendish was officially registered December 21, 1990, and incorporated two weeks later.

He also landed the long-term accommodation he'd wanted, and on December 29, David and Noël Davis moved into a tidy, two-bedroom, furnished garden flat on the corner of Maxwell Gardens and Moore Park Road in the London borough of Fulham. The flat was just around the corner from the Fulham-Broadway tube station. Canada was lost now, behind the fog, the flurries and the fury of winter storms. Canada was moving into memory. London was home.

Barbara Thomson, the agent from whom Albert had rented the flat on Moore Park Road, found David Davis utterly charming the day he arrived to view the property. He'd read the ad in *The Sunday Times*, telephoned, introduced himself as Davis and arranged to view it the following day. Because he was so soft-spoken and courteous and immaculately dressed, Barbara didn't find it extraordinary when he explained that he and his daughter wished to move in "immediately." In fact, he was so polite and poised that when he asked Barbara if she minded him paying cash, she remarked that while it was "highly unusual," she'd check with the owners.

"Of course, you'll need a reference," she insisted.

"Oh, that's no problem," Davis replied with a casual wave of the hand. "My solicitor will vouch for me."

The owners did not mind cash, they told Barbara, provided she found Davis trustworthy. She did, and the next day, David Davis showed up with his daughter Noël, his luggage, a bag containing almost £2,400 in cash—1,200 for a month's rent and 1,200 for deposit—and moved in. So began a curious acquaintanceship.

"Naturally, you'll have to arrange to take over the gas, electricity and telephone accounts," Barbara reminded him, as Davis hunched over the table to sign the lease.

"Oh no, no, no, no," Mr. Davis murmured, shaking his head. "I can't do that, Barbara. We'll have to make some arrangement. You see . . ." and David Davis began to explain why he'd insisted on paying cash in the first place. He and his wife had owned a bank in Canada, he said. There had been a divorce. He was the one who had single-handedly built the bank into an empire before they'd sold it. Now his former wife was pursuing him for a bigger piece of the pie than was her due. That's why he'd fled Canada, he said: to escape his wife.

"She's absolutely impossible," Davis explained. "I'm sure you can understand why I'd prefer *not* having my name on anything. Except this lease, of course." As for the phone, Davis continued, "I've got my own mobile phone, so I won't be needing one." It was a U.K. registered phone.

"Fine," said Barbara. "We've kept the accounts in the name of the landlord before. That shouldn't be a problem. But I still need your solicitor's reference."

"Of course, of course," Davis said assuredly. He was so convincing, so plausible, so polite. Barbara didn't want to nag him. But the reference would never come. There was always some excuse. Albert was a master at feigning forgetfulness.

In the beginning, London was a life of outrageous leisure. There was ballet and opera and films and window-shopping in the antique emporiums along King's Road. And there was the Royal Borough of Chelsea, right next door, with its swish restaurants and expensive shops and Christie's auction rooms—everything that was elegant and tasteful and good in Albert Walker's mind. It was everything that he had read about in Ian Fleming's novels. Fleming himself, the creator of James Bond, had lived in Chelsea. Now Albert Walker was here—not as Albert Walker—but as David Davis.

Albert knew, however, that he'd have to change more than his name. He'd have to alter his appearance as well. He was sure that by now the alarm had been raised in Canada; confident, too, that the police were scouring Switzerland for him. Sooner or later, though, they'd likely look in Britain, he'd spent so much time here in the past. Doubtless, the police would circulate photographs too, probably the one in his passport: that jowly, grey-haired man with a moustache.

So on the last day of 1990, Albert Walker decided to ring out the old and ring in the new in his own special way. He scheduled the first of what would be a series of facials aimed at toning up his face and changing his appearance. He had told a few acquaintances that he and Sheena had joined the Hogarth Club in Chiswick. He undertook a strict gym program aimed at losing weight. Albert had always been vain about his figure, but regrettably, he had gotten out of shape recently. He would turn that to advantage. Once he'd shed the weight, firmed up his face, shaved off the moustache and dyed his hair, he would be quite unrecognizable. If that didn't work, he decided, he'd consider a surgical tuck. The characters in his favourite spy novels had done it all the time.

Sheena, too, had her hair dyed, a soft shade of blonde. On Monday, December 31, Sheena went to the gym at 10 a.m. Walker followed later at noon. Thereafter, at 2 p.m., Albert had the first of his series of facials, and that evening at 10, they made a long-distance phone call.

"Jill? It's Sheena. Happy New Year!"

The ground rules for calls home were clearly laid down by Albert: no mention of an address or telephone number; no mention of location; no mention of tactics or strategy.

Back in Canada the hunt was on for Albert and Sheena. The

RCMP was focusing its attention on Switzerland, exactly as Walker had hoped.

On the bigger canvas, world events continued to unfold. On January 16, 1991, as Albert and Sheena sat down to watch *The Company of Wolves* on television, a dream fantasy film inspired by the Little Red Riding Hood story, a bulletin flashed over Channel 4 announcing that the bombing of Baghdad had begun. The Gulf War was on.

Albert, however, took litte notice. In the seven days between January 14 and 21, he had four facials, visited the gym almost daily and underwent a special hair treatment. He was trimming down his figure and firming up his jowls. By the time he and Sheena went to see Puccini's *Madama Butterfly* at the English National Opera on a Tuesday in late January, Albert Walker was starting to look and feel better than he had in years.

As Albert and his 15-year-old daughter sat back in their comfortable seats, Puccini's opera about a 15-year-old girl who loves and marries a much older man unfolded. Although Butterfly, the young Japanese child, is sadly and ultimately abandoned by Lieutenant Benjamin Pinkerton, there is no doubt that her love is real and pure. After his departure, Butterfly even bears his baby and raises the child with devotion and loyalty. If Walker selected *Madama Butterfly* as part of a strategy of auto-suggestion, he could scarcely have done better.

Albert and Sheena strode out into St. Martin's Lane that evening, and Albert was well pleased with Graham Vick's production. Opera, forever charged with themes of sex and death, remained a passion for Walker, and London afforded him an opportunity to see it regularly as no other city in the English-speaking world can. Albert felt himself to be a man of culture and taste.

That was certainly the way he presented himself to Barbara Thomson, with whom Albert usually dined whenever the rent came due. Albert was keen for company his own age. Sheena, however, clearly didn't like the idea of her father dining alone with someone else. Her discomfort was so obvious that Barbara remarked to a friend one day over a drink that she wondered whether Noël was really David's daughter?

"They just don't seem to have a father-daughter rapport," she said. "Noël was so sullen when I showed up the first time to go to dinner with him, I almost got the impression she was worried I was going to nab her fella."

Barbara and David had only just sat down for a before-dinner drink at the Fulham flat when Noël came in and wouldn't leave the room. She kept hanging around and around. She just stood there, wide-eyed, a white towel on her head, her hair still wet, a svelte, sullen, silent figure, when David suddenly snapped at her.

"Why don't you just get out of here and dry your hair for *God's* sake!" he shouted. Then, turning to Barbara with a mixture of apology and disgust, he muttered, "I'm sorry, Barbara."

There was something vicious in the tone he'd used on Noël; something that didn't seem at all like father and daughter.

That night at dinner, at the Italian restaurant La Famiglia in Chelsea, Barbara and David talked mostly about sailing and food and restaurants. David impressed Barbara as a very keen sailor and keener still to buy his own boat and "get back into it." He'd had his own yacht in Canada, he said, but had had to leave it with his wife when he'd fled. Barbara, an attractive and athletic figure, was an accomplished sailor herself and had sailed the English Channel as well as the North China Sea. She had her own stories to tell. Yet despite the pleasant evening, in Barbara's mind, the disquieting encounter between David and Noël hung on.

Thereafter, once a month, Barbara would come by for the rent, and she and David would head out for dinner. Each time, Barbara would try to chat with Noël in a motherly way, but from that point onward, Noël always seemed "spaced out." Barbara even thought she might be taking drugs and raised it with David over dinner one evening.

"Oh, she's okay," David smilingly assured her, keen to cut the conversation. "Noël is just on a different clock from you and me, Barbara. You know how it is with younger people. You and I sleep at night and are up and active all day long. Noël's just turned it all upside down."

"She does seem rather lonely," said Barbara. "Hasn't she made any friends yet? Hasn't she met anyone at your club?"

"Not yet," David said. "But then she's always kept to herself. She'll get out and about eventually. Please don't worry yourself with it, Barbara. Really."

"But she's always indoors. Why not get her a cat or something?"

David Davis bought Noël a cat: Chloe. She was soft and white and deaf. Later, David told Barbara that Noël was in love with it, and he really couldn't thank Barbara enough. It had been a great suggestion.

Still, Barbara thought, there was something troubling there. David was always the perfect gentleman when they were dining out, and yet there was clearly something not right at home. But then, the same could be said of many parent-child relationships, couldn't it, she thought?

"It's just that—I wouldn't say she's a prisoner or anything," Barbara confided to her friend over a drink one day. "But he seems to have this incredible hold over her. It's almost like, well . . . it's almost as if she's under his spell or something."

Barbara took another sip of her drink and gazed out the window.

She was very close to the truth. Very close. But she did not know it.

10

THE VERY IMAGE

"Where is that bastard?" Barney Lawrence shouted. "I want to know where he is!"

January 16, 1991. Back in Canada, Barney Lawrence, long-time friend and lawyer for Dr. Bill Wilson and wife Leda, was livid. He had gone from office to office looking for Albert Walker and couldn't find him. Throughout November and December, he'd been asking for a meeting with Walker. Now the lawyer was sure Walker had not only embezzled his clients' $80,000 trust fund held for their daughter but probably took another $50,000 in investments as well.

The same day, a half a world away, Walker was settling into the moist cocoon of his posh health clinic in London, having another relaxing facial.

Lawrence had warned the Wilsons about Walker from the very beginning. There was always something phony about that man, but Bill Wilson wouldn't hear of it. Now Lawrence was going door to door in the name of his client, startling staff and demanding to see Walker. First, he had gone to the Walker office in Brantford.

"He's probably working out of the Woodstock office," a staff member told him.

Lawrence drove to Woodstock. "He hasn't worked here since the fall," a lady behind the counter said. "He's been working out of Cambridge."

In Cambridge, Lawrence was told Walker was in Woodstock.

"Been to Woodstock!" Lawrence fumed.

"Ah—maybe Kitchener?" the employee offered.

Lawrence turned and stalked out.

At the Kitchener office on Frederick Street, Lawrence was finally told that Walker "might be travelling out of the country."

"I'll get that bastard," Lawrence said. "Mark my words. That jerk. I'll get him."

By then, the Brantford police, together with the RCMP and Interpol, seemed well on their way to tracing Walker, and more and more information was coming in every day.

In early January, Albert Walker's American Express bill arrived, and the entry for the British Airways tickets purchased from Elegant Tours was on it. So was the $11,556 worth of jewellery from Birk's at the Eaton Centre. A few days later, Walker board member John Moran, by now sensing he'd been badly had, finally telephoned the police to report a fraud.

Barbara Walker visited her estranged husband's Viscount Road home, where Jill was still living, and discovered every piece of Sheena's clothing gone. By mid-January, it was all painfully clear: Albert Walker had fled for good. In time, official and unofficial estimates of how much he may have embezzled would range from $2 million to as much as $10 million.

The tallying would come later. For the moment, John Moran was feverishly combing company records to assist the police in any way he could. The company he had been left in charge of was in crisis. Barney Lawrence soon filed suit on behalf of the Wilsons, demanding an accounting of his clients' $80,000, and word of Walker's disappearance began to seep and spread like the red ink of a bad balance sheet. Clients were coming to the counter demanding to know the status of their funds. For some, it was their life savings. A sense of panic was growing. Staff appealed for calm. The police were on the case, and the entire matter would be sorted out, they said. But the phone didn't stop ringing.

While the authorities searched in vain for Walker, an envelope arrived at the Walker home from Switzerland that mocked police efforts. It was from the Swiss traffic police: there were speeding tickets for Albert Johnson Walker, three of them. He'd been photographed in a speed trap the weekend of October 13 along Highway 355 between Lausanne and Geneva, behind the wheel of a rented Ford. No one could locate Albert Walker, and yet an automated machine was delivering information as to his recent movements. What had he been doing there, the police wondered?

The speeding tickets were high-grade fuel for the rumour mill. People were certain now that Albert was living in a chateau near Bern and that Sheena was attending a Swiss finishing school. By summer, *The Financial Times* of Canada insisted he was in France. It published a cartoon of Albert stretched out on a beach, apparently on the Riviera, with bills blooming like flowers from his toes. "Albert Walker on French leave," the "Informed Sources" column said. Albert was said to be in France. In time, British police, the RCMP, Walker's lawyers and Walker himself would say that he never left Britain. But apparent sightings would be made around the world.

Back home, they were still sifting through the ruins of the corporation he had ruthlessly gutted.

John Moran had turned up something in the Walker company records that puzzled him. First, there were two American Express receipts for cosmetic surgery paid to a Toronto surgeon in the sum of $2,800. They were dated December 1988, on the same date that Barbara Walker would say her daughter Jillian had had breast implants. There was something else too: a cheque for $35,000 made out to someone named David W. Davis. It was written

December 1, 1990, just days before Walker fled. Moran telephoned the police. "Does this name mean anything to you?" he asked. No, the officer replied, it didn't. But they'd look into it.

In time, they tracked the real David Davis, who explained it had simply been a loan from Walker. The details of the repayment of the principle were supposed to have been worked out later, on Walker's return from Switzerland, but then Walker had disappeared. It was another brilliantly clever move by Albert. He had calculated that sometime in the future, Davis might put two and two together and realize that it was Albert who had stolen his birth certificate. But if Davis went to the police, he might also have to tell them about the $35,000. He couldn't bribe Davis outright. That would have given the game away. But maybe, just maybe, that $35,000 "loan" might make Davis reluctant to come forward. The police did track Davis, and he was made to pay. But Davis himself hadn't yet realized that his birth certificate was missing. He didn't yet have the knowledge to put two and two together. That would come later. Much later. For now, everyone forgot about David Davis.

Back in Britain, Albert, who was by now passing as David W. Davis, attended the annual Harrogate Antiques and Fine Arts Fair in February. He met Elaine Boyes and her boyfriend, Ron Platt, who approved of Elaine's decision to join Mr. Davis's new art and antiques venture as his special assistant. Afterward, when Albert returned to London, he grew anxious to get his money laundering operation up and running. He telephoned Elaine and invited her and Ron down to London for the weekend. He made the offer irresistible.

"Hang the cost," Davis said. "I'll look after it. The two of you just get on the train and come along. You *need* it, Elaine. So does Ron. You need some quality time together."

Elaine and Ron did come along and thoroughly enjoyed themselves. Mr. Davis put them up in a decent hotel in Knightsbridge, not far from his flat in Fulham. That Saturday, Ron and Elaine came around for pre-dinner drinks, and they were pleasantly surprised by Mr. Davis's welcome—as though they were long-lost friends. A bond was developing.

That evening, they all dined at the Blue Elephant, a fine Thai restaurant located around the corner from where the Davises lived. The food was "wonderful," Elaine said, and noted that the bill came to more than £200. Mr. Davis paid cash, quite casually. She and Ron were impressed by the generosity and certain that Elaine had made the right decision in joining Cavendish. That spring, 1991, when Mr. Davis paid for Elaine to come to London alone to attend a four-day course with him on getting started in antiques, they took tea at a posh hotel.

It was there that Mr. Davis had first sketched the broader outlines of the tragedy that was his first marriage and how his wife was now pursuing him for alimony. His response was to flee the U.S., he said. Now he'd even changed his appearance, he confided.

"So much so," he boasted, "she could walk into this hotel lobby right now, Elaine, and not even know who I am."

That said, Mr. Davis put his head back and laughed.

Elaine Boyes quit her job at Henry Spencer's in April 1991, and Mr. Davis made her the secretary of Cavendish Corporation, and Ron Platt, too, signed on as an unpaid director. Elaine was to act solely as Mr. Davis's nominee and only under his precise instructions. She would be paid £15,000 annually and would be given five weeks' paid vacation.

Mr. Davis explained to Elaine in detail that because his wife "back in the States" was still vigorously pursuing him for alimony, it was absolutely, vitally important that his name never appear on the incorporation papers or documents of any kind. Not even a cheque should be made out in his name. Elaine said she understood the situation perfectly, and there would never be any problem.

Mr. Davis said it was good insurance, too, to have Ron on the board. "Just in case something ever happens to you," he said. "Of course, nothing will," Albert assured her. "It's just good business practice." It was spring, and the relationship between Ron and Elaine and Mr. Davis seemed set to blossom.

With the May long weekend approaching, Barbara Thomson mentioned, when she came to collect the rent, that she had a business trip planned that would take her north to Nottingham, Leeds and Harrogate. Since David Davis had mentioned he had a "business partner" in Harrogate, she wondered if he and Noël would be interested in joining her? They could tag on a trip to the Lake District and make an adventure of it.

"A fantastic idea," David said. "I'll look after booking the hotels."

The drive up was uneventful, although Barbara found it peculiar that on the few occasions when she had had to stop for an appointment, David and Noël refused to take up her offer of the use of the car. She gave David the keys and encouraged him to "take a drive around the town and do a little exploring." But David and Noël didn't budge. They sat in the car and waited for Barbara sometimes for an hour or more. They never moved. Albert Walker couldn't risk it. The only driver's licence he'd ever had was issued in the name of Albert Johnson Walker. He wasn't about to risk being pulled over for some small mistake and possibly have his identity discovered. He'd wait.

Barbara also found the sleeping arrangements rather surprising. At their first overnight stop in Harrogate, there were only two rooms booked, and Barbara assumed she and Noël would be sharing. That wasn't the case.

"Oh c'mon, David. You don't want to sleep with your daughter, do you?" Barbara innocently chided. "Noël can sleep with me."

"No, no, it's fine," David said. "Don't worry about us. We can stay in the same room. We're used to it by now, with all the travelling we've done." An odd arrangement, Barbara thought. She was a seasoned traveller, and it was her experience that women always shared a room under such circumstances. David's polite insistence, however, seemed genuine. He was concerned that Barbara enjoy a good night's sleep. After all, she was the one on business, and she was doing all the driving. She relented and accepted his generosity, and in the morning, she awoke refreshed and thankful.

She was looking forward to meeting David's Harrogate business partner, of whom David often spoke. Yet David was secretive about her, and Barbara remarked that he never once mentioned her name. Suddenly, David announced that he would be off to attend to his own business affairs and excused himself for a day and a night. That evening, Barbara and Noël dined alone. Barbara found the younger woman pleasant, though quiet. She didn't give off much. But Barbara did learn a little more about the Davis family. Noël had two sisters, she said, one in college who was living with her boyfriend, and the other, a younger one, who lived at home with their mother. Noël said her father had decided to bring the younger one over to Britain to live with them.

The next day, when David returned to the hotel, he gave no details about his business trip, except to say that work had gone well, and they travelled on through the Lake District, to Blackburn, Gretna Green and Windermere. There, Barbara again offered to share a room with Noël. They were standing in the lobby of the Linthwaite House Hotel, a lovely place David had found, again combing through the travel section of a Sunday paper. The hotel promoted itself as "the perfect place to start a love affair," a sumptuous 18-room Edwardian retreat surrounded with some of England's most beautiful scenery and an outstanding dining room. Barbara was delighted and felt it was her turn to return the favour.

"Noël and I can take the same room, David. It's really not necessary that you and Noël share."

"No, no, no, Barbara. It's okay. We're used to it." Such were the sleeping arrangements for the entire four-day trip.

Both David and Noël were well prepared for hiking and brought their well-used gear with them, and the next day, the three set out and climbed Helvellyn, the Lake District's fourth highest peak, more than 3,000 feet high. David made the climb quickly and effortlessly, as though Helvellyn were nothing more than a gentle, rolling hill. So did Noël. Barbara, however, found the climb exhausting. Still, the following morning, she was up and at the breakfast table early while Noël didn't leave her room the entire day.

"Anything wrong?" Barbara asked.

"No, not at all," David said. "It's like I said, Barbara. She's got a different clock."

She must have, Barbara thought. For the rest of the trip and for the drive back home, Noël seemed "spaced out" again, unusually quiet and utterly uncommunicative. She must be using drugs, Barbara thought.

As spring turned to summer, David Davis informed Elaine Boyes that he and Noël would be moving north to Harrogate. He wanted to work more closely with Elaine, he said. He had enjoyed London, but it was busier and "dirtier" than he'd expected. He'd miss the cultural venues, but then, Harrogate, too, had its own theatre and music hall, art and antique shops. He asked Elaine to keep an eye out for a prospective home for him to buy. His enjoyment of London was not quite over, though. It was time, Albert decided, to acquaint himself with the art world.

As a recently registered member of The Friends of the Royal Academy, Albert received an invitation to the gala opening of the Academy's annual Summer Exhibition on the evening of June 5. There, in the Academy's lecture room on Piccadilly, he spotted British painter Olwyn Bowey's *Everlastings*, a complicated modern pastoral dominated by a posy of brilliant flowers. Sipping wine and carrying himself with a bearing that said he was entirely at home in such surroundings, the truck driver's son purchased the painting for £3,000. Later, strolling through Gallery III of the exhibition, he found another, *Sunset at Llangwyfan*, by Kyffin Williams, Order of the British Empire, and he bought it for £2,275.

The entire evening had been a refined experience, the crystal, the formal evening wear, the very way people spoke in those serious, measured tones. Of course, buying fine art was a lovely way of laundering stolen money too. Albert had enjoyed his time at the Academy so much that when he saw an ad in *The Sunday Times* for Christie's "Victorian Pictures, Drawings and Watercolours" auction, scheduled for Friday, June 14, at 11 a.m., he decided he'd attend.

Carrying his auction catalogue with Sir David Murray's *Hampstead's Happy Heath* on the cover, Albert strode down Picadilly, turned south on St. James and entered through the King Street entrance. Signing in, he was handed bidder's card number 67 and he took his seat in the Great Room among the hush of the well-heeled. Albert had already viewed the paintings the week before, and he knew precisely what he wanted: *Norah Creina*, a portrait of a voluptuous young red-haired woman with porcelain-like skin, painted by William Frith in 1846; *A Rest by the Gate*, two rosy-cheeked little country girls posing wide-eyed for artist William Bromley in 1866; and *The Very Image*, by Joseph Clark, an idealized vision of a successful artist-son standing back from a portrait of his mother to which he is just putting the final touches, as his mother, father—a benign figure in the background—and tiny daughter look on in awe and admiration. The front room in which the sitting is taking place, like the front room of his own childhood, is humble: there is a fireplace, a teapot, a candlestick and a clock. The artist-son, dressed in a gentleman's country suit, the colours of which precisely match those of his mother, stands back confidently, his palette poised, a kerchief tucked in his breast pocket, and basks in his mother's joy. She is smiling, astonished and pleased by her son's work. It was Albert's life in miniature—at least the one he'd wanted, but never had.

Albert bought the paintings for £14,425, almost $30,000, and he had Elaine Boyes sign a cheque for them on Cavendish Corporation's behalf. *The Very Image* alone had cost him £7,000. All three works, in their gold-leaf frames, were carefully crated, and he personally picked them up from Christie's on June 24. Albert

Albert Walker, 2,
at the family homestead in Freelton, near Hamilton, circa 1947

Albert was a quiet and shy boy growing up.

Albert, 14,
Christmas 1959

In the house at Woodham Walter, Albert erected a big, beautiful tree like the ones that had filled the front rooms of his youth.

Albert Walker, 21,
believed to have recently
returned from Europe,
Christmas, 1966

*He had seen some of the
world, he said, and he decided
he wanted more of it.*

Barbara and Albert Walker
at a wedding, circa 1971

*He was six-foot one, dark-haired and
handsome. Barbara's petite figure and
beautiful red hair seemed to set his
dashing figure off even more.*

Albert Walker,
a 30-something entrepreneur

For Albert Walker, the 1980s were years of charm and appetite.

Sheena Walker,
a carefree high school student,
aged 14 or 15

*But mainly, it was the "freedom"
her father offered her that
seemed to win her loyalty.*

Ronald Platt, wearing his Rolex Oyster Watch, and sporting a distinctive maple leaf tattoo.

It was in the hope of cleaving to some of that good luck and distinction that Ron Platt strode into the jewellers Carl of Osnabrück and bought his own, and only, Rolex Oyster.

Albert Walker posing as David Davis, July 1993

If Walker's scheme went according to plan, his life as David Davis would be ended, the birth certificate burned. By then, Albert Walker would have become Ronald J. Platt.

Back in Canada, Barbara Walker and youngest daughter, Heather, pose with a photograph of Sheena, who disappeared with her father while on a skiing vacation.

Though badly burned, Barbara was determined to show Albert she could not be trampled on . . .

Elaine Boyes at a friend's wedding

Elaine Boyes blushed. She was shy and a little uncomfortable being complimented so directly by a man who had just arrived at Henry Spencer's for the first time. But this was probably just the American way, she thought.

The Walkers, posing as David and Noël Davis, rented a cottage from Carole Poole (left) and Judith DiMarte.

"Is that the wife?" Carole asked, her high inflection indicating surprise.
"The young blonde?"
"Yes."
"Yes, yes, I know: quite young, right? She is pretty though."
"Pretty young, I'd say."

The house where Albert and Sheena Walker lived in Woodham Walter.

Frank Johnson and Audrey Mossman were the Walkers' neighbours in Woodham Walter

Anyone looking in on the scene at Little London Farm would have found a perfectly tranquil domestic situation: a family of three; two multi-speed Raleigh bicycles out back; the window sills abloom with boxes of brightly coloured geraniums . . .

The *Lady Jane*, Walker's boat—
Constable David Lea stands in the cabin

In early March, the daffodils that line the lane leading to Kestrel Cottage began to bloom and Albert Walker's interests took another turn. He decided to buy a sailboat . . . Albert bought a 24-foot twin-keel Trident sailboat called Peach *which he renamed the* Lady Jane, *Jane being little Emily's middle name.*

Platt's body was found 6 miles from the coastal town of Teignmouth

In that light, from that distance, the operator could make out identifiable markings on the horizon: the red clay known as the Ness, at the mouth of the Teign, the spire of St. Mary's Church . . .

John Copik pulled Platt's body from the water.

"He belongs to somebody," said John. "I'd like to think that if it were me, somebody'd bring me in."

Platt's Rolex watch. The British police would never have identified Platt without the help of the watch's serial number, which linked them to its owner.

"Every Rolex Tells a Story," the Swiss-based company boasts.

Detective Chief Inspector
Phil Sincock

*Sincock first came to
national attention in 1990
when he took a Devon
murder case that had lain
unsolved for 10 years and
conclusively pinned it on a
criminal named Keith Rose.
Rose was already doing 15
years for kidnapping.*

*A lawyer by training,
Turner had taken an active
interest in the case in the
five days since the body
was discovered.*

Her Majesty's Coroner Hamish Turner

Detective Sergeant
Bill Macdonald

Detective Constable
Ian Clenahan

The Platt file, however, was low priority. Detective Sergeant Bill Macdonald and Detective Constable Ian Clenahan had managed to track the deceased's brother, Brian Platt, up in Hay-on-Wye. The dead man was definitely Ronald, he confirmed.

Sergeant Peter Redman

On October 14 Peter Redman, dressed in a civilian suit, set out in an unmarked car from the Chelmsford police station headed for Woodham Walter.

Coroner's Officer Robin Little

*Little dialled Rolex in Bexley, Kent,
and explained the circumstances.
He slipped the watch out of its plastic
bag and flipped it over in his hand for
the umpteenth time.*

Dr. Gyan Fernando, pathologist

*The following afternoon at 3 p.m.,
Dr. Gyan Fernando, the Home Office
pathologist for Devon and Cornwall
arrived at the hospital mortuary and
the meticulous process of examining
the body began again in earnest.*

Gordon Pringle

*Pringle pointed out that they
didn't have an eye witness. The
evidence was entirely circumstantial. Then he began to list what
the crown could not prove.*

Defence lawyer Richard
Ferguson

*In the end, Albert Walker chose
Richard Ferguson, Q.C., a former Northern Irish MP, whose
flinty accent and street-fighting
skills in the courtroom had
earned him one of the finest
legal reputations in the United
Kingdom. There were some who
said that in criminal law he was
the best in Britain.*

Prosecutor Charles Barton (left) and Richard Ferguson

*After two weeks of intense testimony, it came down to this: two be-
wigged barristers coolly arguing the guilt or innocence of Albert
Walker before a judge and jury in England. There were no great theatrics, no prancing about the courtroom, no fingerwaving, no shouting, no gavel thumping. Just reason and persuasion . . .*

"That man is a murderer," prosecutor Charles Barton said.

"Where is the burden of proof?" Ferguson replied.

Elaine Boyes after testifying

She seemed helpful, especially helpful, and—was it her nature or was it simply part of the job of receptionist?—she seemed subservient to the every need of others.

Barry Hall (left), and Patrick Gill after a day in court—Hall is carrying an anchor similar to the one that held Platt's body to the seabed

On July 8, Albert Walker walked into Sport Nautique, a busy sporting goods store specializing in yachting supplies. Patrick Gill, the manager, approached. "Can I help you with anything?"
Albert Walker was looking for a number of supplies, he said, but the key thing he wanted was hanging from the ceiling in the middle of the shop. Anchors.

PAUL LEVIE

Walker shields his face from photographers as he leaves a courtroom in March 1997

He seemed sophisticated and sincere, and after a while, the female court attendant decided it didn't seem quite right that such a man should suffer the indignity of being brought into the courtroom in handcuffs.

COURTESY OF *THE TORONTO STAR*

Albert J. Walker

Convicted of the murder of Ronald J. Platt, July 6, 1998

Walker was living the life he had dreamt of, and he wanted to live it for the rest of his days.

To ensure that, he'd have to cover his tracks again. The move to Harrogate would be kept hidden from Barbara Thomson. Albert simply lied to her. As July began, he informed Barbara that he and Noël had planned "a six-week vacation" to explore Devon and Cornwall.

"How marvellous," Barbara said. "The west country is beautiful this time of year. Noël, you'll positively love it."

"My older sister's coming!" Noël told Barbara with all the excitement of a 15-year-old. "It's going to be great! I haven't seen her for so long. She's going to vacation with us!"

It was the first time Barbara had seen Noël truly excited about anything. Seeing her sister was probably just what she needed. The girl was so desperately lonely.

The Davises were gone only a few days when Barbara got a call from Tina, the woman who cleaned the flats at 41 Moore Park Road.

"They're gone," Tina said.

"I know they're gone—they're gone on holiday. They'll be back."

"No, Mrs. Thomson, I mean they're gone for good."

"Tina, what would *ever* make you say such a thing?"

"The cat's gone."

"Of course, the cat's gone. Noël's besotted with that cat. She wouldn't go without it."

"No way," Tina said. "They're gone. We won't be seeing them again. And I'm not getting paid." Still, each week, according to Mrs. Thomson's instructions, Tina continued to dust. Weeks later, Tina phoned again.

"Every single thing has been cleaned out of the wardrobe,

Mrs. Thomson. Everything except a pair of shoes, and they're not his. I told you they weren't coming back."

"What do you mean they're not his shoes?"

"Come on, Mrs. Thomson, you know how he dresses. He only ever wears handmade leather shoes from Jermyn Street. These shoes—these shoes are beat up bad. They're not even his size. And there's a brief case too."

Barbara was now intrigued.

"Anything in it?"

"Hang on, Mrs. Thomson, I'll check."

Tina was away from the phone for only a moment when Barbara could hear a crash.

"Mrs. Thomson? I think you ought to come over here right now."

"Is there anything wrong?"

"You'd better come over Mrs. Thomson. I've got something to show you."

Barbara hung up, got in her car and raced over. Tina led her into the bedroom.

"What's this?"

"I just went to pick it up, and the whole thing fell apart in pieces. I'm telling you I didn't do anything wrong, Mrs. Thomson."

There, on the floor, was the briefcase. It was a very expensive case of rich black leather. It had completely collapsed. Every lock on the case had been broken; every hinge, unhinged. They picked up the pieces and examined them carefully. What did it mean?

"It was just set there on the table," Tina said. "It was just made to come apart when anyone touched it."

"Bizarre," Barbara said. "Very bizarre."

From what book or thriller Albert might have lifted this scene isn't known. But what is known is that Tina was right.

Neither she nor Barbara would ever see the Davises again.

That summer, London was abuzz with what promised to be the biggest musical event of the season. Luciano Pavarotti was set to give a free, open-air concert in Hyde Park in late July. Free, that is, to those who would stand in the distant reaches of London's most famous royal park. The glitterati of London would pay up to £350—more than $700—for seats in a special VIP enclosure.

Police were expecting 270,000 to pour into the park, but weather forecasters predicted thunderstorms. Consequently, only 130,000 people showed, but among them were Princess Diana, as well as Charles, the Prince of Wales, Prime Minister John Major, Andrew Lloyd Webber, Eric Clapton and others. No one was disappointed by the performance, but everyone was soaked.

As Princess Diana shivered in a front-row seat, her flimsy jacket drenched, Jeremy Isaacs, the head of the Royal Opera House, leaned across to give her his plastic hat. Diana declined. She declined, too, the offer of a white towel brought down from a Pavarotti aide, draping it instead over the shoulders of the Prime Minister and laughing in her wonderfully radiant way.

The al fresco concert was a triumph. Pavarotti, standing on a shocking-pink stage beneath the tempest, sang with a robustness equal to that of any of his great performances. He seemed inspired by the elements, and he dedicated *Donna non vidi mai* to Princess Diana, because, Pavarotti said, looking down from the stage, "I never saw a woman like her." Diana blushed.

By the time Pavarotti sang his signature grand finale, *Nessun dorma*, from Puccini's *Turandot*, the crowd felt itself to be lifted not only to its feet but to the heavens. The applause rolled like thunder down across the lawns, down toward Hyde Park Corner and beyond.

According to Albert Walker, he was there too, applauding with vigour amid the torrent.

11

"WHAT A MAN SOWS, THAT HE SHALL REAP"

"And how much do you want for the stove?" Albert Walker asked politely.

It was mid-July 1991, a sunny Saturday afternoon in the posh Yorkshire town of Harrogate. Albert had taken the train some 200 miles north of London. He was standing now in the kitchen of 45 St. Leonard's Oval, a comfortable, out-of-the-way, three-bedroom brick home, discussing the final details of his new house purchase with owner David Emmett.

The Emmetts had just listed their home for £122,000, hoping for around £115,000, when Walker appeared introducing himself as "David Davis, a retired merchant banker from New York," and entered a generous bid of £120,000, which was gratefully accepted. Now he was pitching for appliances.

"It's a cooker," David Emmett gently corrected him with a smile. "You Americans always insist on calling them 'stoves.' They're cookers—used for cooking, not heating," he chided.

"Of course," Walker grinned. "I should know that by now, shouldn't I? And the price?"

Emmett looked at his wife, Anne. She was leaning up against the doorway making small talk with Davis's daughter, the slim, blonde-haired teenager who had introduced herself as Noël. He turned back to Davis.

"Four hundred pounds?"

David Davis promptly reached into his trouser pocket and pulled out a large bundle of £50 notes. He counted out eight and handed them over nonchalantly.

Emmett laughed. "I see you came prepared."

"I never carry less than £1,000 cash," said Davis. "It gives you the freedom to make those impulse purchases."

Looking on, Sheena smiled. She didn't talk very much, the Emmetts noticed, but seemed to hang on her father's every word.

David Davis explained to the Emmetts that he and his wife, a medical doctor still living in New York, had recently divorced. It had been a bad split, and having "made his pile," he'd decided to move to England and Noël had chosen to come with him. Another daughter had remained with her mother in the States, he said. Ultimately, his dream was to settle down somewhere in the French countryside, a dream he'd nurtured for years. But first, he wanted to satisfy another long-held yearning to buy and sell art and antiques, and Harrogate, an old Victorian spa town with broad, tree-lined avenues and a large number of dealers, seemed an ideal setting. After all, the town played host to two internationally famous fine art fairs per year.

He liked the Emmett home: an anonymous house on a quiet street, a house that looked like any other on the block. He especially liked the study the Emmetts had built, a room filled with natural light that overlooked the garden. It was here, Davis told Emmett, he would hang the paintings he'd recently bought from Christie's and the Royal Academy in London. He would have security bars fitted for the windows and maybe install a built-in swimming pool in the garden. He had grand plans, and even before the house deal was completed, he had a design consultant come by and take photographs of the house, inside and out, just to see what further enhancements might be made.

The location was ideal, Davis told the Emmetts. Since he did not drive, he could walk up St. Hilda's Road and cut across The Stray—200 acres of parkland at the heart of Harrogate that have been preserved for more than two centuries—and be downtown in minutes.

Not being able to drive would be a nuisance, Albert thought, but it was better to be careful. It was also a good excuse to buy a couple of bicycles for him and Sheena and concentrate on staying fit.

He'd pay cash for the house, he told Emmett. No need for a mortgage. He'd have the money transferred from one of his Swiss bank accounts, and the whole process needn't take long. The Emmetts handed over the keys on September 12, 1991.

Albert selected a stunning *Lit Bateau*-style bed from Harrods in London, for which he had Elaine Boyes sign a cheque, and had it delivered to Harrogate together with a settee and some small end tables. The bill came to more than £5,600, about $11,200. The bed was a magnificent piece of furniture made of rich, lustrous mahogany.

Albert and Sheena were pleased with their new home and in love with Harrogate. But living there would also bring risks. It had been easy to remain anonymous in a city the size of London. Here, however, was a much smaller community, and people were expected to fit in. The challenge for Albert and Sheena was to be accepted—but not known.

The town was filled with good restaurants, there was an old established tennis club and a fitness centre nearby, and the new house was within easy walking distance of elegant and stylish shops. Connections to London were also excellent: three direct trains a day could take Albert Walker there in just over two and a half hours. In fact, after having looked at Emmett's house, Albert did just that, shooting back down to London by train to attend the Pavarotti concert. So he told his neighbours, with some pride.

Harrogate was a good place to hide: it had a reputation for it. In December 1926, Agatha Christie vanished from London and hid there for 11 days. The disappearance captivated the nation. Like the Walkers, she too took an assumed name for her stay, booking into the Old Swan Hotel as Theresa Neele, using the surname of her husband's mistress. Some historians speculated her stay was the result of a nervous breakdown. Christie had simply wandered aimlessly into Waterloo station, fell under the spell of a poster advertising the spas of Harrogate and boarded a train north. Others suspect a more romantic reason: Agatha Christie was having an affair. The truth remains a mystery.

For Albert Walker, there was little mystery as to why he had chosen Harrogate. The town was home to Ronald J. Platt, Elaine Boyes' boyfriend. Walker knew from his very first meeting with Boyes, at Henry Spencer's Antiques, that if he could befriend Platt and either coax or steal his identity from him, he would have a cover that would last a lifetime. If he executed his plan properly, he would have legal status, bank accounts and mobility— none of which he enjoyed now. His current cover was based on the slimmest of possible threads: David Davis's birth certificate. He might be able to use it in limited situations, but he could never risk building a complete identity around it.

Sooner or later, the real David Davis might need it and call police to say it was missing. They might see the connection and a worldwide manhunt for Walker, living as Davis, could be launched. But by then, if Walker's scheme went according to plan, his life as David Davis would be ended, the birth certificate burned. By then, Albert Walker would have become Ronald J. Platt.

In Canada, meanwhile, the search for Walker had stalled. No one had yet made the Davis connection. Still, working with the Walker family, the Brantford police were able to confirm a few key details. Sheena's sister Jillian was indeed getting calls, although she had no telephone number with which to reach her father and sister. Switzerland, however, was out. That much police knew. They also confirmed that both Albert and Sheena were living under assumed names. Whether they had altered their appearances or not, neither Jillian nor anyone knew.

When the Ontario Provincial Police appointed Staff Sergeant Joe Milton in October 1991 to lead a joint-forces investigation into the whereabouts of Walker and the missing millions, all of this information was passed on to him. He concentrated most of his efforts on interviewing the dozens of people whose money had been embezzled.

In England, the challenge that lay before Albert Walker was to establish a plausible personality and fit into Harrogate society. The starting point, he knew, was obvious, so obvious, in fact, that he had already cased it out.

Harrogate's Baptist Church is located in the heart of the town along gracious Victoria Avenue, behind an old-fashioned marquee that announces, "Whatever a man sows, that he shall reap." Shortly after moving in, David Davis began showing up every Sunday in a right-hand pew, about halfway up the centre aisle. His dark-haired, debonair figure, dressed in a neat blue blazer with a striped tie and grey flannel trousers, caught the eye of the Reverend David Hoskins, and outside the church after service one Sunday, he greeted him warmly.

"Welcome," Hoskins beamed, extending a hand. "Attending a conference? Or is it a new posting at Menwith?" Menwith is Menwith Hill, the U.S.-staffed, high-security international listening post west of Harrogate. It was one of the most important CIA stations during the Cold War and is still believed to gather intelligence from around the globe. As a consequence, Harrogate's citizens are accustomed to Americans.

No, he wasn't at Menwith, David Davis explained. He'd just retired and planned to make Harrogate home. He loved the town, he said, and on selling a bank in New York and surviving a divorce, he'd decided to retire here and indulge his passion for trading in art. He'd bought a home in the Oatlands area.

As the months passed, Hoskins, an open and trusting cleric, grew comfortable with Davis. The new man seemed to know his theology. He was at ease in the church, and in time, Davis gradually began to open up to Hoskins, telling him of how he'd been born in England but raised in Vermont, how he'd made his own way in the world, despite difficult circumstances. Here, thought Hoskins, was a man with real savoir-faire, a wealthy, self-made, international jetsetter who still held dear to the Christian principles of tolerance and charity. He was a liberal in a conservative church: Hoskins' favourite kind of congregant. Why at coffee after the service, Davis even offered to share his financial expertise with members of the congregation interested in investment tips. Such a generous man.

When the Reverend Hoskins announced he was organizing a night of counsel and support for members of the church recently let go by their firms during the recession, David Davis was the first to volunteer help. Sitting around Hoskins' table one Sunday evening, he lectured them on the importance of "remaining upbeat" about their prospects.

"You have to sell yourself," he said. "Draft a resumé. Establish a budget. Get on with your life!"

Molly Mountford, whose husband had been laid off from a local firm, was unimpressed. In fact, she was highly suspicious.

"He's a phony," Mrs. Mountford told Hoskins later. "There's something about that man that just doesn't add up." What it was, Mrs. Mountford admitted, she couldn't quite put her finger on. He had a brashness that made her bristle, an air of self-confidence that seemed misplaced. He spoke authoritatively, yet his vocabulary was strangely simple for a man who claimed to know so much about seemingly everything. And he was evasive about his own personal circumstances in a meeting where others were expected to be open about theirs. Mountford and Davis clashed at Hoskins' table that night and traded insults.

"Imagine him telling me I ought to consider seeing a psychiatrist just because I didn't agree with him!" she fumed to Hoskins over the phone. "The nerve!"

Hoskins, however, liked Davis's self-assurance and easy manner, and by springtime, Davis had even begun teaching Hoskins' 11-year-old son Ben how to play tennis over at the

Harrogate Sports Club, where Davis and his daughter Noël were members. In no time at all, it seemed that David Davis had become a mainstay in a tiny corner of the Harrogate community: he belonged to the church, the tennis club and the Tangerine Fitness Club over on Beech Avenue, and he and his daughter could often be seen pedalling their mountain bikes down to Betty's, the elegant old tea shop and restaurant that is one of Harrogate's best-known landmarks. From here, Harrogate's famous tea merchants, Taylors of Harrogate, exported English-ness worldwide. Albert Walker loved it.

"Who was Betty?" the write-up on the back of the menu rhetorically asked. "The identity of Betty still remains a secret, and although many tales are told and explanations offered, some mysteries are better left unsolved." How true, Albert Walker mused as he sipped a bit of afternoon Darjeeling and listened to the pianist. How true.

The retired couple who lived next door on St. Leonard's Oval, Douglas and Jean Clarke, thought the Davises were neighbours sent from heaven. No sooner had the Davises moved in than Jean and Noël were exchanging gifts of baked goods and Mr. Davis was bringing over bottles of wine. "There was a special promo-tion for it at Sainsbury's supermarket," he'd say. "Tell me if you like it." He even brought the Clarkes as his guests to see the Bolshoi Ballet at Harrogate's Royal Hall in the International Conference Centre. "Oh, Mr. Davis, you're just too generous," Mrs. Clarke said.

"Please," Albert implored, "call me David."

David had, it seemed to Jean, an almost poetic quality about him. He was able to appreciate not only the finer things in life, like ballet, opera and classical music—Vivaldi's *Four Seasons* was a favourite—but also those natural things that so many take for granted: "the mist on the heather in early morning" that he'd told the Clarkes about after he'd returned from a trip to Scotland. One early-winter night, there was a knock on the door, and when the Clarkes went to answer it, there was David in a pullover sweater, standing in the darkness, his hands over his heart.

"You've got to come out and see the moon!" he said in a tone approaching rapture. "It's absolutely beautiful!" The Clarkes moved out onto the lawn and gazed up, and yes, the moon was beautiful.

In fine weather, David would continually chat over the back fence to Douglas Clarke about everything from the dangers of creosote ("I was once badly burned by it as a kid," David said) to the price of French real estate ("Have a look at some of these properties," David insisted, waving some French real estate pamphlets at Douglas, "and tell me which one you think we should buy. We're going to move there some day").

Not only were David and Noël generous and thoughtful, but they were Christians, and their devotion to the Christian calendar was obvious. When Palm Sunday arrived, Noël came back from church with a small cross of woven palms and gave it to Jean as a present. At Christmastime, the Davises invited the older couple over for paté and toasts and claret. The Davises had a large and beautifully decorated Christmas tree in the front room, and Jean brought over her little grandaughter Sarah one afternoon to see it. David played with her and gave her two pretty red-and-white-striped candy canes. He must have been the perfect father, Jean thought, he was so affectionate with children. "You can bring her over any time," he told Jean.

The Walkers' Harrogate hiatus, however, was about more than good neighbourliness. It was about business. To the neighbours, it appeared David Davis filled his days by playing tennis and working out at the club, taking French classes in the afternoon and art lessons in the evening. Painting had become a new passion for David, and he submitted one of his own canvasses to the Academy's summer '92 exhibition ("Artist: David Davis. Title of work: *Black in White #1*"). Ultimately, however, it was rejected.

Undeterred, Albert decided to turn his nascent artistic talent to forgery. If he couldn't fool the judges of the Royal Academy, he decided, then perhaps he could fool the buying public. So he diligently propped up one of the paintings he'd bought by Olwyn Bowey, *Everlastings*, and painted his own version. Later, he copied the other by Kyffin Williams, OBE, *Sunset at Llangwfan*. Albert was feeling quite invincible now. No challenge seemed too grand, no fantasy beyond reach. He'd been both a wizard of finance and a master embezzler. Why couldn't he be a master forger?

In between canvasses, however, his real work continued. Unbeknownst to his neighbours, David Davis was busy laundering money. Vast quantities of it. And the devoted and somewhat naive Elaine Boyes was helping him do it.

David Davis had again explained to Elaine that his divorce had been bitter. His wife would try to track him down and get at his money. Security and secrecy were crucial, and there were to be no slip-ups. His wife should be given no advantage.

Elaine had a strong incentive in following instructions to the letter. For by now, Davis's generosity far exceeded the original proposal when they'd met at Henry Spencer's the year before. Not only was Mr. Davis paying her £1,250 a month now, tax-free—almost twice her taxed monthly salary at Spencer's—but he had also arranged for her and Ron to leave their tired little flat at 15 Rutland Road and move up the street and upmarket to 31 Howard Court, Rutland Drive, a smart, two-bedroom apartment in a modern, yellow-brick building. Mr. Davis, or "Mr. D.," as Ron Platt now called him, had put up the money for the £55,000 purchase, and Ron and Elaine had moved in late in 1991, just three weeks after the Davises had moved into their new home. There was a sense of partnership in the air—although it was always clear that Mr. Davis was the boss. More extraordinary still, Ron and Elaine confided to friends, Mr. D. had rented premises for Ron up on King's Road and set him up in his own business, a television and video repair shop so he could keep busy while Elaine was away for work. Mr. D. even helped Ron fill out the incorporation papers for the new enterprise, which Ron called Rutland Radio. He also lent Ron the £13,000 he needed for start-up costs.

It all seemed so wonderful. Mr. Davis was like a guardian angel. One moment they were always strapped for cash, the next, Mr. Davis arrived and suddenly their world was transformed. As for the work Elaine had to do, it wasn't onerous at all; in fact, it frequently left her with time on her hands, time to visit Henry Spencer's once a week, where her former colleagues were worried and curious.

"Come on, Elaine, what exactly is going on?" her previous boss Nigel Smith, who headed up the fine art department, teased her. "Are you running drugs for this man?"

"No, no," Elaine laughed. "It's nothing like that. Nothing like that at all."

"Well what, then? We're all quite concerned."

"I go to art and antique sales and gather information for Mr. Davis," she said, "pieces he might be interested in buying. I look at properties in France, visit estate agents, bring him back information on listed homes, that sort of thing. Mr. Davis wants to move to France, he says. He says he's looking for a country property, something sort of 'far from the madding crowd,' if you know what I mean. He says he wants to get away."

"But Geneva? Why did he send you to Geneva? What was that all about?"

"He wanted me to do a photographic essay on the fountains of Geneva," Elaine said brightly.

Smith was flabbergasted. The fountains of Geneva? Elaine could take reasonably good photographs, she'd taken a course at the local college, but she was hardly ready to publish a coffee-table book. What in God's name was Mr. Davis getting her to do?

What Mr. Davis was getting Elaine Boyes to do was to mule money he had brought with him from Canada and stored in safety deposit boxes in London and deposit it in banks on the continent. Each month, David Davis would take the train down to London to visit one of his deposit boxes there and withdraw cash. Sometimes it was in pounds, sometimes Swiss francs and other times French francs. He also had some gold bars stored there, the very bars he'd bought from Friedberg & Co. on Bay Street in Toronto. At his safety deposit box at a NatWest Bank in the city's financial district, or at Chester Mews in Belgravia or another at Metropolitan Safety Deposit in Knightsbridge, he'd withdraw the cash, secure it safely in a briefcase, hail a taxi for London's King's Cross Station and board the train back home. If everything went well, he might be able to stop for lunch at a café in Soho. In fact, if he took the 7:15 out from Harrogate in the morning he could complete his business, have lunch and be back in time to take Noël out for a late-night dinner at Gianni's, Harrogate's fashionable Italian restaurant. Or if he had a hankering for London nightlife, and he sometimes did, he'd stay for a day or two.

A week or so later, after these regular London visits, he'd send Elaine off on a trip to France, Italy or Switzerland, where he'd ask her to have a look at this or that antique sale, these or those properties and—while she was there—deposit the cash in different accounts she was to set up under her own name, as secretary of Cavendish Corporation. Throughout most of 1991 and all of 1992, the operation worked smoothly: Elaine would return home to Harrogate after jetting across Europe, and a week later, a deposit slip would arrive by mail at her home on Rutland Drive. She'd bring it around to Mr. Davis, and he would have her transfer some of the same money back into Cavendish's accounts in Harrogate. The idea was that, if the authorities ever did catch up with him, the web of transactions back and forth, up and down across Europe would be so confusing and complex, they'd never be able to unravel it. They'd never be able to say for certain whose money had gone where. In time, eight accounts were set up, one each in Paris, Milan, Florence and Lausanne, as well as four other accounts all clustered in banks around the Quai de L'Ile in Geneva. One was opened by Ron Platt in his own name at Mr. D.'s request. He had accompanied Elaine on a trip, as a bit of a vacation, and had also converted some cash for Mr. Davis. The banks that were used represented the upper echelon of the international banking establishment, including the Union Bank of Switzerland, the Credit Lyonnais and the Credit Italiano, among others.

Elaine would jet out of Manchester or Gatwick with a briefcase full of money and land in Geneva or one of her other destinations, usually for three or four days, then jet back and report to Mr. Davis. In all, police believe she may have helped Walker mule as much as $1 million.

Not all transfers had to be done in person, of course. Albert Walker cleverly asked Elaine if she could also move money from one bank to another by fax and by mail. Much to his delight, that worked equally smoothly. Elaine even faxed a letter in Italian once to the Credit Italiano in Florence, using the tiny bit of Italian she'd learned when she had worked as a nanny in Italy years before. The money was promptly transferred.

In between her trips, Mr. Davis would regale Elaine with his stories of the rich and famous. He always seemed to be "bumping into" people while he was down in London, Elaine remarked to Ron—Kevin Maxwell, for example, one of the sons of the infamous newspaper baron Robert Maxwell, who had slipped from his ship and drowned in the Mediterranean after having raided his employees' pension fund. Kevin was in the papers and on the evening news almost every day now. Was it an actual meeting with Kevin Maxwell or just a sighting, she wondered? Mr. Davis never offered, and Elaine never pushed. Mr. Davis mentioned that he'd sat next to the rock star Rod Stewart on a Concorde flight from New York once during the 1980s, and they'd shared a bottle of champagne.

"A great guy," he said. "I always fly the Concorde, of course. It gets you there refreshed."

Elaine never felt confident enough to press Mr. Davis for details on his extraordinary encounters with greatness. Mr. Davis once said that he had even had dinner with Ronald Reagan. To ask whether he had dined alone with him or with others, or whether it was a business meeting or a friendship, might have communicated that she doubted him, and she certainly didn't want to annoy Mr. Davis, not the man who was paying her way, providing her with a mortgage and keeping a roof over her head. Besides, whenever she did ask a question, he always seemed to change the subject. On one occasion, however, something strange did happen that made Elaine wonder. Something small. Mr. Davis led her and Ron into one of the bedrooms on St. Leonard's Oval to show them a magnificent quilt draped over the bed.

"Marvellous, isn't it?" said Davis, obviously seeking approval.

"Oh it's stunning, Mr. Davis," Elaine said politely. "So intricate, so colourful. Wherever did you get it?"

"It belonged to my grandmother," Mr. Davis explained proudly. "She made it herself, and it was handed down to me."

"Really?" Elaine replied, feeling the obviously new fabric in her fingertips. "How lovely."

Later she raised the conversation with Ron.

"You didn't go along with *that* story, did you?" she asked.

"About what?" said Ron.

"About the quilt. It couldn't possibly have been his grandmother's, and it couldn't possibly have been handed down to him. There's an identical one in the window at And-So-To-Bed, that linen shop off Montpelier Parade. Why would he lie about such a thing? It's so small."

"Oh you know Mr. D. He tends to exaggerate sometimes. Don't *worry*, Elaine."

"You know," Elaine said, "sometimes I feel he's not telling us the truth. Or all the truth. Just the other day, he let slip that he had a house in Switzerland. In Geneva. I can't understand why he didn't tell me before. The company could save a lot of money instead of having me stay in hotels. But he'd never offered."

Elaine was annoyed. Still, Mr. Davis certainly wasn't the criminal type or anything like that, she thought. Quite the opposite. He was a perfect gentleman in the old-fashioned sense. Whenever she and Mr. Davis walked along a street, Mr. Davis always took care to walk on the outside, between her and the street, and she liked that. She also liked him taking her to fancy restaurants. She had never really been treated so well. Sometimes Mr. Davis would even confide in her. Occasionally he would tell the story of his previous life back in the States, about how he had been raised on a farm in Vermont, how he'd met his wife, Barbara, while the two were still students at the University of Edinburgh, he in English literature, she in medical school.

"She had such lovely golden-red hair in those days," Mr. Davis said, with apparent fondness in his voice.

His wife had gone on to become a prominent, internationally known surgeon in Long Island, while he had made his fortune in finance and banking, but the strain of two professionals living under one roof with three children, daughters Jillian, Noël and Heather, took its toll, and he and Barbara eventually grew apart. He had suffered serious stress in mounting his own successful career, he explained. He had been born poor, into a home lit by coal-oil lamps. His father had been a truck driver, and he himself had sold vegetables at a roadside stand to raise money to go to school. He was entirely self-made, he said. He'd made his fortune and come to England after a messy divorce to lead a quiet life. His wife might want alimony, he said, but she wasn't going to get it. He'd see to that.

He was especially proud of his daughters, though. "And they adore their father," he told Elaine. He hoped soon to bring his youngest, Heather, over to join him, but he didn't say how he would accomplish that. Nor did he say how his wife might react.

It was hard for Elaine not to notice how Mr. Davis doted on Noël, regularly buying her special gifts. He always wanted her to look good, and it pleased him, he said, that whenever he and Noël had walked by a construction site in London, the workers would whistle at her slim good looks. One evening when he fell asleep before the fire, with Frederick Forsyth's latest thriller lying open on his chest and his glasses slipped down on his nose, Noël turned to Elaine and said in a low murmur, "Gee, but Dad looks old sometimes." There was affection between them.

Elaine once remarked to Mr. Davis that Noël actually looked after him "like a wife," with all the cooking and cleaning she did.

"Of course she does," he said. "I want her to know how to do all these things so that when the right man comes along, she'll make a good wife." He wanted her to able to speak French as well, and he and Noël and Elaine attended afternoon French classes for two semesters at a local college. Elaine was surprised at how Mr. Davis, such a well-travelled person, could perform so miserably at languages. He couldn't even distinguish between *il* and *elle*.

"Remember the woman's magazine *Elle*, Mr. Davis," Elaine would say. "*Elle* is she, *il* is he."

"Yes, yes, an excellent way to remember, Elaine. Thank you."

Albert Walker was not at all proficient in languages. It was the key reason he had had to stay in England. His true talents, however, lay in the territories of deceit, guile and manipulation. In springtime, when Elaine was about to set off on one of her frequent trips to Switzerland, he asked her to post a package from Switzerland to London. It was addressed to Barbara Thomson, and in it was the equivalent of nearly $10,000 in Swiss francs, cash. A note was attached, "Dear Barbara, Sorry I had to leave without saying good-bye. Enclosed is the rent I owe you. Yours sincerely, David."

Albert Walker had had a bit of a rethink on his hasty and surreptitious departure from London the previous fall. He didn't want anyone looking for him because of a measly $10,000 in rent owing, agreed upon under the one-year lease. Moreover, should any police ever appear at her door looking for him, she would tell them authoritatively that he was in Switzerland. She had proof.

In mid-April 1992, David Davis ordered another £4,200 worth of furnishings from Harrods, small pieces mainly, and summoned to his home an interior decorator from Ottaway's of Harrogate, explaining that he wanted his bedroom renovated. The decorator found it strange that a single man should wish to spend so lavishly on his own bedroom when the rest of the house was still so sparsely furnished. But Mr. Davis was unequivocal. He selected a regal-looking green and burgundy pattern, *Salignac*, from the Paris-based textile manufacturer Channée Ducroq. It was the most expensive pattern in the decorator's sample book and cost £92 per metre, $200 a yard. Mr. Davis surprised the designer further by saying he wanted sufficient material not only to cover his handmade *Lit Bateau*—his elegant five-foot-wide bed—but enough to sweep back behind, up and over the bed into a specially designed canopy that the decorator would first sketch to his satisfaction. When the final quote was submitted, he promptly paid the £1,000 deposit in cash.

"He certainly seems like the lord-of-the-manor type," the designer remarked on returning to the office. "The daughter didn't say a word the entire time I was there."

When the order for the fabric was faxed from Harrogate to Channée Ducroq's London supplier, the supplier was taken aback and immediately phoned to ask the Harrogate designer to double-check his figures.

"Are you sure you have the right numbers?" the supplier asked.

"Perfectly sure," said the interior decorator.

Mr. Davis's design required no fewer than 20 metres of the *Salignac* pattern. When work was completed in May 1992, Mr. Davis was handed a bill for more than £4,000 less his deposit. He paid the balance in cash. The bill was the equivalent of almost $9,000.

A week later, he walked into Austick's Bookshop in the centre of Harrogate and bought a paperback edition of Fyodor Dostoevsky's *Crime and Punishment*.

Close to a year after Albert Walker had shown up in Harrogate, he began to think about getting rid of Elaine Boyes. She had proven useful. Accounts throughout Europe had been established, and the complicated paper trail would be difficult for anyone to untangle. Walker was now ready to launch stage two of his Harrogate plan: sending Elaine and Ron to Canada and then seizing their identities for Sheena and himself to use. As part of Walker's plan, he had already clawed back £30,000 by making Elaine take out a mortgage with the Halifax Building Society and handing the money over to him. Now he began to allude to further, unspecified "cash-flow problems." After weeks of references to "money being tight," he told Elaine the balance of the money he'd put up would have to be called in. He needed it for another business deal. Elaine was not happy.

"Surely there's some kind of arrangement we could make, Mr. Davis?" she said during an afternoon meeting at the Davis home. Davis was seated at the dining room table with a vast array of papers spread out before him.

"Elaine, I don't think it's possible. It's unfortunate, I admit. If there were two people in the world I'd really rather *not* have to do this to, it's you and Ron, believe me. But I don't see any way around it."

"But Mr. Davis—what if we sell the flat to you? Sell it outright? That way, you could hold on to the property, and we could pay you rent?"

"It's not a question of income for me, Elaine. It's a question of commitments I have to meet. I know it's sudden, and I've done what I can. But it's time you called an estate agent and start thinking about putting the flat up for sale. I'm not in a hurry now, but I soon will be. You and Ron will be heading off soon to Canada anyway."

"But what if we come back? We'll need a place."

"It would be prudent if you acted now, Elaine."

Mr. Davis's tone had turned serious, and Elaine knew the conversation was over.

Later, when Elaine told Ron about the exchange, he was unfazed. Mr. D. had always been a straight shooter and more than generous, and he would be again when he could, said Ron. If Mr. Davis said he needed the cash, who were they to argue? Elaine and Ron had the property listed for sale at £62,500. Maybe they could turn a difficult situation into a profitable one, Elaine thought, and salvage a bit of money in the experience. But at £62,500, there were no takers.

Some weeks later, Mr. Davis also informed Ron that he could no longer pay the rent for Rutland Radio. Ron would have to go it alone; money was now incredibly tight.

With the onset of fall, Mr. Davis's interest in antiques seemed to fade. He had bought an expensive mahogany wardrobe, a few paintings and two bronze statues from a dealer down in Nottinghamshire, but there was precious little else. He began to speak now of possibly opening his own tea shop, like Betty's, but furnished with antiques. Later he spoke of perhaps buying a news agent's shop—the British were positively addicted to newspapers, he said. But it was idle talk. Albert Walker was growing impatient to move on. In October 1992, when it came time to renew his and Sheena's membership at the Tangerine Fitness Club, he signed on for six more months only. It was his own arbitrary deadline. He decided that by spring '93, his mission would be accomplished: Platt and Boyes would be shipped off to Canada, and he and Sheena could then leave Harrogate with new identities.

On Christmas Day 1992, the final steps of his plan were set into motion. He invited Ron and Elaine to Christmas dinner and presented them with a card in which he had written: "Two air tickets to Canada. Valid until the end of February." Platt was overwhelmed.

"I think it's time you and Elaine seized the dream, Ron," Mr. Davis said, smiling broadly.

They poured wine, there was a toast, there was a sense of celebration, and Ron and Elaine thanked Mr. Davis profusely. They were committed and they were going, although Elaine would later extract from Mr. Davis a return ticket, just in case.

"Not for me," Ron told her. "I'm never coming back." This would be different from his other attempts to settle in Canada—two times during the '80s—this time he'd succeed, he said.

It had been a difficult year, but Mr. D. had still come through, just as Ron had predicted. Mr. Davis, however, had a favour to ask in return. Naturally, he would be sad to see Ron and Elaine go, he said, but their departure would also work a hardship for him. He still had to operate Cavendish Corporation and access his money. Could they possibly see their way to making two rubber stamps each of their signatures? For Ron and Elaine, the beneficiaries of so much of Mr. Davis's generosity, the request did not seem unreasonable. How would Mr. Davis access the various accounts otherwise? It seemed wrong to refuse the request. So they complied.

Once Boyes and Platt were gone, the stamps would allow Walker to continue to operate as usual. He could access everything by fax and by mail. In those rare instances when he actually had to go to a bank counter, he'd simply have a presigned cheque at the ready, or in a pinch, he could even forge one. He'd get by, especially since he would now have credit cards and British bank accounts as well. That was easy.

"I'll pay the balance owing and close them down for you, Ron. No need for you to worry. Leave 'em to me."

The signature stamps would also allow him to apply for replacement copies of Platt's driver's licence and birth certificate and even get a new set of credit cards. When the documents and cards came in, he would sign them R.J. Platt in his own hand. Albert Walker's calculating plan was falling into place nicely. Ronald Platt had been stripped clean and never even knew it.

On February 11, 1993, Elaine signed over a sweeping power of attorney to Mr. Davis, ostensibly so that Davis could finish up the sale of the Howard Court property for her after their departure. In effect, though, the power of attorney gave Albert the legal right to take over all of Elaine Boyes's affairs. Everything. The document, the signing of which was witnessed by a neighbour, gave Mr. Davis the right, "to deposit money . . . to draw money . . . to sign my name . . . to receive mail on my behalf . . . generally to act in relation to my personal affairs . . . in all respects as I myself do." He couldn't complete the sale of the house unless Elaine signed it. She did. It was a stroke of genius. Henceforth, who could possibly say that anything Albert Walker did in Elaine Boyes's name was illegal? He held the document in his hand.

Finally, as his last generous gesture, Mr. Davis organized an account for Ron Platt at the Royal Bank of Canada's main branch in Calgary, Alberta. Into it he transferred $7,250 so that Ron and Elaine would have sufficient funds to look after themselves when they arrived. That very week back in Canada, police investigators had finally tracked Albert Walker's old safety deposit box at the Bank of Montreal at King and Bay and drilled out the locks. The door fell to the floor with a hollow metallic sound. Peering into box number 7277, a hole in the wall 24 inches deep and just big enough to put your arm into, investigators saw that there was nothing. An estimated $700,000 of assets had passed through this space: gold bars, Swiss and French francs, British pounds. It was all gone. The police were late again.

Weeks later, they would hold a press conference and issue a Canada-wide arrest warrant for Walker. Later still, Ontario Provincial Police Staff Sergeant Joe Milton would appeal to the Attorney General for provisional arrest warrants for Walker to be issued overseas. Not a chance, came the reply; not until there was convincing evidence as to where Walker was hiding. The police hunt for Albert Walker was going nowhere. In desperation, Barbara Walker engaged the services of a part-time private investigator. Perhaps he could help. Meanwhile, on the other side of the Atlantic, Albert was preparing to move on.

Harrogate had served his purposes perfectly. He had achieved all of his goals: he had organized and successfuly operated his money-laundering operation; he had acquired the necessary documents from Platt to launch a new and more mobile identity—getting rid of Platt and Boyes in the process; and lastly, he had successfully and comfortably fit into the town's life without being found out. His acting skills had served him well.

On February 15, only eight days before their departure, Albert Walker convinced Ron and Elaine to accept an offer of £50,000 for their Howard Court flat, £5,000 less than what he had paid for it. He'd close the deal in April. Later the same day, he quietly dialled an estate agent saying he wanted to list his own property as quickly as possible.

He had good reason: he and Sheena were also leaving Harrogate. Sheena Walker was pregnant.

12

BIRTH AND REBIRTH

On the evening of February 22, 1993, after a farewell dinner in Harrogate, Ron Platt glanced down at his watch and looked up at Elaine's mother, Joan. "By this time tomorrow, I'll be there," he said. "I'm going home."

The next day, Ron and Elaine boarded a flight in London for Calgary and were gone for good. At least, this is what Albert Walker hoped.

Once again, Walker's patience and planning had paid dividends. He had, or would soon have, the complete cover for a life on the run: a driver's licence, a birth certificate, credit cards, bank accounts, and all of it in the name of Ronald J. Platt. He also had signature stamps in both Ron and Elaine's names.

The baby was due in mid-September, and Albert Walker knew that they had to leave Harrogate as quickly as possible. It would not be long before Sheena's pregnancy would become obvious, and that would raise uncomfortable questions among the neighbours. Sheena was only 17, and no one in Harrogate had ever seen her in the company of any man except her father. Walker had the feeling their French teacher was suspicious about their relationship. He was right. The French instructor had remarked to colleagues that maybe Mr. Davis and Noël really weren't father and daughter after all. She thought they might be older-man-and-younger-girlfriend. Through two terms of a conversational French course, Mr. Davis had always been noticeably protective of the young woman he had introduced as his daughter.

"He never lets her out of his reach," the teacher had said to a fellow staff member at the photocopy machine one day. "She's never attended a single class without him. Don't you find it peculiar that a 17-year-old should attend afternoon French classes with daddy when everyone else her age is either working or in college?"

Mr. Davis had explained to staff that he was thinking about buying property in France and his daughter Noël would have to learn French in order to attend college there. That sounded logical, the teacher thought. But he did seem awfully young to be retired as he claimed to be.

In the short term now, Sheena's pregnancy would complicate matters. It would certainly have to be hidden. When Sheena first told Albert that she was pregnant, there had been a deep and emotional conversation and the possibility of abortion had been discussed, Sheena would later reveal.

"I'll stand by you," Albert said, "no matter what choice you make, you can count on me for support. I'll stand by you both emotionally and financially."

Later, Sheena visited a doctor on Harley Street, London's avenue of expensive private physicians. She introduced herself as Elaine Boyes, although she had no I.D. in the name of Elaine Boyes. Albert hadn't organized that yet. Afterward, Sheena decided to keep the child. In the long term, of course, a child would have the effect of enhancing their cover. With a newborn, neighbours and acquaintances at their next destination would be more inclined to believe they *were* husband and wife. Albert decided he and Sheena would wear wedding rings to complete the illusion. All of that, however, lay ahead. For the moment, Albert and Sheena Walker would have to leave Harrogate soon, and yet their departure could not seem hasty. Undue speed would raise further suspicions. Everything had to be done smoothly.

Typically, Walker had set his departure plans in motion early by listing his own house for sale even before Ron and Elaine had left the ground. He also told his neighbours, the Clarkes, that come fall, Noël would likely be leaving for the U.S. to pursue a fine arts degree at a posh Ivy League college.

As for the closing of Ron Platt's television repair shop out on Kings Road, it had gone off without a hitch after Ron and Elaine had departed; better, in fact, than expected. Walker used the opportunity to dish a little dirt on Platt. Albert could never resist the chance to weave his web a little finer.

"Just up and left for Canada suddenly," he explained to Alfred Batemen, the landlord of Platt's Kings Road property, "and left me holding the bag."

Bateman was surprised.

"You're having me on," Bateman said, incredulous. Bateman knew the story of Mr. Davis's generosity with Platt well. Davis himself had explained it to him more than a year earlier, the day Davis had first come to look at the Kings Road premises on Platt's behalf. Davis said he'd met Platt by chance in a pub up by Summer Bridge, not far from Pateley Moor, and was greatly impressed by the soft-spoken man and his avowed expertise in electronics.

"I think all he needs is a bit of Christian charity and some financing to get him going," Davis had said, introducing himself to Bateman as an American banker-turned-art-trader recently retired to Harrogate. Davis had even arranged to pay Platt's rent through Cavendish Corporation.

Now it looked as if Davis had been had.

"Took his girlfriend with him and left me with rent owing and £200 in telephone bills!" Walker said, standing in the middle of the abandoned storefront, waving his arms and bristling with annoyance. "Can you imagine a guy like that?"

Bateman shook his head in disgust. "And after all you did for him. Who would've thought?"

Walker was secretly thrilled at his own acting skills and his talent for duping others. He could always count on the gullibility of people of goodwill, and Alfred Bateman was no exception. Shortly after leaving Bateman's Kings Road address, Walker went into a print shop and had brand-new business cards made up in the name of Ronald J. Platt, Cavendish Corporation Limited, 45 St. Leonard's Oval, Harrogate. Albert Walker's new life as Ronald Platt was beginning even as his old one as David Davis wasn't yet cold in the ground. He put his newly acquired driver's licence to immediate use, buying a little second-hand Austin Metro. Now he was mobile. No longer would he need to take cabs around Harrogate. A pity, he thought. He'd miss stringing along the local cabbies, making them think he was a CIA agent working with his fellow Americans over on the base at Menwith. He had loved that, he once confided to the Clarkes.

The sale of Ron and Elaine's flat also went well, and using his power of attorney, Walker handed over the keys to the new owners on the April 2, 1993, the same day a harmless Canada-wide arrest warrant was issued in his name. The same week, Walker went to the Tangerine Club for his last workout, telling the manager he and Noël wouldn't be extending the membership, as they were moving shortly.

Then an unforeseen problem arose: the sluggish real estate market wouldn't cooperate. It should have picked up with the arrival of spring but hadn't, and Walker was getting nervous. On April 15, in the hope of stimulating offers, he called his real estate agent and told her to slash the list price on his house from £122,000 to £105,000. He had to get moving.

Complicating matters further were the constant calls from Ron and Elaine in Canada. They seemed reluctant to let go. It had been a rough landing in Calgary, they told him on the phone. When they had touched down, it was 30 degrees below zero, with winds gusting up to 30 miles an hour. For Elaine Boyes, who had lived almost all of her life in gentle Harrogate, that pleasant gateway to the Yorkshire Dales, Calgary in February was a harsh point of entry. As the jet had taxied to the terminal, she peered out the window and wondered what she had got herself into. Neither of them had jobs, so they were forced to look downmarket for an apartment, and as a couple accustomed to the quaintness of north England's leafy spa town, it was a demoralizing experience.

"Well, it doesn't have to be Calgary, does it?" Walker asked Platt during a long-distance call.

"No. No of course not," said Platt. "It's just that this is what I'm familiar with. Or *was* familiar with. It doesn't seem the same any more. We're thinking about driving to Vancouver."

"Great idea. Try to do the Rockies and the little towns along the way," Walker encouraged. "Give yourself time. You'll love them. It's a marvellous country, Canada. A wonderful place."

The Rockies were spectacular, and along the way, they stopped in Harrogate, British Columbia, explaining to a local merchant that they had come from "the original Harrogate." The merchant was mildly amused. As for Vancouver, Ron didn't like it. It was too congested, too expensive, and they drove straight back to Calgary. They finally found a little basement apartment in the northwest sector of the city and moved in. Neither could find work. At night, they lay awake in bed and listened to the rumble of trucks on the Trans-Canada Highway a block and a half away. On Sundays, they'd drive out to Lake Louise and walk across the frozen lake in silence. Calgary was not at all the wide open, friendly frontier town of Platt's memory. It seemed dark and cold now, and Ron began to brood and grow morose. Elaine worried about him, but she also worried for herself. Ron's dark moods were beginning to drag her down. She was glad she had insisted to Mr. Davis that she have a return ticket in her pocket before leaving England. Her sister Gillian's wedding was scheduled in Norwich in July, and Elaine decided she would give the current arrangement until then. If it didn't sort itself out, if things did not improve, she would return to England and stay.

On May 15, in "the original Harrogate," Albert Walker had good news. A potential puchaser by the name of Yves Laurent Brown put in a bid of £100,000 for the St. Leonard's Oval house. It was £20,000 less than what Walker had paid, but it was progress. Walker told his agent he was prepared to saw off at £103,000, and on May 24, he accepted the revised bid. The Browns paid the customary 10 per cent down as a sign of their commitment, and Walker informed them he wanted to hand over the keys "as soon as possible." He'd lost £17,000, almost $35,000, but it was worth it, provided he could close the deal promptly and find a place where Sheena could give birth to the baby in relative obscurity.

One day in mid-June, Albert Walker drove his small Austin Metro south through Somerset to look for a new place to live. Upon entering the green geometry of deepest Devon, a county of endless hedgerows, undulating hills and clear trout streams, Walker knew he'd found it. The hedgerows lining both sides of a labyrinthine network of country lanes gave him a deep and comforting sense of cover. This was well out of the way, a warren-like world of secrecy in which he could hide with Sheena as Ron and Noël Platt. He would have to move quickly, though. She was in her fifth month. Soon she would start to look notice-ably pregnant.

That night, he booked into a farmhouse bed and breakfast near the streamside village of Bickleigh, telling the proprietors, Len and Barbara Fullilove, that he was looking to buy into the area.

"A new wife and a new life," he offered, by way of explana-tion, immediately addressing Len and Barbara by their first names, a habit the English regard as manifestly American. He gave Barbara one of his new business cards, and she pencilled in "Platt" in the registry book, adding the note, "looking for prop-erty." It was June 20. Mr. Platt spent two days visiting local estate agents, and though he did not find a house immediately, he told the Fulliloves he would definitely return. He loved the mid-Devon countryside, he said, "the way the early-morning mist nestles among the hills."

It was only when he returned from Devon to Harrogate that the Clarkes, the next-door neighbours, noticed something odd. It had always been David and Noël's habit in fine weather to take their evening meal outside in the garden with a nice bottle of wine. These days, the Clarkes noticed, David always dined alone. Where, they wondered, was Noël?

"Oh she's headed off to the States," Davis explained to Douglas Clarke one evening, as they chatted over the fence. "Surely she said good-bye? Do you mean to say that she—?"

"Didn't mention a word," said Douglas, obviously hurt.

"Oh Douglas, I'm *sorry*. I'm *so* sorry. I'll definitely have a word with her on the phone about this. Believe me, Douglas, I will. I can't imagine her having left without saying good-bye!"

"Oh well," Douglas said quietly. "It was probably just the excitement of leaving. Young people do get swept up about going off to college. I'm sure it wasn't intentional."

Jean Clarke was surprised and a little peeved when Douglas came in from the garden and told her the news.

"Can you imagine that Noël," she said, "up and leaving without so much as saying 'Cheerio'?"

Noël had gone up to Scotland for a period. No one in Harrogate ever laid eyes on her again.

June dragged into July, and finally, the Browns announced they were ready to move; and Albert Walker prepared himself to hand over the keys and move on. Then the Browns stalled: first they wanted to take a holiday, then take possession on August 27. Walker was apoplectic. He had a pregnant 17-soon-to-be-18-year-old on his hands with a baby due in eight weeks, and now his real estate deal was unravelling. More worrisome still, he had just received a call from Elaine Boyes. She was coming home for her sister's wedding, she said. The arrangement with Ron was growing more difficult. Suddenly, it seemed, everything was going wrong. Despite his best planning, Albert Walker's world was becoming complicated.

There was, however, one piece of good news out of Canada: Ron was staying on. Although he was still in a deep funk and remained without work, he would not budge. How long would it last, though? Albert Walker knew he had to speak to Elaine as soon as she landed back in Britain for her sister's wedding. He had to convince Elaine to get back on the plane and return to Calgary as soon as possible. If Ronald Platt were ever to decide to come back to England, Walker knew, three years of careful planning and hard work would evaporate. He could not allow that to happen. He would gladly pay for Elaine's return to Canada. First, though, he had to sort out his real estate problems.

"I can't wait forever!" he shouted at his estate agent over the phone.

"But Mr. Davis—"

"I've contacted my solicitor and we're agreed: if the Browns won't take the keys, we want the 'Sold' sign taken down and the property shown immediately. I've got to get on with my life too!"

The bluff worked, and the Browns promised to take the keys August 9, Albert's birthday.

But there was more trouble ahead. Elaine returned from Canada to announce she wasn't going back. Walker was not pleased. Not surprisingly, he was somewhat preoccupied at the Boyes' family wedding. Even Elaine remarked on it. From the very first moment when he picked her up, he seemed on edge and was irritated that photographs of him were being taken during the reception, a petty annoyance Elaine found strange.

Mr. Davis was impeccably dressed as always, wearing a natty blue blazer, a silk tie with coordinated socks and taupe dress slacks. He apologized to the family for Noël's absence.

"She had to fly off to New York to celebrate her sister's sixteenth birthday in Long Island," he said, drawing on a small Davidoff cigar. "She would have *loved* to have been here, though." The trip to New York, he explained, had been planned months in advance.

The family understood. They were just so pleased Mr. Davis had decided to come on his own anyway that they pinned a beautiful white carnation on his lapel, and everyone regarded him as Elaine's official escort. Elaine had always thought of him as suave and good-looking, not to mention rich, and during the reception later in the garden, they sat close to one another and shared an intimate conversation.

"What really seems to be the problem with Ron, Elaine?" Albert asked, holding a large crystal goblet of red wine while surveying guests in the garden.

"Oh Mr. Davis, if you only knew. It was terrible. Ron can't find work; I couldn't even look, because I couldn't get papers. Ron failed his driver's test. Then he got depressed—deeply, deeply depressed. I just couldn't cope, Mr. Davis. He'd go for days without talking. It was like living with someone who wasn't there."

Ron had remembered Calgary the way it was when he was a young boy, Elaine said, when it was still becoming Canada's oil capital. It was booming then, bright and promising, Ron said. And there was work to be had, plenty of work. But now, Elaine said, there were few jobs and Calgary had changed. It was a much more "mixed" city than Ron had recalled.

"Ron's not a racist or anything like that, Mr. Davis."

"Of course not, Elaine."

"But it's as mixed a city as, say, Manchester or Birmingham. Or Leeds."

"Multicultural," Mr. Davis corrected her. "That's the term they use in North America, Elaine: 'multicultural.'"

"I can't go back there, Mr. Davis. I can't. I've got myself to think about. It would break me. It nearly *did* break me. My doctor has me on medication even now."

"But what about Ron?" Mr. Davis offered gently. "He needs you, Elaine. He needs your support. The poor guy can't face it alone. It sounds to me as though he's really trying, Elaine. Giving his best. He just hasn't got a break yet."

Elaine went silent.

"I think you should give him a second chance," he said. "Every man deserves a second chance."

But Elaine Boyes would not be moved. She had been with Ron for 13 years. She wasn't going back to Ron, she decided, not now, not ever. Walker sensed it and knew he would have to live with

Elaine's decision. It wasn't a perfect set of circumstances by any means, but he could manage it if he had to. And he would.

In August, Albert Walker arranged for movers, handed over the keys to the Browns and left Harrogate at last. Harrogate was history. Or so he thought.

Days later, he and Sheena re-emerged together at the Fullilove's bed and breakfast near Bickleigh, signing in as Ron and Noël Platt. Sheena was very pregnant, only a month from delivering. They took an upper room for two weeks at the Fullilove's Lodge Hill Farm set back off the highway, and while there, Sheena took a taxi to see a doctor at a local clinic. There she presented herself as Elaine Boyes "from America," explaining that she had lived in Britain for three years, and she was subsequently issued a National Health Service card.

During this time, Albert, now Ron, resumed his search for a new home. He found it in the classified section of a local newspaper. It wasn't for sale, only for rent: "Quiet, secluded, three-bedroom barn conversion in tranquil setting. 15 minutes Tiverton." It sounded perfect and was.

The owner, Judith DiMarte, was a small, friendly blonde woman of about 40, a widow who managed her own sheep farm and raised horses. Her teenage daughter, Kit, was an aspiring jockey, and Judith's sister Carole, an outgoing French teacher with short brown hair, lived in her own half of the farmhouse duplex.

Judith rented out three cottages on her premises and was accustomed to foreigners. She herself had married an Italian gentleman who had recently died. One of the cottages was rented to an Australian family, so an American with a young, pregnant wife was not so extraordinary. On August 23, Ron and Noël moved into Kestrel Cottage, a sunny, many-windowed building set on a ridge overlooking a valley. Albert always preferred the company of women, finding them nonthreatening and, generally, susceptible to his politeness and charm. The absence of men at the DiMarte spread in the tiny village of Oakford suited him fine.

"I thought you said you rented it to a couple?" said Carole, staring out the window into the garden as she washed dishes following a late breakfast one morning. "I did," said Judith, sipping coffee and studying bills. "I thought I'd told you about them?"

Carole kept washing dishes, staring into the yard. Across the way, a young woman was hanging clothes on a clothesline. A light morning breeze was blowing. These were the last days of summer, and the sisters' schedule of teaching—Judith taught Italian to adults in the area—had just begun, signalling the start of fall. *La rentré*, the French called it, Carole thought, the autumn ritual, the re-entry into the rigours of real life after a leisurely summer.

Standing at the sink, she could just barely see the young woman's head bobbing up and down behind the line as she hung out the wash. She was blonde and pretty in a young way, a girl really, maybe 18. That was strange, Carole thought, because Judith hadn't mentioned anything about the new couple having any kids. Carole herself had exchanged greetings with Ron, the new man, only the day before and thought him friendly, American and apparently in his 40s. As Carole stared dreamily off into the yard, the wind picked up and flapped at the clothing on the line, pulling back a set of sheets and exposing the young woman at length: she was wearing a flower-print shift and pumps and was pregnant, very, very pregnant.

"Is that the wife?" Carole asked, her high inflection indicating surprise.

"What?" said Judith, looking up from her bills a little annoyed.

"Is that the wife?"

"The young blonde?"

"Yes."

"Yes, yes, I know: quite young, right? It's the way of the world, Carole. That's men these days. She *is* pretty, though."

"Pretty young, I'd say," said Carole. "How old do you think?"

"Kit's 14, and she thinks she's no more than 18 maybe?"

"My God, she's pregnant. She must be ready to deliver any day."

"Ron, the husband, says it should be a couple of weeks, mid-month, I think. Her first, obviously."

"What exactly does Ron do for a living?" Carole asked.

"I'm not really sure," said Judith. "He mentioned something about 'finance' and 'the City.' I think he's into share trading. But semi-retired in a way. He wasn't very specific, really. They both seem to love art, though. He paints quite a bit apparently. I think she does too."

"He seems *awfully* young to be retired, semi or otherwise. What could possibly have brought them here?"

"Don't know, really. Second wife. Fresh start. That sort of thing. I'm not sure. He certainly gives the impression that money is no problem. So—as long as the rent's paid on time . . ."

As time went by, Albert Walker told Judith and Carole a fair bit about his life. He said he had been born in Britain, in Wallasey, Merseyside, and that he had crossed the Atlantic to Canada with his mother and father in the '50s, when he was still a young boy. His father was a teacher, he said, and as a result of his father's fixation on Canada and its wide-open spaces, he had spent his formative years there. It was the Ron Platt story in its entirety. Walker had abandoned the David Davis cover now completely. Sheena remained Noël in the transition—but Noël Platt now, no longer Davis—and she called him Ron. A few months after they moved to Devon, she bought him a softcover collection of Gary Larson cartoons for Christmas and inscribed it: "To Ron, with love, Noël, Christmas 1993." Albert had lectured her again and again: their use of each other's names, in public and in private, had to be rigorously consistent. That was the safest way, he said. That way, there would never be any mistakes.

It was fall now, and the Walkers had migrated and metamorphosed yet again. It was as if this had become their autumn ritual.

They had picked up and moved three times in four years, not just geographically but psychologically, moving further and further away from their ever more distant Canadian reality. All of that southwestern Ontario flatness, once so familiar, was growing dimmer, hazier and a little more out of focus. Albert was skilfully removing Sheena from her past, creating a tightly controlled present, one from which she could not escape and, hopefully, from which she would not *wish* to escape, provided he could make it attractive enough and exciting enough, provided he could make her believe that they were partners engaged in a common enterprise—but partners in a plan in which she would always defer to him. He made the plans. He set the rules. He was the mastermind capable of achieving anything.

The English say people come to Devon to die, but that once they get there, they forget why they came. Albert Walker knew exactly why he had come: to start a new life as Ronald Joseph Platt. Devon would be a place of birth and rebirth.

Inside Kestrel Cottage, with its beamed ceilings and French doors through which sunlight shone in early morning, Walker installed his big French *Lit Bateau*, his computer to keep track of his money dealing and share trading and, of course, his paintings—his own, those he'd copied and those he'd bought—carefully wrapped in bubble paper. In the kitchen, he fixed his favourite French calendar to the wall, the "Hidden Corners of France." Yes, Albert thought, he had found his own hidden corner right here in Britain. Now everything would be fine.

On Wednesday, September 22, 1993, at Tiverton and District Hospital in the County of Devon, Sheena Walker gave birth to a girl. They called her Emily Jane Platt. A month later, Albert filled out the birth registration form: "**Father:** Ronald Joseph Platt. **Place of birth:** Wallasey, Merseyside. **Occupation:** Artist. **Mother:** Elaine Claire Boyes. Artist. **Place of Birth:** America." In the space allotted for the two signatories of the form to identify themselves was written: "Father, Mother."

The real Ronald Joseph Platt was far away and living quietly in Calgary. Elaine Boyes was still in Harrogate. Albert signed the certificate in visibly shaky handwriting, and the form was then handed back and shipped off to the General Register Office at St. Catherine's House in central London, where it was filed among the millions of other certificates kept there. No one, Albert Walker thought, would ever find the birth certificate or even think to look for it.

Albert Walker brought Sheena and the baby home from hospital to Upcott Farm in Oakford with all the trepidation and youthful excitement of a first-time parent. They crossed the threshold of Kestrel Cottage and carried Emily up the wooden staircase to a room on the second floor that Albert had equipped with a special new crib, a humidifier and a small musical mobile. For Sheena, it was the most extraordinary experience of her young life. For Albert, it was all very familiar.

13

I THANK THE LORD

"Oh Ron, Noël, she's so beautiful," said Carole. "And the dark hair!"

"She *is* beautiful," said Ron, cradling the newborn baby in his arms and glancing up with a glittering smile. This was Emily, his pride and joy. It was October 1993.

They were all seated in the front room of Kestrel Cottage on a bright and brisk fall day: Ron and Noël, Carole Poole, her sister Judith DiMarte and tiny Emily, a little more than a week old.

It was the first time Ron and Noël had shown off Emily to visitors, and Ron was especially proud.

"And will your mum and dad be coming from the States to visit, Noël?" asked Judith.

"Oh probably," Ron said. "Yes, yes, they likely will."

"Wonderful," said Judith. "Is this their first grandchild?"

"Yes, it is," said Ron.

"Well that settles it," said Carole. "They'll positively *have* to come, won't they? But where to put them? You've hardly room here. Have you looked at any hotels?"

"Yes, we're actually thinking about the Tarr Steps," said Ron.

The Tarr Steps is perhaps the loveliest country hotel in the region, a Georgian mansion tucked among the wooded slopes of the River Barle in the heart of Exmoor, a glorious national park filled with wildlife.

"That would be smashing," said Carole. "They'd love that." It would be typical of Ron, too, she thought. He revelled in his sense of good taste. It was always the best of everything. Nothing was too good or too expensive. God only knew where he got his money, Carole wondered. He was forever using a kind of corporate vocabulary: "capital," "the City," "investment." It was very vague.

"We were up to the Tarr Steps just a few weeks ago, looking it over," Ron continued. "Noël's parents would love it. The dining room is supposed to be fantastic."

"That's what we've heard," said Carole. "Though, of course, we've never been."

Time passed, and Noël's parents never did arrive to welcome their first grandchild into the world. At first, the sisters thought it most unusual, but then, they thought, perhaps Noël's marriage to an older man had caused friction in the family—even more so, since Ron was actually an old friend of Noël's father, or so Ron said.

"Noël and I met at an art school she was attending up in London," Ron explained one autumn afternoon. "Her father was a college classmate of mine, and when he heard I was coming to England, he asked me to look in on her and make sure she was okay and, well, what can I say? These things happen. We fell in love." It sounded like something out of a book. Doubtless, Noël's parents had found it unsettling.

Still later, Ron also revealed that Noël's mother and father had actually separated a few years back. It was a nasty break-up, he said, and that was another factor making a visit unlikely. In time, Carole and Judith let the subject of the impending visit drop.

As the weeks and months unfolded, Ron Platt presented himself to Carole and Judith as a model father and threw himself into his new role with relish. One would have thought that, as a man in his late 40s, he was a bit old to contend with the 24-hour demands of a newborn. Yet Ron was invigorated by it. In fact, he appeared to do almost everything. He cooked, he cleaned, he changed diapers, he played with Emily, he cooed to her, tossing her up in the air and teasing "Dada" from her again and again. From their perspective, he was every inch the image of the new man: sensitive, caring and unafraid to pitch in and do what other men of his generation might consider women's work.

He did so much, there were times it seemed as though he were looking after two children.

"It is remarkable," Carole said to Judith one day, "I mean he *is* old enough to be Noël's father."

True. That probably explained why Ron went to such extraordinary lengths to appear young. The sisters noted his hair was dyed black, with occasional patches of embarrassing grey bursting in from time to time; and there were always those tight jeans. Far too tight for a man his age, they felt.

"He's such a nice man," said Carole. "But swaggering about with his thumbs in the pockets of those trousers, I mean . . . he doesn't need to do that."

"It's a bit sad, really, isn't it?" Judith added. "But with such a young wife, he probably feels the pressure."

"Probably," Carole agreed.

To the sisters, Ron and Noël were "jeans people." In posh Harrogate, Albert Walker had taken care to keep to the local code of jackets, ties and flannel trousers. Here, too, he made sure he kept to the local country character. He and Sheena rarely dressed in anything but jeans. Albert was a chameleon. He knew how to blend in.

He also knew how to adapt. In Harrogate, he'd fostered his image as Noël's caring and protective father. In Devon, he was Noël's romantic older husband.

"Would you like to see our bed?" Ron enthusiastically asked the sisters one day, before leading them up the staircase to see the massive mahogany *Lit Bateau* he'd managed to squeeze into their pine-panelled bedroom. It was the same one he'd brought from Harrogate. He did seem romantic.

Often, when Carole went out in the evening to walk the dogs, Ben and Charlie, a candle shone from Ron and Noël's dining table. Inside the glowing ambience of Kestrel Cottage, Carole imagined, all was well. There was wine, a cosy fire and the over-all impression was one of comfort and happiness. What a life, she thought.

But behind that door, there was planning going on.

"The money I've earned isn't going to last forever," Albert carefully explained to Sheena one day. "Eventually I'll have to get a job. We've got to face up to it."

Albert told Sheena he was interested in becoming a counsellor. In Britain, counsellors are a blend of social workers and psycho-analysts, trained to help others to deal with problems; marital difficulties, anxiety, anything really. Albert knew that a small and respected school, the Iron Mill Institute, was located in a deep, oak-lined valley only a 20-minute walk from his Kestrel Cottage door. In time, the institute would unwittingly assist him in making his next, great metamorphosis. Another autumn would come 'round on the calendar. Albert Walker wanted to be ready.

On Christmas Eve, Ron and Noël decided to attend midnight mass at a church in nearby Tiverton, and they asked Judith's dark-haired daughter Kit to babysit. She arrived on time, was given a tour of the house and was left careful instructions about how to care for Emily and how to contact them in the event of an emergency. Emily liked piano sonatas, Mr. Platt explained. Kit should play some sonatas on the CD player if little Emily had difficulty sleeping.

As Mr. Platt led Kit upstairs to see the baby's room, she noticed a large painting on an easel in the landing, directly beneath the louvred Velux skylight. It was modern and abstract and dominated by four heavy blotches of thick, jarring yellow.

"Interesting," Kit offered politely. "Very interesting."

"Do you like it?" Ron asked.

"I think so. I'm not sure I understand it, though."

"It's called 'Friends,'" Ron said, his baritone burgeoning with pride. "It's mine. I painted it."

Kit felt a little uncomfortable. She didn't like it but didn't want to say so. Then she noticed the signature.

"Why is it signed 'David'"? Kit queried.

Albert Walker paused. "David is what my friends called me in art school," he said. "I signed all my paintings 'David' in those days."

Albert knew that David Platt is the name of one of England's most famous footballers, and he was naturally prepared for the next question.

"Are you any relation to the real David Platt?"

"Cousin," Ron said proudly. "But I only see him at birthdays and funerals."

The following day was Christmas 1993, and Ron Platt gave Judith, Carole and Kit a wonderful Christmas hamper filled with goods from Fortnum and Mason's, the Queen's own supplier of provisions on Picadilly in London. This, they thought, was truly special. They had never had a tenant quite like Ron.

In the coming months, Kit often babysat Emily, usually when Ron and Noël went into town for dinner or to catch a movie at the Tiverton cinema. Kit found Emily developing into a bright and responsive girl and believed Ron and Noël to be very good parents. Their bookcases were lined with various baby manuals, and whenever Kit arrived, she was always given precise instructions about Emily's care. Ron would give Kit the telephone number of the restaurant or theatre where they could be reached, show her where the Coke and cookies were kept and always tell her to "make herself at home." Each time, Kit would learn a little more about the Platts.

"What are you seeing tonight?" she asked Ron.

There was a film with Danny DeVito in it in Tiverton, Ron said, and he loved Danny DeVito.

"Absolutely hilarious," Ron told her. "And you know, even though he's just a short little guy, he always gets what he wants."

They chatted about DeVito's various roles, then Ron Platt asked her, "Did you ever see *The War of the Roses?* That film with Michael Douglas and Kathryn Turner, where DeVito plays the lawyer?"

"Oh yes," said Kit. "Kind of a strange film."

"Not strange to me," Ron told her. "You know the marriage between Douglas and Turner? That's exactly what my first marriage was like."

About Noël, however, Kit remained puzzled. Though Kit was only 14, she was certain Noël was very close to her own age.

"She's not 20 yet," Kit told her mother. "There's no way she's 20."

"How can you be so sure?" Judith asked.

"I don't know. I can just feel it."

Kit found it strange, too, that even though she and Noël were relatively close in age, it was Ron who did all the talking. Noël almost never spoke. Carole and Judith agreed. To them, Noël remained an enigma.

"For the life of me, I can't understand how she can be so self-contained," Carole observed to Judith one day. "Whenever Ron has to go into London on business for a few days, she just shuts herself off."

"It is odd, isn't it?" said Judith. "When I go to Minehead for my Italian classes, I always ask her to come along, but she never does. She could bring the stroller, do some window-shopping, have a bit of tea. A change of scene, a break, whatever. But she never comes."

It was a conundrum for which there was no rational answer. How could an unassertive young girl, in a foreign country, newly married, with her first child, who was so utterly dependent upon her husband for seemingly every single thing, suddenly become strong and independent when her husband went away?

"No thank you. I'll be fine," Noël would say, whenever invited for tea or shopping by Carole or Judith. She didn't need to go shopping. The catalogues for OshKosh B'Gosh and Sally Parsons and other smart shops in Chelsea came to her door by mail. That was looked after. "And Ron will phone," she'd say. Ron always did.

In a day or two, Ron would reappear. He'd been up seeing his bankers and brokers in London, he said. Being a retired banker himself from New York, he still liked to keep a close eye on his investments. The sisters mentioned that Noël appeared to be rather "isolated" whenever he left.

"Oh she's okay. She's fine," Ron would dismiss them, in a friendly fashion, of course. He appreciated their concern, but Noël had to learn to get along on her own.

While up in London, he'd visited art dealers too, he confided. He seemed preoccupied with art. Whenever Ron took the family away for a weekend together, Carole and Judith were asked to keep a close eye on the cottage, because there were expensive paintings inside, wrapped in bubble paper, waiting to be shipped to Christie's or Sotheby's for auction. It seemed an utterly different kind of life from anything Judith and Carole were accustomed to. Once a month, Ron wrote out his rent cheque on his National Westminster account in Harrogate. It was an unhurried life of quiet quality—detached and discreet.

On January 24, 1994, Albert Walker filed the obligatory annual report with the British government for Cavendish Corporation, once again using the rubber-stamped signature of Ronald J. Platt. The real Platt was still in Calgary, working for an electronics company north of the city. He'd finally applied for Canadian citizenship, and he'd have it within a month. For the real Ron, it would be a dream fulfilled.

Meanwhile, on January 29, while making his way to London

alone by train, Albert Walker purchased a copy of the *Daily Mail* in Exeter at St. David's railway station. He caught the connecting Great Western from platform five, and as the train rumbled toward the city, Albert settled into his comfortable seat and opened the paper to the women's pages. "Learn to solve all your problems in just a day," the headline read. Albert had begun to nurture an interest in psychology, and he read the article about a totally new form of therapy with interest. The headline read like one of those amazing offers Albert had sometimes seen on the matchbook covers of his youth: "Learn to hypnotize your friends in six simple steps!" Only this article was serious.

"Dave Hawkes and Ron Wilgosh believe in miracles," the piece began. "Neither faith healers nor religious fanatics, they are simply therapists whose brand of psychotherapy can have dramatic results."

Albert was intrigued.

The piece went on to explain how Hawkes and Wilgosh had embraced a new kind of "wonder therapy" developed in the United States by a researcher named Steve de Shazer. It was called "Brief Therapy." De Shazer's research revealed that while traditionalists believed psychotherapy had to be a long-term process, most patients only attended seven sessions. If patients could resolve problems in just seven sessions, he reasoned, why not in one, two or three sessions? The secret, de Shazer felt, lay in focusing not on the problems of the past but on the solutions of the present. Hence, some began to refer to de Shazer's technique as "solution-focused therapy."

"It sounds very American and airy-fairy," the British writer skeptically intoned, "but in fact, solution therapy has a solid structure for plotting change. . . .

"Although the technique sounds deceptively simple, its results can be highly complex."

Albert began to calculate: if the proponents of brief therapy believed it could be quickly administered, why couldn't it be quickly learned? Why couldn't he, as Ron Platt, become a brief therapist himself?

The article closed with an address for therapists "interested in training in solution therapy." They were instructed to write, including a stamped, self-addressed envelope to, Solutions in Therapy, 175a High Street, Brentwood, Essex. Albert Walker carefully tore the page from the newspaper, folded it over and slipped it into his briefcase. The train rumbled along. He'd be writing soon.

Albert enrolled in a counselling skills course at the local Iron Mill Institute and his occasional conversations with Carole over a glass of wine now turned from his love of France—"We're definitely going to move there"—to counselling and solution-focused therapy. Though Carole was an accomplished French teacher, she had an interest in counselling herself and had even investigated the idea of becoming one. She found Ron's conversations stimulating. He seemed well read and was an enthusiastic talker. He was not, however, a very good listener, and counselling was very much about listening.

"Why don't you hurry up and get your qualification, Carole, and we could go into practice together," he'd encourage. "You'd make a brilliant counsellor!" With teaching and looking after two sons, Carole had her hands full.

Ron was always flashing books about from something called the Counselling in Action Series: *Gestalt Counselling in Action*, *Experiences of Counselling in Action*, *Person-Centred Counselling in Action*, *Training and Supervision for Counselling in Action*. He spoke of another new book, entitled *Dissolving Wedlock*, recently reviewed on the cover of the *Sunday Times'* book section. And he spoke of Colin S. Gibson's *Reclaiming the Inner Child*. Ron was always interested in wounded-child theories.

Whenever he spoke of books, however, he seemed always to zip along the surface, like a stone skipping on water. There never seemed to be any depth to such discussions, and the bindings of his books rarely seemed to have been cracked, even though his apparent passion for all books was unbounded. Lined along his shelves beside John Grisham's *The Chamber*, which was very well-thumbed, were *All Quiet on the Western Front*, a selection of writings by Henry David Thoreau, *The Carl Rogers Reader* by the eminent psychologist, and Dostoevsky's *Crime and Punishment*, among others. Ron certainly had the time to read. His seemed to be the ultimate life of leisure.

In early March, the daffodils that line the lane leading to Kestrel Cottage began to bloom and Albert Walker's interests took another turn. He decided to buy a sailboat. Relying on a little advice from Len Fullilove, an experienced sailor and the proprietor of the bed and breakfast he and Sheena had stayed at in August, Albert bought a 24-foot twin-keel Trident sailboat called *Peach*, which he renamed the *Lady Jane*, Jane being little Emily's middle name. He purchased it through Simanda Yacht Sales in Totnes. It cost £4,500 and fulfilled a lifelong fantasy.

First, though, before any sailing could be done, the vendors advised that he would have to organize marine insurance. Albert did so, improvising his own remarkable sailing history as he filled out the insurance forms. Name: Ronald Joseph Platt. State the last two craft owned/sailed by you: 21 ft. homemade plywood sailboat. Period: 1975-1995. Cruising areas: Long Island, New York, USA.

To the question asking what crew would be carried, Albert wrote the words "my wife." Then there was a detailed list of Yes or No questions to fill out. After replying to seven or eight of these, Albert was fed up. Will the vessel be used for single-handed sailing in any capacity whatsoever? "Yes," Albert wrote. If so, please give full details. "Whenever I feel like it." He had never realized there were so many regulations involved with sailing. He signed the form "R.J. Platt" and bought the insurance.

Finally, he enthusiastically set about having the *Lady Jane* prepared for its launch. He had the engine and the sails checked, and on March 24, the boat was lifted from the water and a new Apelco Global Positioning System for navigation was fitted and installed along with a matching aerial. Despite his boasting of 20 years of sailing experience, he was strongly advised never to wander out without a GPS, as the system is called. A few additional cables, clips and plugs, and he was ready to begin.

A Trident is actually a fine boat for beginners. Its name has mythic connections too. A trident is most often associated with Poseidon, the Greek god of the sea, known, as were many of the Olympians, for his ability to change form to further his amorous desires. Albert had always been good at that.

Indeed, throughout this period, Albert Walker had been visiting a hairstylist at a beauty salon, called Centre Stage, in Exeter for a colour and cut every three weeks. It was fitting for a thespian like Albert, who had honed his craft for years, that the salon's insignia bore the theatrical masks of comedy and tragedy. Each time Albert appeared at Centre Stage, an attractive young stylist named Paula Winsor would seat Albert back in her chair and, using a brush, carefully apply L'Oréal's Majirel hair dye number two. It was a darker shade than Paula recommended. But that was what the client wanted.

When Sheena came in, Paula would show her swatches from the L'Oréal folder, and she would select a soft shade of blonde.

The women at Centre Stage were always puzzled by Noël's reserve and thought she was simply snobby. She had an older American husband who was obviously wealthy, and she seemed not to have a care in the world except for her new baby, Emily.

Ron, on the other hand, was friendly and chatty, and the women in the salon found him fascinating. Paula, Julie Bridges and Angela Kelland thought Ron a wonderful man, outgoing and witty. He'd always show up on a quiet Monday or Tuesday, they'd serve him coffee, and they'd all make small talk. They were intrigued by the British-born American who had lived in Canada and eventually headed up a bank in New York and who, despite his wealth, was so down to earth. He made them laugh and always tipped well, and he even had the nerve to drive the most humble-looking, blue-grey Austin Metro. Once he told Julie that if she had "an extra couple of hundred pounds" he could "double it" in no time at all, but sadly, Julie and her husband didn't have a couple of hundred extra, and the offer was forgotten.

There was one morning, however, the women would never forget. Ron came into the shop on his own and said hello but seemed unusually quiet and introspective. Julie, Paula and Angela had grown to feel quite comfortable with Ron, and they were concerned.

"Anything troubling you this morning, Ron?" one asked, as they poured him a second cup of coffee.

"No. No, not really," Ron said, looking up, his eyes welling with tears. "It's just that—I don't know. I got up this morning and I just thought, 'My God. How lucky I am. I have a lovely wife, a beautiful child, I have as much money as I need, and I should just thank the Lord for being so fortunate.' I just felt like crying." And with that, Ron did.

All the women, too, got equally choked up. That day when Ron left, they all stood at the window and waved good-bye.

"What a very special man," one of them said.

It was sometime after that, in the spring, that Ron began growing a beard. He asked Paula if she could recommend a dye for it as well.

"It's a lot of work, Ron," she warned him. "A head of hair, you might need to dye once every two or three weeks. But a beard is different. Facial hair grows much more quickly. You'll have to tend to it almost every day."

"Oh I don't mind," said Ron.

Paula recommended another L'Oréal product and gave him a special little brush for applications. As well, she insisted he take a professional stylist's hand cleaner, Handsoclean, since the dye invariably tended to get on your hands and was very difficult to get out. Thereafter, Ron religiously dyed his beard on an almost daily basis, making sure it looked as natural as possible.

"So what's this—some sort of disguise?" Carole Poole teased him one day, noticing the new look. "Or have you just got tired of shaving?"

"Just tired of shaving," Ron replied nonchalantly. "I always wanted to grow a beard, and now with the boat, it just seems right."

Albert got a mooring near Galmpton Creek on the River Dart, tucked in a tiny bay overshadowed by a cliff. High up on that cliff, surrounded by tall stands of oak, was Greenway House, the mansion where Agatha Christie had lived and written productively for years. Rosalind, Christie's daughter, lived there still. Whether consciously or unconsciously, Albert Walker seemed to be moving about in Agatha Christie's shadow.

It was tough sailing at the beginning, learning how to manoeuvre the boat down the Dart to the "ocean," as Albert insisted on calling the sea. On the first occasion he pulled up anchor and headed out, the weather was a bit rough, and he gave himself quite a fright, he told Len and Barbara Fullilove, the bed-and-breakfast proprietors who had now become friends. Much more distressing to the Fulliloves, however, was the fact that Ron had had baby Emily on board. After that experience, Ron was much more cautious and tended to venture out only on calm days.

Devon weekends now became dominated by boating, and every Saturday that summer, Carole and Judith would watch Ron pack everything into his little Austin Metro—the baby carriage, the dinghy, the pails, the shovels, the hats—and head south to his mooring on the Dart. When the weekend was over, he'd return, empty the car and entertain Carole with stories of Emily on the boat.

"Emily just loves the boat," he'd say. "She's a regular little sailor. Here, look at these pictures." There would be little Emily, wrapped in an oversize orange safety jacket, squinting into the sun. With the car unpacked, Ron would pull a rug from inside the cottage and lay it out on the lawn, and they'd all sit out and have a cup of tea and watch Emily struggling to stand, wobbling about, giggling and falling over. Ron, beaming, would video the scene. Home life seemed so important.

But he was talking to Carole about moving again. His course at the institute had ended. He'd actually had to re-write his final assignment, he carped to Carole, and he'd recently attended a workshop with Solutions in Therapy, based in Essex, east of London.

"It's run by a couple of interesting guys," he told Carole. "It's a whole new approach they've got going. I'm thinking about putting a little money down and joining them. We're in the middle of discussions now."

When Ron had an idea, Carole thought, he certainly moved quickly. By fall, little Emily was taking her first steps, and Ron and Noël were moving on. They left Judith and Carole a forwarding address: Suite 633, 2 Old Brompton Road, South Kensington, London, and said good-bye.

Months later, a letter arrived at Kestrel Cottage, where Carole now lived. Through the little plastic window of the envelope, Carole could see it was clearly addressed to "Elaine Boyes, Kestrel Cottage, Upcott Farm, Oakford, Devon."

"It's got to have something to do with Emily, I think," Carole told Judith. "It's from the Health Trust."

"But how odd," said Judith. "*Elaine Boyes?*"

"Oh, maybe it's just Noël's maiden name."

"If it's her maiden name, I might understand it," said Judith. "But why Elaine? Why not Noël Boyes?"

"Well it could be Elaine Noël, or Noël Elaine, couldn't it?" Carole reasoned. "I mean Daddy was Henry George, and half the family called him Harry and the other half called him George."

"I don't know," said Judith. "Should we send it along or toss it? Do you think it's important?"

The two sisters looked at one another. There really was only one way to find out.

Inside the envelope, they found a notice from the local surgery reminding Emily Jane Platt's mother that the baby's regular checkup was coming due. Down in Essex, the sisters were sure that Ron and Noël, or Elaine, were certain to have registered with the local clinic. They wouldn't need this reminder after all. But the envelope got them wondering.

"Do you really think they were married?" asked Carole. "I mean legally married?"

"Don't know," said Judith. "They always did wear wedding rings, though, didn't they?"

This was true. But both agreed there was always something just a little peculiar about it all. Ron and Noël seemed romantic in their way, but they never touched each other in public.

"Did you notice that we never saw any photographs of just the two of them?" asked Carole. "No wedding photos? No pictures of parents, siblings? No photographs of families?"

"Strange," said Judith, clicking the envelope on the table and gazing out the window.

On the wall of Kestrel Cottage was the calendar Ron had left behind as a souvenir, "The Hidden Corners of France." It was October 1994.

"I wonder if they'll ever really move there?" asked Carole.

14

"I'VE BEEN HELPING
PEOPLE FOR YEARS"

"Frank!" Audrey Mossman called up the stairs. "Frank, there's a removal van next door. New people are moving in."

Down the staircase of Little London House, in the quiet Essex village of Woodham Walter, came Frank Johnson, tall, dignified and younger looking than his 83 years. He and Audrey had known each other for decades, and when their respective spouses passed away within a short period of time of each other, the surviving spouses decided, for convenience, economy and friendship, to move in together. Frank's rambling 18th-century cottage at the far end of Little London Lane was big enough for the two of them. They had always got on well with one another. So why not, they'd decided.

"I wonder where they've come from?" Frank said, stepping toward the front door and opening it. A chill rushed in as he and Audrey moved out to the porch and down the sidewalk. It was a typically overcast autumn day, but the arrival of new neighbours seemed to brighten it. The house next door, a two-storey stucco structure known locally as Little London Farm, had been empty for months. Now men were moving in furniture. It was a large van with "Tiverton" written on it.

"They've come from Devon," Audrey said, a little breathlessly. There was a certain excitement in her voice. An air of anticipation. Woodham Walter was a lovely village, but it could get lonely down at the end of Little London Lane, a quiet cul-de-sac flanked by fields of grain at the edge of the community. New neighbours ought to liven things up a bit, she thought. Audrey, a round-faced, bespectacled woman in her seventies was a very sociable sort—and blessed with a Miss Marple-like curiosity.

The next day, she and Frank walked next door to extend Woodham Walter's hospitality. A smiling man with a beard answered the door.

"We just wanted to welcome you to the village," Frank said, extending his hand. "Frank Johnson."

"And I'm Audrey Mossman. We live right next door. In Little London House."

"How awfully nice of you," Albert Walker said. "I'm Ron." Then, turning and calling over his shoulder, "Noël!" a young blonde woman appeared behind him—an *awfully* young blonde woman, Audrey later remarked—carrying with her a little auburn-haired girl.

"Hello," Noël said quietly, shaking hands and smiling.

"And this is Emily," Ron said proudly. "We'd invite you in, but we're busy unpacking."

"No, no, no," Frank said. "We don't want to disturb you. But do come along for a drink whenever you can."

"From America are you?" Audrey asked.

"Yes, we are," Ron said. "I come from Vermont, though I was born in England. Noël is from New York. Woodham Walter seems like a lovely village. We're sure we're going to like it here."

"Oh it is. You will. It's a friendly village," said Audrey.

"We'd be pleased to help in any way we can," Frank added as they waved good-bye.

That was how it began.

The village was friendly and, in a villagey way, quite curious about newcomers. Albert could see it in their eyes. He and Sheena sat down and carefully reviewed their history. Consistency was essential, Albert stressed.

The curiosity was the same at work, at Solutions in Therapy, once a few colleagues had met Noël.

"I'm sure you're wondering about the age difference," Albert casually told Dave Hawkes, a psychiatric nurse and partner at the practice.

"Well I—"

"No, no it's fine to say it," Albert interrupted. "Many people *do* do a double take when they see us. They wonder what a man my age is doing knocking about with a young blonde."

He then recounted the story of how Noël's father had asked him on his way to London to look in on Noël at art school and he did and they fell in love.

"But I think we're living proof that, despite the age difference, it really *can* work. Age doesn't matter."

Hawkes was impressed with such openness. It was typically American, as were Ron's optimism and visions of opportunity.

He had first shown up in the summer of 1994 at a two-day Solutions in Therapy workshop. He'd come fresh from a counselling course at the Iron Mill Institute in Devon, and he'd brought with him a compelling proposal.

The potential for the practice was enormous, the bearded Platt explained. It only needed to be managed. That was what Solutions in Therapy required, in fact: a practice manager. Someone who could organize more workshops, help them expand and shape them into a more professional organization. The existing partners had the psychoanalytic skills, he said. What they lacked was business acumen. With Ron's business experience, his university degree and his own knowledge of counselling, *he* was what Solutions in Therapy needed. He sweetened the offer by saying he'd even loan the practice several thousand pounds from his own investment company, Cavendish Corporation, to bankroll expansion.

Hawkes and partner Ron Wilgosh were convinced. It was a great idea. Platt was signed on, and the Solutions letterhead was soon adjusted. The fact that they were "Winners of the Queen's Nursing Institute Award for Innovation, 1993" and "Members of the British Association for Counselling" stayed the same. At the top of the partnership list, though, the new practice manager was now listed: Ronald Platt, B.A. In his new guise, Albert Walker had conferred upon himself a degree, from the respected University of Edinburgh, no less.

The entry into Woodham Walter was the easiest of all transitions, since Albert and Sheena had arrived as a family with Emily. Who could possibly have dared to think the unthinkable—that he and Sheena were actually father and daughter? Their age difference may have jarred, but the presence of Emily gave the apparent marital union a seal of respectability that placed it beyond questioning. Sheena, too, was a loving and caring mother. Neighbours would see her walking the country lanes with tiny Emily in her little red boots, fussing over her and showing her obvious affection. Albert was proud too. He was a family man again.

In the days leading up to December 5, 1994, Sheena telephoned Audrey Mossman next door and asked whether she knew anyone who might be able to babysit for them? It was her and Ron's anniversary, she said—the anniversary, if Audrey had only known, of their flight from Toronto with millions in investors' money and the beginning of their new life. They were going out for a special dinner, Noël said. Oh, they did seem romantic, Audrey thought.

But the old habits still gnawed.

Neighbours Martin and Vickie Emmison invited them over to a Christmas buffet on December 10. Martin, a corporate lawyer, had met Vickie in Cambridge, and their home, The Ravens, at the end of Little London Lane, is a wonderful piece of architecture built in 1480, replete with leaded windows and hand-carved beams. To the festive Christmas gathering, Martin also invited a professional colleague, Biggs, his wife, Anna, her nephew Mark and Mark's girlfriend, a lovely model by the name of Nadia. Albert spent most of the evening making a brazen play for her.

"Could you believe that man Ron?" Anna said to Vickie the next day. "Sitting there with his 22-year-old wife, making such an obvious move on Nadia?" Sheena was 19 at the time. "I've never seen anything like it," Anna went on. "The nerve of that man."

Nonetheless, it had been a fun-filled evening with laughter, much wine and good food. Ron had explained to Anna how he headed up a local partnership of psychotherapists and helped train others, and he delivered snippets from his and Noël's stock history. He had "another family" in Vermont, from his first wife, with three daughters, he explained.

"One is actually about Noël's age," he said. Then he sat back and smiled.

During the course of the evening, Martin casually offered that he and Vickie had travelled all across North America in the 1970s and knew it fairly well. They'd actually settled in Toronto for a time, in 1976, where he'd worked for a law firm, and he and Vickie lived in a flat near St. Clair Avenue and Bathurst Street. In fact, he still did regular business with a firm there, he said.

Albert made a mental note: never mention Toronto or Canada in Martin's presence. Some things should never be toyed with. This was one of them.

Christmas 1994 came, and Albert erected a big, beautiful tree like the ones that had filled the front rooms of his youth, where his mother and father and siblings crowded around; indeed, like the ones he'd erected in his own living room on Watts Pond Road for Sheena and his other children. There seemed to be a strong sentimental streak in him. But this was his new family's Christmas. It was actually Emily's second. Albert was creating and re-creating, weaving his magic, becoming a kind of master builder. Reality was whatever he said it was. Whatever he made it.

By January 1995, Albert and Sheena were well installed at Little London Farm. They had a group of friendly neighbours: the Emmisons—who had chosen to overlook Albert's unsuccessful flirtation with their young dinner guest—Marion and Ed Jones, who lived at Orchard Bungalow, and the genial Frank Johnson and his delightful and curious friend Audrey Mossman. Albert and Sheena had become part of the peaceful, safe, enclosed world of Woodham Walter.

Then it happened.

In March 1995, a letter arrived at one of Albert's London post boxes. In the upper left-hand corner was the real Ron Platt's return address: 9-1410 First Street N.W. Calgary. On opening it, Albert read the news: Ronald Joseph Platt was coming home.

It was the day he had dreaded in his dreams. It had always been a possibility, of course. Yet he had taken such care and trouble with Ronald Platt, given him money, bought him air tickets, pointed the way. In the end, though, this very generosity had created a problem. Ronald Platt found himself in a bind once again—and to whom should he appeal? Who had always helped him and never let him down? Naturally he turned to Mr. D.

Platt's homecoming was a *fait accompli*. Ron had already informed his mother of his imminent return, Albert learned, and though she didn't have room for Ron, she was expecting him. As for Calgary, Ron was fed up. He was living on odd jobs and had little money. He needed help.

Albert's whole new life was on the line. Under pressure, he had always relied on logic, reason and an acute skill for organization. No problem coolly approached, he felt, was insurmountable. These were the tools that had brought him this far. They would have to bring him through this crisis too. There was no percentage in panic.

There were other developments as well. Sheena Walker was pregnant again. Thankfully, it wasn't like the last time. Things were different, for the community had already accepted them as a family. There was nothing to hide. Quite the contrary: it was cause for proclamation.

When warm weather arrived and the Emmisons invited Ron, Noël and Emily for a barbecue, Ron said he had "an announcement" to make. He was always comfortable with the Emmisons, a lovely couple whose relationship was marked by affection and playful teasing.

"Noël is going to have another baby," Ron said.

"Oh congratulations," said Vickie. "That's great news." Noël seemed pleased, and when Martin offered his congratulations, Ron remarked on what a fine thing it was for a man his age "to have such a young wife." Another child about the house would definitely keep him on his toes.

Indeed, he already was. As Audrey Mossman observed, he did almost everything: cooked, cleaned, did the shopping and went into the office three days a week. He had a set routine for everything. He was compulsively orderly about such things.

Beyond this, the Emmisons noted that he also seemed a good father. On sunny days, Ron would come strolling down Little London Lane with Emily on his shoulders and Noël by his side to see the chickens raised by Brian, a local farmer. The Emmisons' border collie, Holly, would wag her tail and come out to greet them, and Ron would stroke her and maybe throw a stick. Martin would quietly observe the scene from his garden and wonder: a middle-aged man, a young wife, a small child, a new career. He must be starting over, Martin mused. He must've decided to start all over again at the beginning. That was it. That was most certainly it.

It was the next month, April 1995, when Frank Johnson confided to Ron over a drink that he wasn't at all pleased with the rate of return his bank was offering him on a £200,000 investment. Ron had said he was a former banker with Citicorp and had done frequent business in Switzerland and Luxembourg. What did he think? Did he think Frank should be satisfied?

Not at all, Ron said. In fact, three or four per cent for such a large sum of money seemed scandalous.

"You should be making far more than that," Ron offered. "In fact, I could make you 15 per cent per year."

"Really?"

"Oh, with very little trouble at all. I've been helping people for years."

"I'll think on it," Frank said, "and perhaps we'll be able to work out an arrangement."

In time they did: Frank signed over £200,000 to his next-door neighbour on the understanding that Ron would invest it and earn him the aforementioned 15 per cent. Anything above that return, Ron could keep himself. Ron said he was up to the challenge, provided the "loan," as he proposed to call it, was for three years, until April 24, 1998. That way, he'd have sufficient time to work out an investment strategy that would pay them both dividends. Then they signed a document and shook hands. There were no guarantees, Frank knew. He trusted Ron.

It was spring, and Woodham Walter was more welcoming to Albert Walker than he could ever have imagined. Despite the impending return of the real Ron Platt, everything seemed right with the world. Anyone looking in on the scene at Little London Farm would have found a perfectly tranquil domestic situation: a family of three; two multispeed Raleigh bicycles out back with locks and spoke reflectors and a sky-blue baby seat; the window sills abloom with boxes of brightly coloured geraniums; the shed, chock-a-block with a Mowmaster, planting pots and bags of fertilizers; and inside, a wood stove, which Albert had installed himself and which was not unlike the one that had warmed the home of his own early childhood.

In the back garden was a picnic table and sun umbrella and two identical chaise lounges, side by side, where Albert and Sheena could sit quietly and watch the evening sun go down.

"It all seems so frightfully domestic," Audrey commented to Frank one evening. "And yet there's something peculiar about Noël. That girl hardly says a word. I tried to talk to her about art school and art in general the other day, but it went nowhere. She probably thinks I'm just an old woman."

"Oh I wouldn't trouble yourself with it, Audrey," Frank counselled, setting down his *Daily Telegraph*. "She's quite young. There's probably not an awful lot of experience there."

"Quite. When I knock on the door, she just leaves me standing there. Never invites me in. I suppose she just hasn't learned yet."

"Perhaps not."

"I asked her the other day, 'What did you do before you were married?'"

"And?"

"She just stared at me. Rather vacantly, I must say."

What Noël did before she was "married" no one could ever know.

The arrival of spring meant the commencement of outdoor sports, golf and tennis, and the Joneses in Orchard Bungalow introduced Ron and Noël to the Little Baddow Tennis Club off Spring Elm's Lane. Marion Jones was a keen plant person whose back garden was a kind of Shangri-la. Once a week or so, Noël would come along with Emily, to feed the fish in the pond and take tea. It was a beautiful English garden filled with eucalyptus and Russian vine, pampas and waterside plants, plum, pear and quince trees.

However lovely the Joneses' garden, though, it was the special little tennis club itself, with its two clay courts, completely hidden in an oak forest and dotted with broom, rhododendrons and silver birch, that was the real stuff of fantasy. Nothing but sunshine permeated that enclosure.

Albert and Sheena joined the club in April 1995, attending the drink and buffet spring social. The club provided an idyllic scene: the "pawf" of swatted tennis balls amid shouts of "40-Love," and the slim Albert and Sheena scurrying about the courts like longtime companions trying to settle old scores—in a friendly way. In between strokes, the air would fill with the sound of songbirds, thrush and wood pigeons. There mightn't be a prettier pair of courts in all the world.

But reality beckoned. In May, Albert Walker prepared to meet his namesake, the real Ron Platt, and as usual, Albert had done all of his meticulous planning ahead. Control was key.

He had broached the subject with Sheena of Ron's staying with them for a period, but Sheena was against it.

"There's not enough room," she said. "And when the baby's born, there'll be no room at all."

Albert drove out alone to Heathrow and welcomed Ron home, and after a brief reunion, the two men drove on to Reading, where a room had been booked for Platt at the Russell Hotel. Albert paid, of course. It was important for Albert to assert his control.

The re-entry went remarkably smoothly. Albert's organizational skills had set Ron up quickly and nicely. He found Ron a job at a security company just outside High Wycombe, where Ron could be near his mother. The town was safely distant from Woodham Walter—High Wycombe was west of London, Woodham Walter east. Though only 100 miles apart, London would act as a buffer. Their paths should never cross. Albert gave Ron money to open an account on June 6 at the Midland Bank, and on June 12, Ron started his new job. On June 23, Ron moved out of his mother's tiny lodgings on Sycamore Road, where he had had to pitch up for a period, and into his own place nearby, at 83 Mendip Way. Albert could relax.

Summer turned to fall, and fall to winter. Albert Walker ensconced himself in his work and workshops and his comfortable life in little Woodham Walter. There was no need to move on. He had everything under control, including Frank Johnson. In December, he gave Frank a cheque for £25,000, telling him this was "the profit" that he'd already earned on Frank's £200,000. Frank was mightily pleased, as well he should have been.

That year's Christmas cheer, however, was short-lived. In December 1995, Ronald Platt lost his job. He announced that he wished to move to Chelmsford to be closer to the person he now regarded as his only friend: Mr. D.

Albert Walker was not a happy man. What did he have to *do* to rid himself of this man? Until he could more fully develop some plan, he would have to accept Platt's decision. It was risky: Platt would be just six miles away.

On December 22, Albert Walker, once again assuming his David Davis guise, helped the real Ron Platt find accommodation at 100 Beardsley Drive in Chelmsford, just west of Woodham Walter. He paid the deposit and gave the landlord his name and mobile telephone number: David Davis, 0589-972726.

On Christmas Day 1995, exactly three years since he'd presented the surprise gift of tickets to Ron and Elaine Boyes in Harrogate, Albert and a now very pregnant Sheena Walker welcomed Platt to dinner again. Albert had a little explaining to do about Sheena's obvious condition. He told Platt that he had once met the father of Emily, and he left it at that. He was supportive of Noël, that much was clear. He was upbeat, too, while Platt was increasingly morose. He was struggling with depression.

Dinner was awkward. In the middle of it, Emily grabbed a bunch of coins from a little purse Albert had given her and swallowed them. She choked and turned blue, and Sheena had to put her fingers down Emily's throat and induce her to vomit. The entire scene upset Sheena. It had been a close call. She apologized to Ron and cleared the table.

After dinner, Albert drove Ron back to Chelmsford. It had been a miserable evening. On his return to Woodham Walter, Albert Walker was pulled over by police in a drink-and-drive road check. The police officer asked for his licence. He produced the one with Ronald J. Platt's name on it, and there was a moment of high tension. Any contact with the authorities had its risks for a man on the run. Had the traffic officer stopped him on his way into Chelmsford, with Platt in the car, he would have had to reveal to Ron that he was using his licence. As Sheena would swear later, Platt never knew that her father was using his name.

The traffic officer looked Albert in the eye, handed back his licence and sent him on his way. Albert had reason to feel cocky.

Back in Canada, though, trouble was brewing. Barbara Walker hadn't given up the search for her daughter, nor the pursuit of her now-divorced husband. The part-time private investigator she had engaged was gathering sightings of Albert and Sheena. Two in the U.S. were widely reported—both bogus, as it would turn out. But they were enough, together with a burned U.S. investor on Walker's creditors' list, to get Albert wanted by the U.S. Marshall's office. Further, Interpol finally paid serious attention to Ontario Provincial Police Sergeant Joe Milton's file on Albert Walker.

Ten days after Christmas 1995, on newsstands in London and across Europe, a banner headline appeared in *The European* newspaper: "Interpol puts missing financier on 12-most-wanted list." There on the front page were photographs of Walker and his daughter Sheena, the way they used to look—before Albert's beard and dye job, before Sheena's pregnancies and her own hair change.

Albert Walker never saw it. He was utterly unaware of the newspaper piece. Had he known of it, some say that what happened next might never have happened at all.

15

SOWESTER: THE NAME TO GO TO SEA WITH

Despite the depressing Christmas, the month of December 1995 hadn't been all bad. In fact, for Sheena, it came not with a silver but a golden lining. December 5, 1995, had marked the fifth anniversary of the Walkers' flight from Canada together, five years of an entirely new life. Albert gave Sheena five gold bars. It was the stuff of fairy tales, strengthening and solidifying her loyalty—a loyalty that was remarked upon by several acquaintances as something resembling outright subservience. Except for Emily, Albert was everything to Sheena now: provider, teacher, father, husband—Lord. He had created their world out of almost nothing—out of paper and his own vivid imagination: some stolen legal tender, some air tickets and his own extraordinary talent for dreaming, planning and lying. He continued to have a powerful, almost Svengali-like hold over her. In truth, Sheena could have been made to do almost anything. And did.

On January 14, 1996, in St. Peter's Hospital in Maldon,

Essex, only a few miles from the parish where former obstetrician to the Royal Family, Dr. Peter Chamberlain, invented the forceps in the 17th century, Sheena Walker gave birth to Lillian Clare Platt.

On the birth certificate, "Ronald Joseph Platt," whose occupation was listed as "counsellor/lecturer," was registered as the father, and "Elaine Clare Boyes, otherwise Noël Platt," as the mother. Noël's occupation was not filled in this time, but her place of birth was again noted as "United States of America." The couple's British address was registered as "Little London Farmhouse, Woodham Walter," and in the box noting the qualification of those submitting the information to the registrar were the typewritten words "Father. Mother."

Lilly was brought home from hospital. Emily had a sister.

All the neighbours remarked on how the new baby looked "just like Ron," and Audrey Mossman was naturally anxious to see the newborn too. With Noël being as retiring as ever, Audrey had to push, but eventually she got an invitation, and yes, she observed, the neighbours were right.

While Sheena settled in to look after the needs of two small children, Albert continued to busy himself with his burgeoning counselling business at the Solutions in Therapy office in nearby Brentwood. He and practice partner Dave Hawkes, who lived near Basildon, were taking their solution-focused therapy workshops all over the country, and during February and March, Albert scheduled several in Scotland. He and Hawkes got on well. Hawkes was a wickedly witty man, and in no time at all, Albert began calling him "the Ben Elton of Basildon," after the well-known British comic writer. A Hawkes workshop on solution-focused therapy was as much about entertainment as it was about learning.

Albert was quite a talker too. "I've got a lot of money invested in Eurotunnel shares," he boasted to Hawkes over dinner one evening at the Erawan Express, a Thai Restaurant on Rose Street in Edinburgh. The two had booked into A Haven Townhouse for two nights on Thursday, February 1, and on Friday, they decided to catch a late-night dinner. "It's a magnificent piece of engineering, the 'Chunnel,'" Ron continued, "and I'm looking to buy something in France, you know. With the speed that you can cross the Channel now, buying property there makes a lot more sense."

A waiter came over, and as Ron took the menu in his hands, Hawkes cringed a bit. The new practice manager had an annoying habit of always scanning a menu and asking for something that wasn't listed. It was an obvious ploy to communicate that he knew something about food and expected to be treated with special attention. Ron seemed to need a lot of that, Hawkes noted. He also noticed that occasionally the office would get calls from people asking for Ron by the name of "David." Ron explained that this was an inside joke with some of his friends who liked calling him "David," after David Platt, the famous footballer and cousin of his.

At the restaurant table, once the ritualistic duel with the waiter was over and meals were finally ordered, Ron settled in to discuss his "problem" with Dave.

"I've got this cousin who moved into Chelmsford over Christmas," Ron began. "He's a Canadian and a complete no-hoper. A nice enough guy, but he just keeps hanging around. I'm meeting with him once a week, trying to give him a bit of counselling, but he's got no job, no money and no apparent prospects."

"Why not hire him to do a bit of scouting for you for this property in France?" Hawkes suggested. "If he finds something and he's good with his hands, maybe he could renovate it for you? That would keep him busy—and give him a sense of purpose."

Albert Walker's eyes lit up.

"That's a marvellous idea, Dave. Brilliant. Why didn't I think of that? Of course. He's got nothing but time on his hands. That's great. I'm going to phone Noël straightaway."

Hawkes didn't think his suggestion was that brilliant. It was just small talk. Ron's reaction was completely over the top. But Ron was often like that: given to drama and exaggeration.

Ron reached over and pulled his mobile phone from his jacket and dialled Noël.

"Noël? Everything fine? . . . Dave and I are just having dinner in Edinburgh, and he's come up with a wonderful idea . . ." and he proceeded to tell Noël all about what Dave thought they should do with his "no-hoper cousin."

It was February 2, 1996.

That very same day, at counter number 12, at the Banque Cantonale de Geneve at 17 Quai de L'Ile, overlooking the Rhone River in downtown Geneva, the real Ronald Platt, Albert's so-called "no-hoper cousin," made a cash deposit into account number R3205.57.94 in the his own name. In truth, he was already back on Albert's payroll. Ronald was doing a little continental banking for Albert. The deposit was keyed in through computer terminal 51 and registered as order number 03023. The teller who took the deposit was identified by operator code number 21. An automated receipt was produced, which was then signed by the teller, who slid it back across the marble counter into Platt's waiting hand.

For Albert, having a Swiss account under his control in Platt's name was a good investment, and it made particularly good strategic sense. All of Albert's other European accounts were in Elaine's name. Now, if he ever had to, he could go directly to a counter himself in Switzerland. He could never do that with the accounts he controlled in Elaine's name. The new account was an added piece of insurance, another new escape hatch, should he ever need one.

Albert Walker was weaving his web finer and finer. He was juggling at least three different personalities now—Walker, Davis and Platt—and by this time, he was overseeing a vast network of bank accounts, some of which were active, some dead. Ronald Platt's account was, at the very least, Albert Walker's thirty-fourth, and they were distributed over at least six different countries. To British friends and colleagues, however, he was just Ron Platt, practice manager for Solutions in Therapy, the American starting over with a young wife, two small children and a comfortable home at the far end of a quiet cul-de-sac in sleepy Essex.

When Albert returned to Woodham Walter in late March from another round of workshops in Scotland, he was exhausted, but he still continued to meet with the real Ronald Platt once a week, on the same day Albert took little Emily to do the shopping. Such meetings were vital. Albert had to monitor Platt's movements closely and keep him under control. If Ronald were ever to venture outside the dark circle of Albert's influence, everything Walker had worked for would be at risk. Bringing Emily along helped keep the visits limited, controlled and risk-free. In an atmosphere where there weren't other adults around, Albert never had to explain his relationship with Ronald to anyone. He didn't have to introduce Platt by name or explain who he was. This was key.

"I think you're spending too much time with him," Sheena told Albert as he prepared to meet with Ron one Thursday afternoon. "You've got so many workshops on the go. You need time to relax." She was genuinely concerned. Albert was under stress, and it was showing. He was tired. The Solutions job was only supposed to be three days a week, but the hectic travel schedule was beginning to take its toll. She worried about him.

Yet despite his schedule, Albert still had time for his neighbour Frank Johnson. Albert could always call on a reserve of energy when there was money to be made. In April, Albert carefully wrote out a cheque to Frank for another £5,000, then presented it to him over a drink at Frank's place. It was a year since he'd "borrowed" Frank's £200,000, a legacy Frank intended to leave for his grandson. Now Albert had returned to Frank £30,000, exactly 15 per cent, just as he'd boasted he would.

"Thank you very much indeed, Ron," said Frank, thoroughly impressed and pleased.

"Think nothing of it. The investment strategy is working well, Frank."

Albert Walker walked back to his home and family at Little London Farm. Soon, it was Easter. Sheena had helped little Emily put together a card for Albert. She wished him a happy Easter. She called him "Daddy."

Still, the problem posed by the presence of the real Ronald Platt continued to linger. In the short term, it meant added costs. Albert was paying Platt's rent at 100 Beardsley Drive as well as a regular fee. But it was the longer-term risks that concerned Albert most: the longer Ronald was around, the greater the potential for error. Platt was living only six miles away. Everything could be exposed; everything could collapse. What *do* you do with a "no-hoper cousin"?

In late May 1996, Albert Walker told Sheena that he was going down to Devon to check on his sailboat, the *Lady Jane*, just to make sure the boat was ready for the new sailing season. He'd take Ron with him, he said. Ron wanted to have a look at a cottage in the Hartland area. He was thinking about buying and renovating it.

"He's getting more and more depressed," Albert told Sheena. "The trip will do him good."

By June, Albert announced to Sheena a new, more promising development. Ron was going to go to France to start his own business. It was a little like the plan Dave Hawkes had suggested that night over dinner at the Erawan Express, Albert explained. Ron would scout for homes to buy, renovate and sell. While there, he'd keep an eye out for something for them too. Albert said he'd decided to give Ron a few thousand pounds to get started.

"He's seen an estate agent there already," Albert said, "and he brought back some leaflets and even some French fashion magazines for you." And with that, Albert handed Sheena a handful of the magazines.

Once Ronald's plan was revealed to Sheena, things seemed to move quickly.

Platt's landlord was notified that Platt would be leaving Beardsley Drive on June 21 for good. He was heading off to France.

The local council tax office in Chelmsford was informed. Then Platt's mail was redirected to Little London Farm—where Albert was already living as Ronald Platt. New mail in the same name wouldn't raise any suspicions. Albert then booked a moving van for June 21. The "no-hoper" plan was set to go. Soon, Albert wouldn't have to deal with his problematic "cousin" anymore. Albert had been his usual fastidious self. Not a detail had been left to chance. He booked a room for Platt for two weeks at the Tanunda Hotel in Chelmsford, an inexpensive hostelry across the street from BBC Radio's Essex offices. On the morning of Friday, June 21, Albert picked up the van and drove to Platt's Beardsley Drive address, and together the two men emptied out the contents of Platt's modest flat.

From there, they drove to Chelmsford Storage, a commercial storage facility in the town's warehouse district, where they caught the attention of manager Ed Mitchum. For what seemed like a very long time, the two men stood in front of storage compartment number 56, discussing and debating whether or not to put three Samsonite suitcases inside. Albert Walker seemed anxious to get them in and get going. Ronald Platt was reluctant. He didn't want them put in the container.

Inside those cases were clothes, various documents, cameras, photographs, some Canadian souvenirs and special memorabilia Platt had collected over the years—his life, in small pieces. Finally, Mr. Mitchum observed, the smaller man's stubbornness held sway. The Samsonite suitcases were removed from compartment 56 and carried back to the van.

That evening, Ronald Platt checked into the Tanunda Hotel and there he stayed over the next two weeks, occasionally visited by Walker. The proprietors noted that every morning of Platt's stay, the wastepaper basket in his room contained another emptied bottle of sherry and sometimes an emptied bottle of wine as well. Platt always slept late, kept to himself and seemed troubled.

On July 1, 1996, with Platt safely ensconced in the Tanunda Hotel, Albert packed up Sheena, Emily and five-and-a-half month-old Lilly and headed down to Devon in his tiny Austin Metro, where the *Lady Jane* was to be launched for the new season. There was a natural excitement surrounding the Devon trip. It marked the beginning of real summer and a re-entry into that nautical world which by now they all so much enjoyed. With its rolling hills and sweeping woodlands, Devon was so much more beautiful than Essex.

For Sheena, a trip meant restaurant dining and generally getting out. Albert was still extremely cautious about her mixing with people on her own. She had come to superficially know a few young mothers at the Tadpole Nursery in Woodham Walter that Emily now attended, and Marion Jones, the neighbour, continued to invite Noël on outings. Frequently, though, after Noël would commit, she would phone back and cancel. Albert still didn't really trust Sheena on her own. She made mistakes.

Once Marion had organized a tea so that Noël, who claimed to be an artist, could meet an American friend of Marion's who was also an artist. But the visit had gone badly. The American woman was extremely chatty and inquisitive, and in no time at all, she deduced that Noël knew nothing about art.

"She doesn't know a damn thing. She's no artist at all," Marion's friend later said laughingly. "I wonder what she's really up to out here?"

Out in Devon, Albert could keep a close eye on Sheena. Along the way, he told her that he had seen Ron off to France and wished him well. Albert had booked the family suite at the Steam Packet Inn in Totnes, an old inland port about 10 miles up the River Dart. Conveniently, it was a two-minute walk from Simanda Yacht Sales, where Albert had bought the *Lady Jane* and where it was now ready and waiting.

When Ron and Noël had first shown up at Simanda in 1994, John Ross Foale and Simon Baker thought they were a bit of an odd couple. Noël had braces on her teeth and looked like a little girl, really. Yet Ron led them to believe she was his wife, which made Foale and Baker suspicious. However, the Platts began showing up with two children in tow, and the staff at Simanda realized they really were husband and wife.

"The boat's all ready, Ron," Foale announced as the Platt family approached. "Speedometer's been repaired, new locker lids installed, and there's a new 20-pound anchor."

"Wonderful," Albert said. "Ready for a trial?"

John Ross Foale, a handsome, square-jawed, dark-haired man of 30-odd years, stepped into the boat, took the controls and pointed the *Lady Jane* downriver, showing his bearded client the ins and outs of the new control panel. A new engine had been installed since last summer. The original engine had broken down. Now there was a new 10-horsepower two-cylinder Vetus in place.

"That other engine was a pile of rubbish," Foale said. "I just wish I'd known it when we brokered the sale to you."

Everyone knew that Ron Platt didn't know much about boats. His triple-keel, 24-foot Trident was a good beginner's vessel, but not a boat for an experienced sailor, despite his claims of 20 years of sailing experience in New York. But Platt seemed a harmless type—a bit full of himself, but harmless, they agreed.

Foale guided the *Lady Jane* back to Simanda, stepped nimbly onto the wharf, waving good-bye as Platt and his family pushed off down the Dart, heading for their mooring in a stretch of water known as Galmpton Creek, mooring number 29, just beneath Greenway House.

That evening, they returned to their suite at the Steam Packet Inn and wound their way through the hallways to number five. There, they had a peach-coloured master bedroom with lace curtains and an ample king-size bed overlooking the water. On the other side of the hallway was a room with twin beds for the girls. Down a white-railinged staircase was a second level with kitchenette and living room, and there, in the living room, on the wall by the window, was a sad little print by Charles Burton Barber. It showed a little girl of perhaps four, dressed in a frilly Victorian dress, leaning up against the corner of a room. She is in tears. A crushed white rose lies fallen on the floor, and sheltering sympathetically beneath her is a small black and white puppy looking off, fearfully, to some present but unseen danger. The print's title reads *In Disgrace*.

Albert Walker drove back with his family to Woodham Walter, Essex, and on Saturday, July 6, saying he was leaving for business, he said good-bye to Sheena, picked up Ronald Platt at the Tanunda Hotel, where he had stayed for two weeks—not one, as he had told her—and the two men headed off for the Steam Packet, where Albert had booked two rooms.

The pretence Albert used to convince Ronald Platt to accompany him to Devon is not known and may never be known, but they checked into the Steam Packet together that night, July 6. On July 8, at about 10:30 a.m., Albert Walker walked into Sport Nautique, a busy sporting-goods store in the heart of quaint Dartmouth specializing in yachting supplies. A bell attached to the door tolled his entry, and Patrick Gill, the manager, approached.

"Can I help you with anything?"

Albert Walker was looking for a number of supplies, he said, but the key thing he wanted was hanging from the ceiling in the middle of the shop. Anchors. He strolled through the centre aisle, gazed up at the anchors and then down at the shelves below. There, stacked neatly, were anchors of every different shape and size. He reached down and picked one up. It was a plough anchor, about two and a half feet long, with a stem that swivelled 180 degrees and a rather sinister-looking plough-shaped end.

"Sowester," the label read, "The Name to Go to Sea With." Beneath the company's motto was a detailed explanation in bold print: **"This is a high holding-power anchor which will grip the seabed and continue to dig as the strain increases. Each anchor is bench-tested before it leaves the factory to loads indicated on the table."**

Beneath that was the table and the specifications of a half-dozen anchors ranging from 5 to 35 pounds. The one he was holding was 10 pounds. The table indicated that it had been tested to a holding power of 730 kilograms. It was recommended for boats up to 15 feet only.

"I'll take this," Albert Walker told Gill.

"Would you like a bit of chain for it?" Gill asked. "I'd recommend some chain link here."

"Not necessary," Albert said.

"If you're going to use it properly, you'll need chain," Gill insisted.

"No. I'll just take some rope," he said.

Albert selected about nine metres of three-strand Marston rope about 10 millimetres in thickness, tested to approximately 980 kilograms in strength.

Then he wandered over to a rack of expensive yachting apparel, with jackets by Lloyd, Musto and Gill, all quality British names. He pulled a yellow Southern Cross jacket down with a Douglas Gill label. The price tag indicated that it was £129.95. Albert gathered up a few other items and moved to the cash counter. There were seven items in all: the anchor, the rope, some grease, a tin of varnish, some green duct tape, a roll of black duct tape, and the jacket. The entire bill came to £206, and he handed over his MasterCard in the name of Ronald J. Platt. The card was slipped into the credit card block, a form was placed over it, an impression was made, and Walker signed it. All of his goods were placed in a white plastic bag with the Sport Nautique insignia on it, and Walker thanked them and said good-bye. The bell tolled as he left.

Albert walked down to his boat in Dartmouth harbour, and he and Ronald Platt set off up the ancient Dart, one of England's most remarkable rivers, one that Roman generals had led troops up almost 2,000 years ago. It is rich in history and wildlife, and sometimes, when a light afternoon drizzle mixes with summer sunshine, rainbows will stretch from bank to bank. Walker guided the boat past the Britannia Royal Naval College on the left, where generations of officers have been schooled for the Royal Navy, and he steered it up beyond Sand Quay and past Philip and Son Ship-yards on the right. There, suddenly, the river opens up, and its habitable banks give way to magnificent English landscapes, the kind that drew Turner here with his easel. The oak-lined valley is filled with waterfowl: herons and egrets and cormorants.

Presently, to the right appeared Sir Walter Raleigh's historic boathouse, part of Agatha Christie's estate now, with Greenway House above and the wharf down below, where the local ferry-man, Captain Kirk, carries passengers across to the village of Dittisham and back—lovely Dittisham, with its pretty cottages and well-heeled citizens. Finally, Totnes came into view, and the two men were almost home, the river teeming with life.

That evening, Albert Walker and Ronald Platt were seated at the bar of the Steam Packet, waited on by young Paul Thomas, the owner's son. Thomas thought the two a peculiar pair. He knew the tall, brash American drinking brandy. He'd been there only days before, but the shorter English gentleman was a bit of an oddity. He insisted on being called a Canadian and had a maple leaf tattooed on his right hand. Paul Thomas also noticed he wore a Rolex watch.

"Is that a Scottish accent I detect?" Albert inquired of two older women seated at a table in front of the window.

"I believe it is," said Etta Barr, smiling at the tall, handsome man.

"Do you mind if I join you for a drink?" he asked, leaving Platt at the bar. "I used to live in Scotland, you know."

"Oh, we don't mind at all, do we, Mrs. Thompson?" Geral-dine Thompson, Etta's friend, smiled her agreement. "And whereabouts did you live there?"

"Oh, I lived all over," Albert said, pulling up a chair. "I graduated from the University of Edinburgh, but I've travelled all across Scotland. I'm a psychiatrist," he said.

"How interesting," Mrs. Barr said.

"Yes, yes, I've been giving workshops up in the Orkneys, Inver-ness, Aberdeen. All over. Have you ever been up to the Orkneys? Do you have any friends there?"

"Matter of fact, it's one of the few places I haven't been," Mrs. Barr said.

"There's a Mrs. Flett up there in Kirkwall who runs a bed and breakfast, and she makes the most fantastic homemade marmalade. It's out of this world."

"And what brings you to these parts?" Etta asked innocently.

"Oh my people come from the Totnes area," he said. "They were farmers originally and emigrated to America after the war. They're still farming today in the Oklahoma corn belt."

The American seemed like a pleasant chap, open and friendly, Etta thought. His friend at the bar, however, seemed sullen, almost secretive, and intent on keeping to himself.

"And are you just on a holiday?" Etta continued.

"No, no, not really. My friend at the bar here is a Canadian, and we've just bought some land in France. It's sort of a joint venture we have going. We're going to farm it in fact. We're just about to sail there to see it."

"How ambitious," Mrs. Barr said.

The following night, the night of July 9, the stars were brilliant off the south Devon coast. The constellations were so obvious, so beautiful and so connected that it was easy to understand how the ancient mariners had come to set their instruments according to their movements. Beneath those stars, far out at sea and gently rolling on the water, was the *Lady Jane* with Albert Walker and Ronald Platt on board.

The telephone at the Royal Seven Stars Hotel in Totnes rang late, just before 11 p.m. It was Walker. He was out at sea, he said, phoning on his mobile phone, waiting for the tide to come in. Did the Seven Stars have a couple of rooms available? He and a friend should be able to make it to the hotel in about 45 minutes, he said.

At 11:30, Albert and Ronald Platt came walking through the front door.

"My God, what a night," Albert told the proprietor, as he signed in as Ronald and David Platt. "Stuck out on the sea, and now, driving up from the quay, we just ran over a cat."

What Albert Walker and Ronald Platt were doing in the *Lady Jane*, out there in the dark, late at night, on the black-mirrored surface of the sea with the stars' reflected light dancing on the waves, is anybody's guess. But to this day, there are police who believe that Albert Walker tried to kill Ronald Platt that night—tried to, but didn't. They think he lost his nerve.

16

50.29.62 N LATITUDE
03.27.00 W LONGITUDE

The two men were exhausted, the barman would recall. It was a quick drink, then the sleep of the dead in adjoining rooms.

The next morning, July 10, Albert and Ronald rose early, had breakfast and booked a room for Ronald back at the Steam Packet Inn for 10 more nights, until July 20. Albert said goodbye and was off again, alone down the highway, wheeling his way back to Woodham Walter in Essex, a four-hour journey.

He had already informed his colleagues at Solutions in Therapy that he intended to take the family on a Devon vacation until July 19. Consequently, as soon as he arrived back at Little London Farm, the packing for the holiday began. Sheena arranged to have Chloe, the cat, put up at the vet's, cancelled the newspapers and alerted Audrey to their departure. On Friday, July 12, at about 12 noon, less than 48 hours after he had arrived, Albert set off again back to Devon. It was the fifth time in 12 days he had driven this stretch. Albert Walker was once again demonstrating his extraordinary energy. At times, he was almost like a racehorse, stretched, muscular, pounding toward a finish line.

They picked up groceries in Totnes on the way, skirting the fringes of the neighbourhood, where—unbeknownst to Sheena—Ronald Platt was staying at the Steam Packet, and arrived 20 minutes later in Dittisham at their prebooked cottage, the Potter's Loft, at 7 p.m.

By morning, the weather had turned miserable: it was overcast and spitting rain. To cheer things up a bit, Albert produced a white bag with a blue insignia and presented Sheena with the bright yellow sailing jacket he'd bought at Sport Nautique. She was thrilled. It was high-quality and smart-looking, and when she tried it on, it fit nicely. She thanked Albert and hung the jacket on a coat rack near the door.

Unfortunately, as badly as the holiday had begun, so it continued. Emily got the flu and Albert caught a cold, and by Tuesday, July 16, it was plain to both Albert and Sheena that it wasn't much of a holiday at all. Albert decided they should stay on beyond the 19th to ensure some enjoyment, and he telephoned the agent. He was told that the Potter's Loft was already booked for an incoming party but that The Old Brewhouse cottage at the water's edge was available on Friday the 19th. That would be good, Albert replied. Then he telephoned the Steam Packet.

Upriver at the Packet, Ronald Platt informed the proprietor's son, Paul Thomas, that he wouldn't be staying till the 20th. He'd be checking out early. He was heading for Dartmouth, that quaint and quiet port town 10 miles downriver from Totnes, just four miles below Dittisham.

Dartmouth's Victoria Road is lined with a number of bed-and-breakfast establishments. One has a small, neatly printed sign out front depicting an anchor with a bit of rope: The Anchorage. The front bell rang late in the afternoon on Thursday, July 18, and Joan Wintle, an outgoing, straight-talking Welsh woman of about 50, with short-cut, slightly greying hair, opened the door to find a man of similar age asking whether she had any vacancies.

"I'm fully booked," Wintle said. "The only thing I've got is my emergency room. A small room at the top of the stairs. A bit cramped. But you can have a look if you like."

Ronald Platt said he would, and he carried his bags into the drab little hallway and set them down, and the two climbed the 31 steps to the uppermost floor. Wintle fished a key from her pocket and opened door number 4 to reveal a very small, pale pink room with a double bed, sloping ceiling and a single window overlooking the sunny street. Down below, to the left, was a playground where children were playing on slides and swings, and off to the right were senior citizens competing on the Dartmouth Bowling Green. It was the sweep of the human cycle, from cradle to grave, or close to it.

"There's a four-piece bath on the mezzanine," Wintle said.

"How much is it?" Platt asked politely.

"How long do you want it?"

"Two nights."

"I can do two nights for £28, bed and breakfast."

"I'll take it," Platt said. Wintle handed him the key, and he went down and got his bags. He reminded her of a friend she used to have in Bristol a long time ago. His face was strikingly similar. This one was quieter, though. At breakfast she sat him alone, because, as she remarked later, she sensed he was "a bit of a loner."

"Where do you come from?" she asked in a friendly way as she served him up breakfast.

He had been born in England, he replied, but was actually Canadian. "I have dual citizenship," he said. Some reference was made to the Canadian west and then it ended. He was no talker.

Mrs. Wintle put him at a table up against the wall, beneath a caricature of a ship sinking at sea, entitled *The Warning Buoy*. Platt wore a long-sleeved shirt and had a watch on, and seated as he was with his right arm up against the wall, she noticed he was left-handed.

When he checked out of The Anchorage, his room was as clean and tidy as when he'd arrived. He climbed down the stairs, and Mrs. Wintle wrote out a receipt to "Mr. Platt, £28" and handed him a copy, saying brightly, "Take care then." She watched his back as he left through the front door, past the little sign with the anchor on it, out into the street and disappeared. It was the last time Ronald Platt was reportedly seen alive. It was Saturday, July 20, 1996.

On Friday, July 19, in Dittisham, the Walkers had gathered up their belongings at Potter's Loft and moved downhill to The Old Brewhouse, a tatty cottage featuring a scarlet spiral staircase leading up to a galleried landing filled with bad art and a rickety double bed. It was an odd place for people with children, but it would have to do.

Albert had been out solo sailing only once during his stay. On Saturday morning, July 20, he announced that he was heading out again, alone. It was one of the most beautiful days of summer, a day of endless sunshine, 14 hours of it, and a wonderfully warm 23 degrees Celsius, a day when the senses are heightened, a great day to be alive. It was the day Ronald Platt is believed to have been murdered, bludgeoned with a blunt instrument, knocked unconscious, fastened with an anchor and thrown overboard.

For Sheena Walker, it was a long day.

As The Old Brewhouse had no telephone, Albert had left Sheena with his mobile phone. Toward 3 p.m., she called the vet to say they were staying on for a few days. Later, she called the newsagents, twice, to cancel the papers again. Then she called Audrey Mossman.

"Ron and I have decided to stay on a bit longer," Sheena said.

"Oh fine, fine," Audrey said.

"We just want you to know so you can keep an eye on the house. And we didn't want you to worry, of course."

"Has it been a lovely holiday dear?"

"Not really," Sheena explained. It had not gone at all well. Ron had been sick and Emily got the flu.

"How dreadful."

Time passed.

The only other day Albert had gone out sailing on his own, he had returned by 6 p.m., but at 6, Albert didn't show. Sheena prepared a dinner for herself and the children. Outside the door, passengers waiting to cross to Greenway Quay at the foot of Agatha Christie's garden would occasionally gong the bell at the water's edge to summon ferryman Frank Kirk. The light was beginning to dim. At 8 p.m., in neighbouring Brixham, the bells of All Saints Church sounded its nightly round of *Abide With Me*. But by 8 p.m., Albert Walker had still not returned.

Little Emily was tired, and Sheena cuddled up with her on the small settee in front of the television. Emily fell asleep. At 8:35 p.m., Sheena watched a program on the opening of the Olympics in Atlanta. By 8:59 p.m., Albert Walker had still not shown.

At that minute, in the failing light far out at sea off the Devon coast, a hand gripped the controls of the *Lady Jane*'s navigating device, the Global Positioning System, and switched it off. In that instant, the GPS automatically stored the last way-point for the *Lady Jane* that had been entered. It was a point two and a half miles off Hope's Nose, between Torquay and Teignmouth: precisely 50.29.62 N latitude and 03.27.00 W longitude. The time, 8:59 p.m., was also stored, exactly 15 minutes before sunset. In that light, from that distance, the operator could make out identifiable markings on the horizon: the red clay cliff known as the Ness, at the mouth of the Teign, the spire of St. Mary's Church, the large, yellow sewer buoy with its flashing yellow caution light. He didn't need the GPS any more. He could see his way home.

The police would argue that the man operating the *Lady Jane* that night, the man who had just murdered Ronald Joseph Platt— smashing his head so violently that blood and bits of his scalp and hair went flying—was Albert Johnson Walker. They would argue that Walker then slid a 10-pound plough anchor over Platt's belt and, with great effort, threw him overboard.

But at 8:59 p.m. on July 20, the police knew nothing. No one saw anything. Whoever killed Ronald Joseph Platt was well on his way to getting away with it.

Back in The Old Brewhouse, tucked dreamily away under blankets on the settee, little Emily slept soundly. Sheena rose and shut off the television set and began cleaning the dishes. It was well after dark that the sound of the door handle caught her attention. She looked up, the door opened, and in walked Albert. He was wearing a blue cap and a sailing jacket, his duffel bag of sailing gear slung over his arm, and he looked, Sheena would remember later, "scruffy and windswept."

Sheena quickly prepared a light supper for him, chatting idly about the opening of the Olympic Games as she did, but Albert didn't seem very interested. He was tired, he said. He wanted to go to bed. It had been a long day, a very long day.

Sheena tended to sleep late, but Albert always rose early. On Sunday morning, July 21, he called Isobel Rogers, a colleague at Solutions in Therapy, at her home around 8 a.m.

"I know I'm expected back to do the workshop at Waltham Abbey, Isobel. But do you think someone could cover for me? I had a little accident out on the boat yesterday, and I don't think I'll be able to make it back."

"Is it anything serious?" she asked, concerned. "Your breathing sounds terrible." Albert was wheezing.

"I just hurt myself pulling heavy things off the boat," he replied.

Isobel said she'd try to reach Dave Hawkes and have him get back to Ron.

Albert, Sheena and the two children left The Old Brewhouse at about 10 a.m., and for about 15 minutes, they lined up with others waiting for Captain Kirk to ferry them out to their mooring. Eventually, someone Albert knew came along and offered them a lift in his dinghy. When Sheena boarded the *Lady Jane* that morning, nothing seemed unusual. Everything was secure. The sail bags were on the bed, the cabin was perhaps a little untidy, but nothing appeared to be out of the ordinary. Albert had wanted to check something on the boat. While he did that, Sheena helped tidy up and changed Lilly's diaper. Then they telephoned Captain Kirk, who ferried them back to the quay, and they settled into The Old Brewhouse for lunch.

Soon, Dave Hawkes phoned.

"Sounds like you've had a bit of a rough go, Ron."

"Yes. Slipped on a bit of varnish and hurt my chest."

"Are you all right?"

"I think it's okay, but I don't think I should really try to drive back, Dave. The whole week has been a nightmare. Do you think you can do the Waltham Abbey presentation for me?"

Hawkes said he'd make sure it was covered. If one of the other partners couldn't, he'd do it.

Sheena and Albert had a quiet Sunday supper and planned to leave on Monday, but Albert slept unusually late and they decided to stay one more day. That evening, they dined at Keith Floyd's pub, The Maltsters Inn, at Tuckenhay, perched on a small bay off the Dart, between Dittisham and Totnes. Albert did have a sentimental streak. Clement Freud had written about this pub in *The Times of London*, December 5, 1990, that lovely morning when he and Sheena had landed in London. His first day of freedom, before the flight to Geneva, the Warwick Hotel, his visit to the safety deposit box, the flight to Paris and the train across the snowbound landscape to London, his meeting with Barbara Thomson and the move to Moore Park Road, Harrogate, Elaine and Ron, Kestrel Cottage and Devon, his reading of the article about Solutions on the train, the move to Essex—before everything. Before Emily and before Lilly. Indeed, before he'd become Ronald Platt. It had all been fun at the beginning. That seemed a long time ago. That seemed a lifetime ago.

The next day, Tuesday, July 23, Albert hurriedly explained to Betty Quick, the letting agent, that he had to leave Dittisham immediately. He had received a telephone call and learned that his father-in-law had suffered a massive heart attack. He thanked her, and Sheena thanked her too—especially for the day's sailing instruction at the Quick's sailing school—and they left. On the way back home, Albert never mentioned anything about a fall on the boat or any injury. He looked as trim and as fit as ever. Sheena noticed he was tired, though. He was tired of Solutions in Therapy too.

"They're getting on my nerves," he said. Maybe it was just a case of personality conflict, he added, but he and Sheena should be thinking about moving on to Birmingham or Edinburgh. Eventually, Albert wheeled the Austin Metro into Woodham Walter and home, and they removed everything from the car. Sheena carried the GPS into the house and placed it in the bottom of Albert's wardrobe.

On July 28, it was Sheena's 21st birthday.

Across the country in Devon, that very same day, fisherman John Copik found a body at sea.

PART III

17

HE WAS MY BEST FRIEND, A KINDRED SPIRIT

"Is that David Davis?" the voice on the phone inquired.

"Yes it is," said Albert Walker.

"Is that David Davis who acted as a reference for a man named Ronald Platt who leased a flat in Chelmsford recently?"

"Yes? Who is this?"

"It's Sergeant Peter Redman, Mr. Davis, phoning from the Chelmsford police station. I'm not quite sure how to tell you this, but—there's been an accident at sea and a body has been found."

"Oh my God," Albert Walker said.

"We believe it may be the body of your friend Mr. Platt."

"Oh my God."

Sheena was standing there, looking at Albert and wondering what in the world could possibly shock her father in this fashion.

"Are they absolutely certain?" Albert asked.

"Apparently," Sergeant Redman said. "But I don't think we should really go into this on the phone. I'm sorry, Mr. Davis, but could you come down to the station and lend us a hand? Tell us a little bit about him? About Mr. Platt?"

"Of course I will," Albert said. "Yes. Of course."

It was Tuesday, August 20, 1996. The appointment was set for Thursday.

"What was that all about?" Sheena asked.

"The police," Albert said. "There's been an accident at sea and they found a body. They think it might be Ron Platt."

"Really?"

"I can't believe it, though. There must be some mistake."

The weeks preceding the call had been relatively calm. Albert had quietly begun cashing in his investments at Fidelity Brokerage in London and moving the money into his Cavendish account. He was consolidating. On July 31, he had also gone to the Chelmsford Storage facility and placed the three Samsonite suitcases, with Platt's belongings, back into compartment 56.

Now it was late August and he was being asked to make a statement to the police. On Thursday, Sergeant Redman, a friendly, round-faced plain-clothes detective with thinning hair, welcomed Albert to the station, shaking hands.

"Sorry to have to pull you in like this, Mr. Davis," he said. "I'm sure it's a terrible shock. But we need your help. The Devon and Cornwall police had a body pulled up in a fisherman's nets off Teignmouth last month. It had a Rolex watch on it. The records say it belonged to Ronald Joseph Platt. You knew him?"

"Yes I did," Mr. Davis said, thoughtfully stroking his beard. "I've known him for a couple of years. He's a friend. A kindred spirit, really. Quiet. But I understood he'd left for France to set up a business there. In fact, I'd loaned him about £2,000."

"When did you last see him?"

"June, I believe."

"Do you know where he was headed in France?"

"I think he mentioned the La Rochelle area."

"Did he leave a specific address?"

"No, I can't say that he did. It was just La Rochelle. But I was anticipating hearing from him."

Davis told Redman that Platt held dual nationality, British and Canadian; that he had once been in the British Army; and that Platt had a special fondness for boats, large boats, and he often went down to the Portsmouth Naval Establishment to watch them.

"Do you remember any distinguishing physical characteristics about him? Any tattoos, birthmarks?"

"No. No I can't say I do."

"Do you remember a tattoo on his right hand? A five-pointed star sort of thing?"

"No. I don't remember that."

Davis confirmed, however, that before Platt had left, he had had his mail redirected to Davis's address, Little London Farm, Woodham Walter.

"Anything come in?"

"Not really. Just a few pieces."

Sergeant Redman asked if he had any photographs of Platt. Davis said he didn't think so, but he'd have a look, and if he found anything, he'd pass it along.

While Davis sat there, Redman called the Devon and Cornwall police in Paignton and got Detective Constable Ian Clenahan on the line. Redman briefed him, gave him Davis's number and then told Clenahan he could speak to him now. Redman passed the phone to Davis.

"He was my best friend," Davis told Clenahan. "I haven't seen or heard from him since June." Davis did remember a tattoo now. Yes. But it was on his arm, not his hand. He remembered an old Rolex watch that Platt owned. Platt's mother was alive and living in High Wycombe. There were two brothers, but he wasn't sure where they lived. All interesting material, Ian Clenahan thought, and he thanked Davis and took down his address. Davis had been helpful, and they were lucky to have found him. Perhaps with a little more luck, they might be able to close the file on this apparent accident and get on with policing. The new detective chief inspector, Phil Sincock, had arrived in Paignton, and he was known to be a taskmaster. Clenahan was hoping to clear the decks of this case.

For Isobel Rogers, the colleague at Solutions in Therapy, however, there was much that was suspicious at Little London Farm. Three days later, on August 25, she arrived there for a visit. Ron Platt introduced Noël as his wife, but Isobel noticed that Noël called him "Daddy" and she was utterly subservient to Ron too. Later, when Isobel mentioned that she had been dating a police officer, Ron became unusually aggressive. He went on and on about how unwise it was to date a policeman, how untrustworthy they were and how she ought to be careful. A few weeks before, Ron had suddenly announced that he was backing out of a therapy workshop he had committed to—the moment he'd discovered it was taking place in Harrogate. "Too far," he said, scowling. What exactly was going on with Ron, Isobel wondered?

There was a lot going on that neither Isobel nor anyone else knew about. The day following Isobel's visit, Monday, August 26, Albert hired a van and, on the pretence of redecorating a few rooms, loaded into it the Global Positioning System, five gold bars and a number of boxes with envelopes stuffed with British pounds and various documents. It was a necessary precaution, he told Sheena. He didn't want decorators stumbling over the money. Better to store it.

He had no intention of going back to Chelmsford Storage, however. These goods he wanted stored in another place, far away. He drove northwest about three hours to Northampton and arrived at Genstar Storage, a facility with easy access, and placed the gold, and everything else, securely inside. The container was rented out in the name of Elaine Boyes and signed by David W. Davis.

Back on the highway, he drove on to Birmingham. There, on Tuesday, Albert strode into Metalor, a precious-metals dealer on Warstone Lane, and negotiated to buy six kilograms of gold—a dozen 500-gram gold bars—signing a cheque for £57,880.50. He would have to wait a week to take delivery though, the manager told him. It was a security precaution to make sure the cheque cleared. By Wednesday, August 28, he was back in Woodham Walter again. No sooner had he arrived than he received a call from Metalor. The head office in London had overruled the sale. Walker was a stranger to them. He had no sales history. He'd have to collect his cheque.

That morning, the 28th, over in Chelmsford, Sergeant Redman went through the early mail, and he found an envelope addressed to him with no return address on it. Inside was a very poor snapshot, taken from a distance, of a man holding an umbrella, standing next to a horse. The name "Ronald Platt" was scrawled on it with an arrow pointing to the man, whose face was utterly unrecognizable. There was no note. Nothing. Sergeant Redman, however, knew where it had come from. He had asked only one man for a Platt photo: David W. Davis.

Back inside Little London Farm, Albert was now talking more and more about moving. He was dissatisfied with the psychotherapy practice, he explained. It was time to move on.

"Maybe we should take a drive north, around Birmingham, and scout some places to live," he said. "But let's not tell people. I'd rather the neighbours didn't know. We'll just tell them your father is ill and we're heading to the States."

That was convenient, Sheena thought. A lot of people had been asking why Sheena's parents hadn't come to visit their latest grandchild, Lilly. She was eight months now. She'd be walking soon.

For much of September, Albert and Sheena were gone from their home in Woodham Walter, not to the U.S. but into the English Midlands. They stayed for a week in a place called Mona Cottage in Leamington Spa in Warwickshire, near Northampton. Then they moved to the tiny crossroads of Manton, in Rutland County, east of Northampton. They continued to move across the landscape looking for possible places to relocate. Along the way, they bought a second-hand Volvo. It was metallic green and cost £2,500. In the midst of their sojourn north, they used the Volvo to slip back, undetected, to see Lilly's paediatrician in Hatfield-Peverell, just outside Woodham Walter. It was Lilly's eight-month checkup, an appointment, Albert decided, not to be missed.

The trip back to Essex brought him close to London again, and Albert decided it was there he would buy gold. On September 5, he visited the Credit Suisse, whose people had been so unwittingly helpful to him in Canada, when he had first transferred $1 million from Toronto to Geneva. There, at the Credit Suisse branch in London's Cabot Square, he bought five more 500-gram gold bars, signing a cheque for £23,723.49.

"I'm afraid I'll have to ask you for some identification, Mr. Platt," the voice from the other side of the counter said. "It's just a security procedure. I hope you don't mind. Do you have a passport or something similar handy?"

"I don't mind at all," Albert Walker said, and he produced a Canadian identity document—it may have been a passport, the bank clerk wouldn't remember—in the name of Ronald Joseph Platt. There, in black and white, was Albert's own smiling face. Yes, he'd managed that too.

That September, Albert made two other gold purchases: on September 11, he walked into J & A Jewellers in Hatton Gardens, London's gold and diamond district, requesting "loose diamonds." He left instead with two 1-kilogram gold bars. On September 25, he bought another five 500-gram gold bars, again at Credit Suisse. The 30-day buying spree netted him 13 kilograms in all, more than £67,000 worth of gold.

Finally, he contacted Blackwater Marine and arranged to have the *Lady Jane* brought up from Devon and wintered in Essex. Albert was taking care of business in a major way.

By mid-September, down in Little London Lane in Woodham Walter, Audrey Mossman was worried.

"Have you heard from Ron and Noël lately?" she asked Vickie Emmison by phone.

"No. We haven't. Seems they should have returned by now."

"Indeed," Audrey said. "They're a week late by my estimation. I hope there's nothing wrong."

Oh, but there was something wrong, as the village was soon to find out. One day, walking along Little London Lane, Vickie Emmison saw a car parked in Little London Farm. Ron and Noël had returned, and who should she meet walking along but Noël and little Emily.

He Was My Best Friend, A Kindred Spirit

"Welcome back," Vickie said. "We were worried."

"Oh we had to stay a little longer in the States than expected," Noël explained. "My father, you probably know, was very ill."

"Did you—did you get to see him?"

"Yes. Fortunately we did. In hospital. Just before he died."

"Oh I'm so sorry, Noël." Vickie felt terrible. "I'm so sorry. Is your mother coping well?"

"Oh yes," Noël said. "She's coping."

"And Emily? Did Emily get to see your father in hospital before he passed away?"

"Yes," Noël said, and she turned to Emily, crouched down and said, "Didn't you get to see grandpappy, Emily? Didn't you?" And Emily nodded and said, "Yes."

Vickie Emmison was so touched that tears began to well up in her eyes.

A week or two later, something else occurred. On a Friday in the first week of October, while Ron and Noël were away, there was a knock on the door at Frank and Audrey's. It was a woman from the electoral registrar's office.

"There doesn't seem to be anyone home next door, at Little London Farm," she said.

"No, dear, they're away for a few days."

"Shame," said the lady. "Would you kindly give them this form and make sure they fill it out? Otherwise, they won't be able to vote."

"Certainly I will," Audrey said, taking the form and waving good-bye. She closed the door behind her and looked at the address.

Ronald Platt and Elaine C. Boyes, it read, Little London Farm, Little London Lane.

"Elaine C. Boyes?" Audrey muttered. "I wonder what this is? Maybe they're not married after all."

On the Monday morning after they'd returned, Audrey came around with the mail and said brightly, "Here's your post, Noël." Sheena invited her in. After a brief chitchat, Audrey pulled out the electoral form.

"What's this Elaine C. Boyes all about?" she asked.

Sheena took the form in her hands and read it, looking at Audrey blankly.

"Well?" Audrey said. "What about it?"

"That must have been the name of the girl who lived here before."

Audrey looked at her. Noël knew Audrey had known the previous neighbours, the Gates family, quite well. She knew that wasn't right. There was an awkward silence, and Audrey felt embarrassed. "Well, cheerio," she said and left. Something wasn't adding up, Audrey thought. Who were these people, really?

Over at Solutions in Therapy, the other partners were already conducting their own kind of inquiry. While the practice manager was away, they'd decided to go over the books. Ron kept such tight control of the accounts, no one really knew how well they were faring. They made an interesting discovery. Ron had boosted their earnings, just as he'd promised—they were making more than three times what any of them had thought—but there was something strange about the ledger. Despite the dramatic rise in revenues, they were still several thousand pounds in the hole. More money was being taken out than coming in. Where was it going? And what was this entry about, paying Platt the practice manager £4,000 for rent? The cheque was signed by Dave Hawkes, but he didn't remember signing it. They decided to raise it with Ron at the earliest opportunity.

There was something else too. New letterhead arrived with a new citation after Ron Platt's name: "Dip. S.F.T." No one could quite comprehend it—Ron hadn't said anything about a new diploma he'd earned.

"Not to worry," Albert said soothingly when he was back. "It's strictly a marketing ploy. I'm in the process of developing a new course for people to earn a diploma in solution-focused therapy. This will just get people interested in taking the course." The partners were furious. It was unethical, they said, and it had to be removed. Albert reacted badly, and in the days-long argument that ensued, he had all the locks on the building changed. A showdown followed and Albert finally relented, removing the citation and giving them all new keys. But as for their account- ing queries, Albert bamboozled them. He had some complicated explanation as to why they were in a deficit position. The same for the rent. It was intentional, just an advantageous accounting procedure for tax purposes, he explained. The figures didn't liter- ally mean what they said, he emphasized. Once again, there was peace in the partnership. Albert Walker held sway.

On the other side of England, in Devon, Detective Chief Inspec- tor Phil Sincock was settling in, getting to know his personnel and having a look at ways in which he might be able to improve effi- ciency, boost morale and keep his people keen. As the new DCI, he was eager to demonstrate to his superiors that their decision to move him into finer surroundings with a much larger comple- ment of detectives had been a good one.

The Platt file, however, was low priority. Detective Sergeant Bill Macdonald and Detective Constable Ian Clenahan had managed to track the deceased's brother, Brian Platt, up in Hay- on-Wye. The dead man was definitely Ronald, he confirmed. Viewing the body wasn't necessary. A physical description, partic- ularly the tattoo, was sufficient. The tattoo wasn't a five-pointed star, Brian explained, but a maple leaf. His younger brother had been raised in Canada and loved it. Consequently, he'd had a tattoo artist emblazon his right hand with the symbol of Canada. As for the Rolex watch, Brian said, turning it around in his hands and examining it, yes, that was Ron's too. One of his prized possessions. Brian told the police that Ron had had a longtime girlfriend by the name of Elaine Boyes. They had lived together off and on for more than 12 years, but three years ago, in 1993, they had broken it off. She still lived up in Yorkshire, Harrogate, he thought.

Brian said he'd pass the news on to his mother. He was the oldest in the family, he'd look after that.

It had been two and a half months since the body had been found. It was still lying in the deepfreeze in the mortuary of Torbay Hospital, where it had been put into compartment B on July 28. The Devon and Cornwall police had identified it, notified next of kin and appealed through the media for extra assistance but had come up empty-handed. At long last, it seemed, it was time to lay Platt's body, and the file, to rest.

Yet Her Majesty's Coroner Hamish Turner and his officer Robin Little, in discussion with detectives Macdonald and Clenahan, finally decided that one final effort should be made to determine how Platt had actually come to be out at sea. An official inquest had been opened by the Coroner, and as things now stood, there was precious little to put into it. Clenahan tried several times to call Mr. Davis to arrange for a more detailed face-to-face statement to be taken, but there was never any answer. It was decided that Clenahan should call Davis and set up an appointment to go out and see him and take a written statement. Davis seemed to be the dead man's only friend. After that, their duty was done. But there was a problem: Clenahan had lost Davis's mobile telephone number. Clenahan decided to dial Sergeant Peter Redman in Essex again. Could he possibly drive out and see Davis and ask Davis to give him a call in Devon?

On October 14, Peter Redman, dressed in a civilian suit, set out in an unmarked car from the Chelmsford police station headed for Woodham Walter. He pulled off the main road and drove up Little London Lane looking for Little London Farm. There, he found four houses: two of them were labelled; two of them were not. Neither of those labelled were Little London Farm. The odds were 50-50, Redman thought. He pulled up into the driveway of one of the unmarked ones and knocked on the door. A tall, dignified gentleman answered it.

"Terribly sorry to bother you, sir, but is this Little London Farm?"

"No, no, no," Frank Johnson said, looking down at Redman, shaking his head. "This is Little London House. That," he said, stepping out on the porch and pointing next door, "is Little London Farm."

"Sorry to have troubled you," Redman said, smiling and starting to move back to his car. "Thank you very much."

"Not at all," Frank said. "Pleased to be of assistance."

Then it struck Redman. He'd better make sure. He turned around.

"That *is* where Mr. David Davis lives, isn't it?"

"No, no, no," Frank said. "Dear boy, there's no Mr. Davis who lives there. You're mistaken again. That is where Ronald Platt lives."

Redman was stunned.

"Ronald Platt?"

"Yes. And his lovely wife, Noël. And their two children. Why? Is there anything wrong?"

"No, no, not at all. But may I ask what this Mr. Platt looks like? I may have the wrong address."

"Oh he's about 50, I guess. An American chap. Outgoing, friendly, dark hair, beard. A retired banker from New York, from what I understand. What else, now? I can't think of anything, really. Except that he's quite a nice fellow, and he spends a lot of time on his boat in Devon."

Redman steadied himself.

"Oh I must have the wrong man," he said. "Terribly sorry." He thanked the older gentleman, got back into his car and drove quietly away. He drove straight to the station and phoned Clenahan.

"Something's up in Woodham Walter," Redman said.

"What is it?"

"I went out to pass your message to that David Davis fellow and found out that he's living in a house there under the name of Ronald Platt."

"*What?*"

"Yes. I knocked on a neighbour's door by mistake, and an older gentleman told me his neighbour's name was Platt. He gave me a precise description of Davis. To a T. It's the very man who walked in here and chatted with me."

"You're having me on," Clenahan said.

"No I'm not," Redman insisted. "And what's more, Davis even has a boat out in Devon."

"Good God," Clenahan said, his adrenaline rising. He hung up and went straight to the office of the chief inspector. Phil Sincock was in the middle of a meeting on an abducted-child case. A 10-year-old girl had just been carried off by a lodger in her mother's building. Clenahan burst in.

"Boss, something's gone a bit funny out in Essex. I've got to talk to you right away."

"Not now, Clenahan. I haven't the time."

"But Boss, that Davis fellow who gave us all the help on the Platt case? The man who said he was the dead man's friend—he's been living under Platt's name out there."

"What?"

"He's been living in a house using Platt's name."

Sincock's eyes fixed on Clenahan. The synapses were beginning to light up.

"We'll talk later," Sincock said firmly. "And Clenahan—thank you very much for that."

That evening, Sincock went on television to appeal to the man who had taken the 10-year-old girl from her home to return her immediately, and for anyone who had information to contact police. Sincock knew the numbers. If the little girl wasn't found in 48 hours, there was a 94 per cent chance that she'd be dead. The next day, the lodger brought her in.

Sincock convened a meeting with Clenahan, Macdonald and about 10 other detectives in an upper room at the Paignton police station. Orders of secrecy were issued. It was Tuesday, October 15. Sincock said they were going to find out everything there was to find out about the man living under the dead man's name. Discreet inquiries of every nature should be made: council tax records, the children's birth records, the electoral register, the National Health Service, anything that could be legally gathered. The U.S. authorities should be contacted concerning Davis to see whether he was wanted there. The French, too, should be called. If Platt had been headed to France, as Davis said he was, perhaps there was a continental connection. The investigation would be going HOLMES, Sincock said: Home Office Large Major Enquiry System. Every bit of information was to be fed into a main computer. Each and every detective working on the case was to have instant access to everything. It was a system adopted in 1987, after the Yorkshire Ripper case. The British authorities had then determined that if the police had had a sophisticated method by which to share information, rather than hoard it, the five-year hunt for Ripper Peter Sutcliffe could have ended sooner. Lives might have been saved.

In the midst of this flurry of investigative activity, unknown to the police, Elaine Boyes called Albert Walker, trying to get some financial advice for her mother, Joan. A family legal squabble had erupted over Joan's possession of her home at 2 College Road in Harrogate. Her brother had lawyers issue a demand to Joan that she vacate the premises.

"Tell her not to move," Mr. Davis told Elaine. "My experience has always been that possession is nine-tenths of the law. She shouldn't budge. Tell her I said so."

Mr. Davis was so knowledgeable about financial matters, Elaine thought. He was always so concerned about her and her family too. Despite the fact that they hadn't been in touch for some time, she was pleased that she could still call on him when in need. Only recently he had included his telephone number in a letter he'd written to her.

"And how's Ron?" Elaine asked. "Have you heard from him lately?"

Elaine hadn't seen Ron since she'd left him in Canada more than three years ago. The last she'd spoken to him was on the phone in May 1995. She'd been wondering about him.

"I saw him off to France in June," Mr. Davis said. "He'd decided to start up a business there."

"Really?" Elaine said. She was surprised. Ron hadn't known a word of French when she knew him. Nor had he ever had any desire to go to France. Surely, she thought, he would have contacted her and the family just to let them know he was going.

It wasn't like Ron. But perhaps he'd changed. She thanked Mr. Davis and wished him well.

On Friday, October 18, shortly after 4 p.m., Albert telephoned Ian Clenahan. Albert was concerned.

"I'm calling from Birmingham, Detective Constable. I'm calling from a pay phone because I don't have a contact number here. I just wanted to check to make sure you're absolutely certain the body you found is Ron's."

"Why do you ask?" Clenahan probed. "Any news?"

"No, but I wanted to be certain before I sent anything to his mother." Clenahan assumed he was thinking about flowers.

"Another thing," Albert added. "I wanted to tell you I remember having a coffee with him in Essex before he left, and I recall he said something about going down to the Tate Gallery in St. Ives, Cornwall."

"Oh that could be helpful," Clenahan said. The detective asked whether he could organize an appointment to come out and see Mr. Davis in person in Essex—"just to get a little more information."

"I don't have my diary on me right now," said Albert. "Why not leave it with me, and I'll get back to you by phone? Say about 7 tomorrow night?"

That would be fine, Clenahan said.

But Albert did not phone the next day or any subsequent day.

By October 22, the Devon and Cornwall police had gathered a fair amount of material, although they had yet to track down Elaine Boyes. They had various pieces of paper with Ron Platt's signature on them, some of which clearly didn't match. Slowly and steadily, they were putting together a strong case, at the very least, for fraud. But Sincock and his team knew that they'd need far more information than they currently had to press a case for murder. That was still only a hunch, and from an evidentiary point of view, completely insupportable.

"I wonder who he's been phoning on that mobile phone of his?" Sincock said during a meeting of his team later. "We'd better check that." Ian Clenahan said he'd call the mobile phone company and summon Davis's records immediately.

As Sincock, Macdonald and Clenahan were meeting with the other detectives, Albert Walker flew to Aberdeen with Dave Hawkes to do another round of therapy workshops. Albert had taken Sheena, Emily and Lilly with him. His wife was lonely, he explained to Hawkes.

Only a few days later, up in Harrogate, the police finally found Elaine Boyes. Detective Constable Clenahan brought with him a photograph of Platt's hand with the tattoo on it. Yes, she said, it was Ron. She was shaken. Elaine began to tell the detective about her and Ron's life together, how they'd met at a party in 1980, how they had a mutual interest in photography, how they'd met David Davis—and eventually went to Canada.

Yes, they'd spoken with David Davis, Clenahan said. He, too, had been informed.

"How long has he known?" Elaine inquired.

"Oh a couple of months now," she was told.

Elaine froze. A couple of months? She had spoken to Mr. Davis only about a week ago and had asked him how Ron was. He'd said he had seen him off to France. He'd said nothing about Ron being dead. She was petrified.

"You've got to question him," she said. "You've got to go back and ask Mr. Davis. Oh my God. You don't think Ron could have been murdered, do you? You don't think Mr. Davis could have— I mean—"

Clenahan calmed her. There was no need to jump to conclusions, they said. They weren't thinking about murder, he said convincingly. It was more likely an accident. It could have been suicide, he said.

Elaine went to a local psychic in Harrogate that week. No, the psychic said, it had not been suicide. That was certain. Elaine should stand back and let the police do their work. Everything would be sorted out, the psychic said.

Phil Sincock had what he believed was a murder suspect, but no evidence yet that would stand up in court. He felt that if he could get into that house on Little London Lane, he would very likely find a treasure trove of it. He'd have to, though—because if he didn't, he knew that the prosecutors would leave him and his team hanging. The prosecutors would have no choice. They weren't about to support charges of murder unless they were sure it could be proven. They had their reputations to think about too. They had respect for Sincock's work, but they had a greater respect for the facts. The chief inspector would have to contend with that after any arrest.

Albert, meanwhile, was getting increasingly curious. He phoned Clenahan, but Bill Macdonald answered. "He's not in right now, Mr. Davis. He's up in Harrogate."

"Harrogate?" said Albert.

"Yes, Harrogate," Macdonald said. "Nothing to do with the Platt file, of course. It's on another matter."

Albert hung up. They've found Elaine, he thought.

The next day, he took the train to the old Victorian spa town and dialled Elaine Boyes at work. He was in the area, he said, on his way back from the Orkneys. He just wanted to pop in briefly and say hello. Did Mr. Davis know that Ron's body had been found at sea? Elaine asked. Yes, he said. He'd just recently learned. It was tragic, he added. Struck with fear, Elaine agreed to meet him, as she so often agreed to Mr. Davis's suggestions when she was in his power.

Elaine hung up and phoned Detective Sergeant Bill Macdonald in a panic. He was coming, she said. Who, Macdonald asked? Mr. Davis. He was coming to visit her. What should she do? Calm down, Elaine. Calm down. Make sure you meet him in a public place where you'll be well observed. Don't panic. He's not going to do anything. He's not the type. Just be calm. Don't say much. Let him do the talking. Call us the instant he leaves.

Albert arrived at the little office where Elaine was now working, and she was called out to meet him. Albert embraced her and smiled as broadly as he had ever smiled.

The chitchat done, Elaine revealed that she had been visited by the police about Ron only yesterday.

"I have to tell you, Elaine, that on the way down in the train, I was thinking about Ron, and my eyes filled with tears."

There was a dramatic pause.

"Which policeman was it who spoke to you?" he asked.

"Detective Constable Clenahan," she said.

"What's he like?" Albert queried.

"He seemed quite serious," she said. "Quite thoughtful, though. Young."

"How old is he?"

"Not very. Maybe 30?"

"They don't actually know what happened to Ron, do they?"

Elaine was nervous. "I don't know," she said. "I don't think so." Then she looked at Albert closely and thought to herself: Am I looking at the face of a murderer?

"Now don't you worry about all that, Elaine. You just march right back in there and get to work. I don't want you to lose your job."

Albert kissed her good-bye. Elaine was shaking. As soon as she could, she called the police. It was October 30.

Sincock and Macdonald were meeting with the police in Chelmsford, and there, with the cooperation of the Essex constabulary, a raid on Little London Farm was planned for the next morning. Under The Police and Criminal Evidence Act, all were agreed: warrants wouldn't be necessary. They had reasonable grounds that an arrestable offence had been committed.

Sincock left for Devon, and Macdonald approached Frank Johnson and Audrey Mossman. Could he, he asked, camp out at their place that night? There was going to be a raid on their next-door neighbours, the Platts, the following morning. Oh, Audrey thought, this is exciting.

It was just about then that Billy Macdonald's beeper went off. He pulled it from his belt. It was Clenahan. The mobile phone records were in. Davis had made all kinds of calls from Devon between July 7 and July 23. He was in the very area Platt was when Platt was believed to have drowned. Macdonald paged Sincock. He was still on the road driving back to Devon when he received the news. He was rivetted. Within minutes, using the mobile phone records, Devon and Cornwall detectives called the Steam Packet, whose owner remembered the two men together there in July. Captain Kirk, the ferryman, also recalled the American with the beard. His boat was moored nearby, he said. He knew it by sight. Arriving back in Paignton, Sincock was now certain. He's been telling us lies, he thought. He was in the area at the time, he was seen with Platt, and he had a boat. Sincock was in his element and had all of his key people in place. It wasn't a fraud investigation anymore. They'd be going for murder. Come morning, they'd swoop.

18

"MUMMY AND DADDY ARE GOING TO SAINSBURY'S, DARLING"

Not yet dawn, 6:35 a.m., Little London Lane, Woodham Walter, Essex, and Detective Sergeant Bill Macdonald looked down on Little London Farm from an upper window in Frank and Audrey's cottage. From there, he could see the headlights of Sergeant Peter Redman's unmarked vehicle as it moved quietly down the lane, passed the front of the house, disappeared, then back, passed again and moved out toward the highway. The lights hadn't come on yet inside Little London Farm. Across the field, other cars were waiting. Inside one, a special police unit armed with guns was poised.

The hour ticked away. Soon, lights came on inside Little London Farm, and Bill Macdonald could see Noël Davis in the kitchen, carving up a pumpkin, making a jack-o'-lantern for the children. It was Hallowe'en. David Davis was nowhere to be seen. It was 9 a.m. and the firearms squad was edgy. It was rare for armed policemen to be called in for an arrest in rural England. It was 9:30 a.m. It was rarer still to be arresting an American— but with the Americans' taste for weapons, the police weren't sure what to expect. It was 9:45 a.m. and still no signal. What the hell was going on, the lead firearms officer wondered. Then a taxi came up the lane, rolled past the house and went all the way to the end. Nothing. It turned around, came back. It was 10 a.m. It stopped abruptly in front of Little London Farm. The front door of the house flew open, and David Davis darted out, climbed into the front seat and sped off. The police scrambled four cars onto the road, fell into line behind the taxi and moved out in the direction of Highway 414, headed toward Danbury.

"Sorry I'm late," cab driver Maurice Cooch said. "I wasn't sure which one was Little London Farm. I went all the way down the length of the lane and came back. Quite a lovely place back there at the top."

"The one with leaded windows?"

"Yes, that's the one."

"That's Raven Hall," Albert said. "It's owned by a barrister, Martin Emmison and his wife, Vickie. If you think it's lovely from the outside, you should see it from the inside."

"Oh you've been inside, have you?"

"Oh yes. Good friends of mine, the Emmisons."

"Dispatch said you're headed to the train station?"

"Yes. Going down to Brentwood."

Cooch looked in his rear-view mirror.

"I don't know what his problem is," he muttered. There was a police car on his tail. Albert turned around and looked straight into its windshield. Then the flashing lights came on, the police car surged powerfully up on the right and motioned to Cooch to pull over.

"What in God's name—sorry about this," Cooch said. "I'm sure I wasn't going over the speed limit. I don't know what this is all about."

He pulled in by a gas station, stopped, slowly rolled down his window, and in an instant, a policeman was there pointing the barrel of a gun—only inches from his face—straight into his window, aimed directly at Walker's head.

For what seemed like a very long moment, nobody moved. Then, as if in slow motion, on the perimeter of Cooch's vision, he watched a host of other men, some uniformed, some not, move in and surround the car.

"Look in my eyes!" the cop with the gun was shouting at Albert. "Keep looking in my eyes and get out of the car! Keep looking!" Cooch's blood was coursing through his ears. There was the muffled sound of dogs barking. "Get out on the pavement!" the cop shouted. "Keep looking!"

Walker opened the door and slid out, hands up. Calm.

"You! Stand back and slowly put your hands in your pockets and empty them. Keep looking at me!"

Walker reached into his coat pocket slowly, very slowly, gripped something in his right hand, then slowly, very slowly began to draw it out. It was an apple.

"Up against the car!"

Walker spread-eagled across the back window as two officers shook him down for weapons and pulled four keys out of a pocket. One of the cops snapped handcuffs on him. Then into the circle of the policemen walked a figure wearing a suit and topcoat.

"Good morning, Mr. Davis. Do you remember me?"

It was Sergeant Peter Redman.

"Yes, of course I remember you. What's this all about?"

"I am arresting you on suspicion of the murder of Ronald Joseph Platt."

Redman then cautioned him concerning his rights, and Walker was led to a vehicle where his head was gently pushed down and in, the door was shut, and he was driven off in the direction of the Chelmsford police station.

It was October 31, 1996, 10:12 a.m.

An hour later, down in Orchard Bungalow, neighbour Marion Jones's phone rang.

"It's Noël, Marion. Can you come quickly? It's an emergency."

"Of course I can. What is it?"

"Just come, please."

As Marion pulled up, there were a number of vehicles parked around the house: squad cars, Land Rovers, unmarked cars, and there were men and women, some uniformed, some not, moving through the house. She knocked on the door. A man let her in.

"I'm a responsible person," Marion said. She had done a bit of social work in her time. She was familiar with the law. "Can I help?"

"Thank you for coming," the man replied.

Noël approached, looking distraught.

"Do you know what this is about, Marion?" she asked.

"No, has there been an accident?"

"No, there has been no accident, madam," the man said.

As they stood there, another taxi pulled up and the driver came to the door. No, the woman of the house wouldn't be needing a taxi now, thank you very much.

"May I ask who you are?" Marion asked the man in charge.

The police officers introduced themselves and explained that they were conducting an arrest. They didn't explain. Sheena went upstairs. She had just been told she was being arrested on suspicion of murder.

"Marvellous views from here, aren't there?" one of the officers remarked, looking out the window. Meanwhile, other officers were trundling through the house, going through wardrobes, boxes, everything. Marion heard the word "gold" mentioned.

"Perhaps you can just have a seat on the chesterfield," she was told. It dawned on Marion now that if Noël was about to be arrested, she would be needed to look after Emily. Little Lilly would have to go with her mother.

Upstairs, Sheena was gathering clothing and supplies for herself and Lilly, when a woman officer saw her stuffing something deep into a diaper bag. The officer moved in and pulled it out. Inside were two envelopes with £4,000 inside and five gold bars. She motioned to Sheena to move down the staircase with the bag to show the other officers. Everything was seized.

Marion was then handed some clothing, and she and Emily were gently moved to the door.

"Mummy and Daddy are going to Sainsbury's, darling," she told Emily. "You and I are going to go to my house. Okay?"

After Marion and Emily drove off, Sheena was taken not to Chelmsford—where Albert was already genially instructing the officers on the use of a camera that had jammed as they were taking his mug shot—but to Braintree station. They were going to be questioned separately.

At Braintree, Sheena's pockets and bags were emptied. She had a birth certificate and medical papers for Emily, and a receipt for the Dittisham sailing school dated July 18. There was a receipt, too, for Genstar storage in Northampton. And there was a good number of documents in Elaine Boyes's name: a telephone bill, a NatWest chequebook, three Barclay's Bank cards, a Royal Bank of Scotland Visa card and a National Health Service card. She also had a man's wallet. Inside it was Ronald Joseph Platt's birth certificate and driver's licence, two NatWest bank cards and various other papers all in Ron Platt's name.

Under questioning, Sheena kept to the Noël Davis script: she was from Long Island, she said, and her husband had been a friend of her father's. He was asked to look in on her while she was at art school. The police looked at the documents. They looked at her and they were skeptical. They questioned her again and again. Finally, she seemed to break: Yes. David Davis was her father, she said. They were hiding from her mother because she was pursuing him for alimony. The Elaine Boyes identity was for the purposes of gaining access to her father's corporate accounts, for a company called Cavendish Corporation—and to ensure British health care for herself and the children.

At no time would she answer questions about Emily and Lilly. Nor did she reveal that her real name was Walker. Her bond to Albert seemed firm.

As for the real Ronald Platt, she said, she hadn't seen him since

Christmas dinner, 1995. She had no idea that Platt was in Devon during July. In fact, she had no idea that he had even been confirmed dead. Not until now.

Up in Chelmsford, Albert said nothing, only, "I want to speak to a solicitor." He was given a list of solicitors and called Gepp and Sons, a local firm, and one of the lawyers there, Roger Brice, was contacted. During a body search, Albert was found with the birth certificate of both David Davis and Ronald J. Platt. Among other papers in his possession were a health-club card, a Friends of the Royal Academy card and another for the National Trust, all in the name of David Davis.

But there was something far more interesting that day, a day of already extraordinary discoveries: Albert had business cards, made out in the name of James J. Hilton, 146 William Favre, Geneva. It was another identity, an entirely separate cover. Under the Hilton name, he had two safety deposit boxes at Belgravia Safety Deposit, a tinted-glass, reinforced repository with heavy-set guards in Chester Mews, tucked away behind the London offices of Merrill Lynch. To David Davis and Ronald J. Platt, he had added yet another layer. Might there be others, the police wondered? Who was this man they had taken into custody, really? He was definitely not Platt—but was he actually Davis? Or was he Hilton? Or was he, in fact, someone else?

Back at Little London Farm, the police were hard at work. As Detective Chief Inspector Phil Sincock had expected, the house was laden with material. There was money, of course, but there was more: the man of the house was a pack rat. Seemingly every piece of paper that had ever passed through David Davis's hands had been kept: bank documents, legal documents, correspondence—even old train tickets. Yet, incredibly, nothing seemed to go back beyond six years. He seemed a man without a substantial history. He was not, however, without money: in boxes, briefcases and suitcases, they found more than £9,600 as well as 8,170 Swiss francs. A Puma carry bag in the second bedroom had two envelopes with close to £4,000, and there was another bit of paper: a receipt dated July 8 for the purchase of seven items at a sporting-goods store in Dartmouth called Sport Nautique. On it was a notation for a 10-pound plough anchor. What significance the receipt might have, the police didn't know. They filed it with the mountain of other documents they'd seized. There was so much inside the house, in fact, that it took a team of police working around the clock for two days to sort through it all.

Papers and keys led them to other locations too. At the Solutions in Therapy office in nearby Brentwood, police found five more gold bars; in Chelmsford Storage, they found a set of Samsonite suitcases with Ronald Platt's personal belongings in them; at Genstar, they found an Apelco GXL 1100 Global Positioning System, more cash and more gold: two 1-kilogram and five more 500-gram bars.

In total, there were 17 gold bars, close to £30,000 in cash and more than 8,100 Swiss francs.

But there were a few other things that police found: a set of what one lawyer would later call "chemises of distinction," as well as "photographs of a kind which one would not normally expect between father and daughter."

Finally, tucked in among an interesting collection of books, which included *The Dynamic Way of Meditation: The Release and Use of Pain and Suffering*, was something eerie: *How to Hypnotize Yourself and Others*, by Dr. Rachel Copelan.

Detective Chief Inspector Sincock and his team of investigators, assisted by the Essex police, had 36 hours to pull the case together. Detainees could be held for an additional 36, provided a magistrate felt the findings of the ongoing investigation warranted it.

As police scrambled through the night to assemble evidence, Sincock ordered that David and Noël Davis be transported back across the country to Devon in separate vehicles. There Albert and Sheena Walker were jailed as David W. and Noël Davis and kept in separate wings of the Torbay Custody Centre.

On Friday, November 1, at 10:10 p.m., Detectives Macdonald and Clenahan visited David Davis's cell and, in the presence of his solicitor, Roger Brice, attempted to conduct an interview. They ran a tape. It lasted eight minutes. Davis said nothing.

The next day, police officer Paul Lavis attended at the prison, again with Brice present, and requested two intimate samples from Davis: a pubic hair specimen and blood. Davis was appalled. His solicitor was furious. Brice wanted to know why intimate samples were being requested and was told that hair had been found. They did not say where. At 3:22 in the afternoon, Davis declined to provide such specimens, and he was cautioned. Lavis indicated that if he refused to comply with the request, without good cause, such a refusal could be entered as evidence against him at a trial and might damage his case. Then Davis was led back to his cell.

At 4:44 in the afternoon, Davis compromised. He submitted to having his fingerprints taken, a hair plucked from his head and a DNA mouth swab. At 5:05 p.m., he was returned to his cell, and the DNA samples were placed in a refrigerator.

By now, calls were going out all across Devon and Cornwall. Sincock was summoning detectives from across the region. Some 70 officers assembled in an upper room at Paignton police station at 8 a.m. on Sunday, November 3. Everyone was curious. What could possibly get them all out of bed and into Paignton on a Sunday morning? A lectern was set out at the front, and a desk. Sincock, Macdonald and Clenahan were seated at the front, and at 8:30, Sincock stood up and welcomed everyone to Operation Ferrier—an archaic term for ferryman.

"There's no sense mucking about," Sincock said. "We're under extraordinary time constraints, and I would appreciate all of your cooperation." And then he began. "On Sunday afternoon, July 28, while fishing a stretch of water known as The Roughs, about six miles off of the coast near Teignmouth, a fisherman by the name of John Copik picked up a body in his nets . . ." There began an extraordinary bit of storytelling that held the assembled detectives spellbound for more than two hours. This, they thought, was going to be work, hard work, but it was going to be exciting too. By 11:30, they began to fan out, not only across the region but across the country, to put together every single shred of evidence they would need.

A couple of detectives went off to Brixham to see John Copik. They found him, sat him down and made him go over every single movement he had made July 28. Copik carefully led them through his recounting of the story: pulling up the nets, coming into King's Quay, and back again to his mooring once the body had been carted off. There, he recalled, a colleague had come along and fished an anchor out of Copik's nets and walked away.

The two police officers looked at one another.

"An anchor?"

"Yes," Copik said. "An anchor. I didn't think it had anything to do with anything. I just gave it to him."

"Gave it to whom?"

"To Derek Meredith. Another fisherman."

They tracked him.

"Yeah," Meredith said. "I took an anchor that day. I was going to use it for my speedboat, but then I found another."

"What did you do with it?" the officers asked.

"I didn't do anything with it," he said. "I gave it to Susan, my girlfriend. I think Susan and her mother put it in a rummage sale—I think."

By midafternoon, the officers were knocking on Patricia Johnson's door.

"Have time for a cup of tea?" she asked.

The officers sat down in the front room, and Patricia Johnson explained that, yes, she had indeed put the anchor in a sale out near Totnes, with a price sticker on it for £15.

"It was on Susan's birthday," she said. "August 4."

"Is there any way you can remember who bought it?"

"Who bought it? I didn't sell it. It's in the storage area beneath the steps. Do you want it?" She fetched the anchor and brought it in. The officers brought it back to the office like a bright, shining trophy.

On Sunday night, November 3, at 7 p.m., a magistrate was called to Torquay's courthouse, and Sincock, his senior officers and Roger Brice all assembled and waited. The police were making an application to extend Walker's detention. They needed more time. Then the doors opened. In came David Davis and, then, Noël. Those in the courtroom that night will always remember the way Davis and Noël looked at one another at that moment. There were smiles of mutual support—and affection, it seemed—a confirmation of loyalty and resistance. For the prosecution, it was especially troubling: without a doubt, he had a hold on her.

Brice wanted his client released immediately. He demanded to know precisely what kind of investigation the police believed they were engaged in. Sincock was put in the box and questioned by Brice for more than two hours.

"What exactly do you think you're looking for, Chief Inspector?"

Brice said he wanted every witness statement, every piece of paper, every detail of everything the police had done and intended to do—everything.

The police handed over a sheaf of witness statements, about a dozen in all. David Davis's continued detention was upheld, but Noël Davis was to be released. She was relieved. She had had tiny Lilly with her the entire time.

The following morning, detectives Macdonald and Clenahan proceeded back to the detention centre to interview Davis. They produced a tape with three more interview segments, 73 minutes in all, which revealed nothing. The tape was filled with huge gaps of silence. The prisoner's only responses were "No comment."

Later that afternoon, Monday, November 4, David W. Davis was called back to court. There, he was formally charged with the murder of Ronald Joseph Platt.

Meanwhile, the police investigation continued, almost around the clock. The *Lady Jane* was brought to the police forensics laboratory in Chepstow, where it was dusted for fingerprints and very nearly torn apart for evidence. Incredibly, the boat did not have a single print anywhere on its surface, inside or out—not even a print of its owner.

Next, the Global Positioning System was retrieved, and police contacted the manufacturer to see whether it might yield some clues. Inside Operation Ferrier, though, Phil Sincock was puzzled. He was certain David Walliss Davis couldn't possibly be the accused's real name. They'd run a search on it and discovered only one David Walliss Davis to have been born in Britain, and he had left as a child to points unknown—in 1949. So who was this Davis, who claimed to have been born here and yet couldn't produce any convincing I.D.? The appeals to the U.S. and French authorities had rendered nothing.

Finally, at a subsequent meeting of team heads, Sincock made the positive identification of the accused the top priority.

"I want the name of every single country on the HOLMES system to be downloaded and the authorities in those countries notified," he said. An information circular on Davis, with his photo, fingerprints and anything else that might be helpful was to be prepared by Detective Constable Tom Brown and sent to each and every country whose name appeared on the computer.

HOLMES had the names of many countries by now: Canada, because Platt had been raised there; the U.S., because the Davises had said they'd lived there; Switzerland, Italy and France, because Elaine Boyes had by now said she had travelled there. From Paignton, the word went out, and the investigation pushed on.

During this time, Sheena was making occasional journeys from Essex to Devon to see Albert. He had access to a phone. He had called, asking her to bring telephone numbers and other information. She was living quietly in Woodham Walter and happy to be back home with Emily and Lilly. Telephoning Marion's house and saying good-night to Emily for those three nights Sheena was in jail had been heartbreaking.

Sheena wasn't at all certain what the future held. She was still living as Noël Davis. She had not revealed her real name and still hoped that Albert would be set free and they would move to the Birmingham area. But the odds were moving against that.

On November 21, Ronald J. Platt's body was removed from compartment B in Torbay Hospital's mortuary, where it had lain, frozen solid, for more than 100 days. It would take four more to thaw. On November 25, a second autopsy commenced, and something new emerged: another bruise on the outside of the left leg just above the knee. The Home Office pathologist, Dr. Gyan Fernando, and a pathologist attending on behalf of the accused cut into it and agreed: it had been an injury inflicted before death.

With Platt's body stretched out on the stainless-steel examining table, a 10-pound zinc-plated Souwester plough anchor, like the one retrieved from Mrs. Johnson's house, was brought in and laid out next to Platt's left side. Photographs were taken, the flashing light bouncing off steel, and the film was quickly developed. The photographs showed the bruises corresponded well— very well—with the contours of the anchor itelf. It looked as if whoever had killed Ron Platt, if he had been killed, may have fixed an anchor up against Platt's left side. But how?

Sincock ordered Platt's belt and the seized anchor to be despatched to the police forensic lab in Chepstow. Over 30 murder investigations had taught Sincock well: circumstantial evidence was good, forensic evidence best. At Chepstow, a slightly hunch-backed, beaky little scientist by the name of Dr. Alexander Ian Grant received the packages in their plastic bags and unwrapped them as though they were living things.

There were, Dr. Grant pronounced, signs of corrosion on the zinc-plated anchor consistent with it having been in seawater, though he could not say for how long. On the eyelet of the anchor were tiny dark deposits of fibrous material, but what they were could not be determined.

Some 20 centimetres from the belt buckle, however, there were several marks at cross angles on the leather. A more detailed examination revealed them to be light in colour. A microscopic examination showed them to be translucent, near-white and impregnated deep into the belt. Grant sent them off for tests. The tests came back: the deposits contained zinc—zinc of the kind that was used to plate the anchor. Forensically, the belt and anchor were linked. The evidence strongly suggested that the anchor, which had a kind of inverted, vice-like V-configuration, had been inserted over Platt's belt, likely to keep the body down in the water.

In another area of the Chepstow lab, other police forensic experts had been scratching their heads over the mysteriously meticulous *Lady Jane*. They had never seen a boat so clean. Then it struck: the plastic bag. The one with the Sport Nautique insignia on it that had been found on the boat; the one that Albert brought back that day and from which he had pulled Sheena's sailing jacket. There, on the plastic bag, they found the finger-prints of Ronald Joseph Platt.

Elsewhere, something else was found: blood. There were three microscopically tiny droplets discovered on the rolled up sails, and on cushions found in another raid, there was a small bit of hair and scalp. They were sent off for further forensic examination.

There was one more extraordinary discovery to come. The Global Positioning System, found at the Genstar storage facility in Northamptom—where Emily's baby tag from the hospital was also stored—was finally given to the experts from Raytheon, the manufacturer. The technicians explained that a feature of the Apelco GXL 1100 was that it stored the precise time and the last way-point registered when it was shut off. It was now well into winter, but when they beamed up the GPS and downloaded the data and date inside, it was still summer. The printout read: 20 July 1996, 20:59, 50.29.62 N 03.27.00 W. The coordinates placed the boat 3.8 nautical miles from where John Copik had found the body. The evidence the police had against David Davis was mounting.

On November 25, at the National Criminal Intelligence Service (NCIS) offices in London, a telex and a follow-up call came in from the Swiss offices of Interpol in Basel, Switzerland. They were responding, the Swiss said, to the appeal for identification of an accused, one David W. Davis, originating from the Devon and Cornwall Constabulary in Paignton. From the package that was before them, the Swiss said, David W. Davis looked a lot like someone they had identified on an Interpol circular.

"We believe this man to be Albert Johnson Walker of Canada."

At the NCIS office in London, Detective Constable Alan Shears telephoned Detective Constable Tom Brown at Devon and Cornwall and passed on the news, and there was a celebration out in Devon—a brief one. They had caught what might be a big fish, or at least an interesting fish, but the investigation pressed on. They were 26 days in from the arrest, and there was still more work to be done.

In the end, more than 70 detectives, some of them working more than 18 hours a day at the beginning, would carry out more than 1,250 detailed assignments, make an additional 1,500 telephone inquiries, take down 784 witness statements, recover 1,150 exhibits and gather an additional 807 documents. It was a breathtaking investigation. Sincock was justifiably proud of his team.

Later on the 25th, NCIS called the RCMP attaché at the Canadian High Commission on Grosvenor Square in London, who relayed the message to Ottawa, and an OPP officer assigned to Ottawa's Interpol office telephoned Detective Sergeant Joe Milton seated at his desk near Toronto.

Milton hung up the phone and emerged from his office shouting, "We got Walker. We got Walker."

In due course, he telephoned Barbara Walker.

"We found Al and Sheena," Milton announced. "Your ex-husband is under arrest. And something else," he added. "Congratulations! You're a grandmother!"

December 5, 1996, marked the sixth anniversary of Albert and
Sheena's flight from Canada. Albert was in jail. Sheena was coop-
erating with the police and preparing to return home to Canada.
Ronald Platt, on that same day, was cremated at the Torquay
crematorium, his ashes placed in a small black urn.

Albert Walker was going to trial for murder.

19

"YOU HAVE TO ASSEMBLE THE PUZZLE"

It was cold in Bristol prison. It was dark.

Albert Walker rummaged through his toiletry kit and seized a tube of toothpaste. Then he placed a chair beneath the window and climbed up.

It was the dead of night, He had clambered out of his bed fully clothed and freezing, wearing his favourite Barbour brand-name shirt on top of everything else to stay warm. The curtains hanging in the window of his cell had been given to him by a departing prisoner— a Muslim, as it turned out—with whom he had had many interesting conversations about religion and belief since his incarceration.

Balancing on the chair, Albert spread the toothpaste like glue around the window's perimeter, then sealed the curtains, firmly tamping them down all around the window with the flat of his hand. There, he thought, that ought to help cut the draught. Then he stepped down, put the chair back in its place, and climbed back into bed.

The curtains billowed. Albert Walker fell asleep.

Before landing in Bristol, Walker had already spent close to four weeks in Exeter prison under the name of David Davis, until he was finally identified, on November 25, 1996, as Albert Johnson Walker, number four on Interpol's most wanted list. "Interpol," he scoffed inside Exeter prison. "What kind of an organization is that? Almost four weeks and no one knew who I was."

Then, on December 9, he was arraigned under his real name in Torquay's Magistrate's Court and whisked to Bristol prison where he was inducted as a Category A Basic prisoner, the lowest of the low in prisoner ranking. For Category A Basics there were no privileges. Albert was up for murder now and he was in one of the west country's worst prisons. Only Her Majesty's Prison, Dartmoor, that legendary hell-hole in the midst of rugged, windswept Dartmoor National Park, was worse. Albert had heard about Dartmoor prison and feared it. Opened in 1809 to hold French prisoners from the Napoleonic War, it had recently bean called the "dustbin" of the Prison Service by a senior government official. Albert resolved that whatever happened, he would never land in Dartmoor. Not if he could help it.

Keenly activated, he quickly established himself as a model "inmate"—"Remember, we're not prisoners," he told an acquaintance, "we're inmates"—and was upgraded from Basic, through Standard, to Enhanced prisoner status within four weeks. A few weeks more, toward the end of January 1997, he was returned to the more relaxed regime of Exeter prison, where the guards welcomed him back as "Dave," the only name by which they knew him. Upon arrival, he was given a pen and a British Telecom telephone card and was shown to his cell in C-Wing. How civilized, Albert thought. There were rewards for good behaviour. He told others that the guards treated him so well that he could rightly call himself "Inmate Number One."

By now Roger Brice, Walker's Essex solicitor from Chelmsford, had contacted Gordon Pringle, a barrister he often turned to in difficult cases. Pringle, a member of a well-known English military family, and a graduate of Oxford, had a rather sympathetic way of putting forward cases on behalf of drug barons, accused murderers and other supposed criminals. He had a razor wit and an outrageous sense of humour, which allowed him to get on well with all of his clients, no matter what their avowed area of expertise in the eyes of the law. He also had a good success record.

Since all Walker's known assets had been frozen, an application was made for legal aid and approved. The British taxpayer would be footing the bill for Albert Walker's defence. If the trial were to run six weeks, the Lord Chancellor's Department estimated it could cost about $250,000.

Meanwhile, back in Canada, Sheena Walker, together with Emily and Lilly, had been welcomed back by Barbara Walker to the home on Watts Pond Road. There was a bit of a media frenzy at the beginning, with film crews camped out. Barbara condemned her husband as a "vicious, horrific person," but stressed that, despite the apparent trauma her daughter Sheena had suffered, Sheena was a very good mother. Beyond that, Barbara wanted to shut the door on the world. The word "incest" was never mentioned. The community then closed around them, the media retreated and a "No Trespassing" sign was erected on the property. In time, the semblance of a normal life resumed.

But Albert was trying to pry his way in. He continued to write to Sheena. He was anxious to maintain his influence. She knew some of the secrets, Albert realized. The question was, outside his grasp, how many would she give away? He had to keep in touch. He had to maintain her loyalty.

In England, Roger Brice and Gordon Pringle provided Walker with copies of every witness statement as they became available, to ensure that Walker could properly advise them in putting together a cogent defence.

It is believed to have been in Exeter, when Albert was reading and re-reading Sheena's witness statement one morning, that he discerned the worst was happening. Beyond his reach, she was telling the truth, the dangerous truth.

A range of other witnesses had said they had seen Walker together with Platt in Devon as late as July 10. Mrs. Barr and Mrs. Thompson had spoken with him and Ronald at the bar at the Steam Packet Inn on July 8. Paul Thomas, now the young proprietor of the inn, had also remembered Walker and Platt checking out on the 9th. He thought he had seen them both come back together on the 10th, when Platt booked in for another 10 days.

In stark contrast, Sheena's statement said unequivocally that her father had told her Platt had gone off to France in June; that Albert had told her he'd lent Platt £2,000 or £3,000 to start up a business there; that her father had told her Ron had spent a week in a Chelmsford hotel in Essex before leaving; and that, subsequently, Albert had seen Ron off to France, wishing him well.

Sheena's statement suggested that Walker had lied to his daughter and tried to keep Platt's presence in Devon in July a secret from her. Such secrecy could be interpreted as a strategy of stealth, planning and deceit. In fact, when seen in light of all the other evidence, it might suggest a plot—maybe even a murder plot. Sheena's testimony could be the most potent fodder in the prosecution's cannon, a kind of smoking gun. Allowed to stand, it could well be fired again, in open court, with potentially fatal effect.

The issue of Sheena's testimony wasn't something that could be left to a letter. Albert would have to make a personal appeal, by phone, and that would incur a risk. A big one.

Above the row of prison phones, a large notice from the Home Affairs Minister was posted notifying users that their conversations *might* be monitored and even taped. To Albert, Exeter had always had a more relaxed atmosphere than Bristol, so he decided to gamble. Albert chose Sunday, February 2, 1997, to roll the dice and telephone Sheena at the old Walker homestead. It was the place where everything had begun. It was the home he and Barbara had bought 20 years earlier, the place where things had come apart and he had finally conceived his plan to flee. Albert's personal narrative was coming full circle.

Albert had to buy £10 worth of telephone cards for the call, each one lasting two minutes. Five should do, he thought. When he had them in hand, he walked down to the phone area, took a deep breath and inserted the first card. He dialled.

"Sheena?"

First there was small talk. Albert always had to express his concern for others' well-being. But he had a limited number of phone cards and had to get to the point. The first card was gobbled up straight away.

Sheena could remember the conversation clearly, "I'd like you to change your testimony," he said, quickly slipping another card into the slot, lamenting the shortness of their duration. The second of five cards went down and now he had three left—six minutes to go. "I'd like you to say that you *did* know that Ron was out in Devon with me," Albert said.

Sheena paused. There was silence.

"Sheena?"

"Yes"

The telephone spat out another card. Now he had two left.

"Sheena, I want you to tell the police that I told you about Ron being out in Devon and on the boat before. Tell them that you'd just forgotten. Tell them you're trying to be helpful."

There was more silence.

Soon another card was gone. There was more silence still.

Albert was on his last card now. He was frantic.

"Sheena?"

Nothing.

"Sheena?"

Finally, Sheena said, "Okay, okay, fine."

The telephone spat out the last card. Albert hung up. He'd done it, he thought. And what's more, he felt certain the conversation hadn't been taped. It was Sunday, the prison was short-staffed and the chances were next to nil.

As history would show, Albert was right, of course. He had gambled and won. It had not been taped. He went back to his cell with a feeling of satisfaction.

Across the Atlantic in Canada, however, Sheena Walker picked up the phone and made her own long-distance call—to the Devon and

Cornwall police. Yes, she said, that's right. Her father had phoned her from prison and asked her to change her testimony. She didn't want to make a statement through the Canadian police. Her mother was displeased with them at the moment. Shortly after Sheena had returned to Canada, Barbara Walker had filed a complaint against a member of the Ontairo Provincial Police who, she said, told her she ought to forget about Sheena, that she'd never be the same kid again. Moreover, Barbara Walker complained that the police had never really listened to her concerns about Walker over the years.

Back in Britain, Detective Constable Brian Slade of the Devon and Cornwall Constabulary was dispatched from London's Heathrow Airport and flew to Canada. There, on March 12, 1997, Slade took down Sheena's statement. It was an explosive accusation. If it were true, it could be a trial clincher.

The Walker defence team of Pringle and Brice decided there was one more avenue of appeal available before trial. The law-and-order Home Secretary, Michael Howard, was re-organizing trial procedures and getting rid of the expensive, time-consuming, old-style committals on April 1, 1997. A committal was roughly the Canadian legal equivalent of a detailed preliminary, in which a magistrate would decide whether there was sufficient evidence to proceed to the high court for trial. It also provided the defence with an opportunity to test the waters, to get a look at a few key witnesses, to identify potential weaknesses in the crown's case. Pringle applied for, and got, a committal date that would come in just under the April 1 wire, beginning March 24. It was to be held at Teignmouth, off the coast of which Walker was accused of killing Platt on or about July 20, 1996, attaching an anchor to his belt and throwing him into the sea.

Albert strode into the Teignmouth courtroom with all the bearing of a barrister. He wore a charcoal-grey suit, blue shirt and tie, and his natural grey hair was neatly clipped. He looked personable and, except for the handcuffs, charming. During breaks in the courtroom before his committal actually began, he could be heard speaking to the court attendants about Pierre Trudeau and the Foreign Investment Review Agency and money matters of various kinds. He seemed sophisticated and sincere, and after a while, the female court guard accompanying him decided that it didn't seem quite right that such a man should suffer the indignity of being brought into the courtroom in handcuffs. They were dispensed with in short order.

The young prosecutor, James Townsend of Bristol, who was also an Oxford graduate, opened the committal by laying out the allegations in precise detail. He painted a picture of Walker as a calculating, wanted man, who induced Platt to go to Canada, then stole his identity. Then, Townsend said, Platt decided he couldn't make a go of it in Canada and returned to Britain "to haunt" Walker. With Walker's new cover at risk of being exposed, he decided to kill Platt. Walker bought an anchor, Townsend said, then took Platt out to sea on Walker's boat, the *Lady Jane*, and knocked him unconscious. Walker then fixed the anchor to Platt's belt and heaved him overboard. But Walker had made two key mistakes, Townsend pointed out: he'd left a Rolex watch on Platt's wrist, which allowed the police to identify him, and he'd unknowingly registered the time and date of his nautical movements that day on the boat's navigational system, the GPS.

Emphasizing Walker's dependence on keeping Platt's identity, Townsend summed up by saying, "it would be difficult to conceive of a stronger motive for the defendant to get rid of Platt." It was true that it was all circumstantial evidence, "but sometimes," Townsend added, "circumstantial evidence is the best evidence."

Detective Chief Inspector Sincock sat quietly in the courtroom and listened to Townsend underline the extent of the evidence assembled by his detectives. The investigation had been impressive—even the defence complimented the police work. It had weight.

But it didn't have enough, Pringle pointed out for the defence on the third and final day of the committal. It didn't have an eye witness. In his refined Oxbridge accent—the accent the British ascribe to graduates of Oxford and Cambridge—Pringle began to list what the Crown could not prove.

It could not prove that Platt had actually been murdered. It could well have been suicide, he said. It could not prove, to any jury's satisfaction, that the anchor, this anchor, had ever been attached to the belt. Indeed the Crown could not prove that the anchor pulled up in John Copik's nets was in fact the same anchor that was found hidden beneath Patricia Johnson's staircase in Brixham, and almost sold at a rummage sale. Nor could the Crown prove that either the anchor pulled up in Copik's nets or the one found in Johnson's house was the very same one Walker had bought on July 8, 1996. It might be of the same *kind* that Walker bought at Sport Nautique—but was it actually the very same one? The manufacturer had made thousands. There was no specific numbering system for individual anchors. The anchor retrieved by the police could have been any one of then.

More importantly, Pringle said, the Crown could not prove that Platt was on Walker's boat on the day when the alleged murder was supposed to have taken place. And, Pringle continued, the Crown could not prove that Walker himself was on the boat on the very same day. According to evidence, the last time anyone had seen them together was July 10. The death by drowning was said to have taken place approximately 10 days later.

Finally, Pringle stated, even the time of death could not be determined satisfactorily. The Rolex watch had stopped at 11:35, but it was not clear if it had been a.m. or p.m. Hence, even if the precise specifications of the Rolex's self-winding mechanism had remained intact, shutting down the watch some 44 hours after Platt's arm ceased to move, there was still no way to go back in time. What was the starting point to be, Pringle asked: 11:35 a.m. or p.m.? The case should not be committed to Crown court for trial, Pringle insisted. It should be thrown out.

He took his seat behind his desk, glanced briefly down at the back of the envelope on which he had scribbled his arguments and stared at Magistrate Phillip Wassal, wondering just how long Wassal would need in chambers. Pringle was pleased. He thought there was a chance Wassall might have been convinced.

Wassall wrote down a few notes. "I don't think I'll be needing any time," he said, looking up.

"It's tempting, when looking at a case where the evidence is circumstantial, to *disassemble* each part of the jigsaw. But to get the whole picture you have to assemble the puzzle . . . and there are parts here which remain unclear.

"It is my considered view that there is sufficient evidence here which could *possibly* convince a jury that the defendant committed a murder, and so . . ."

And so Albert Johnson Walker's trial was committed to the high court for a date yet to be determined, and Albert was handcuffed, bundled back into a holding van and driven back to his cell in C-Wing at Her Majesty's Prison, Exeter.

It is not entirely clear how long he was back there before he sold the *Lady Jane* to a fellow prisoner—the boat which was even then impounded under lock and key by the police as an important exhibit for the trial. But he did. Walker is said to have sold it for £4,000. There was no denying it: he was a gifted salesman.

Albert had thrived in the spotlight of the old-style committal. It had made headlines in Canada and he clearly enjoyed the media attention, as well as being at the very epicentre of the unfolding drama in the courtroom. Back in Exeter prison, he was friendly with many of the guards, and when a couple of them came back from visiting relatives in the States, they'd chat with Dave, as they still called him, about how inexpensive the cost of living seemed to be there. Albert got to know the guards on a first-name basis. He still loved to talk about money. There was a thrill about it.

When anyone ever called him "Mr. Walker" or "Albert Walker" he sometimes didn't respond immediately.

"I'm sorry," he'd laugh. "I almost thought you were speaking to someone else."

Each morning, if there were milk available in the prison canteen, Albert would eat his All Bran in his cell and drink a cup of Nescafé. With his assests unavailable, the money he had inside prison was derived from the sale of some of his furniture—most of the proceeds of which went to Sheena. Or so he told others.

"It was only right," he'd say. "She needs it."

He was left with just enough money now to buy small supplies such as postage stamps, fruit, coffee and telephone cards. He told acquaintances inside that he was left with "about £600."

That was okay, he said. This was just a temporary hiatus.

"I am getting out of here," he smiled.

He spoke of going back to Italy, where he had spent many months as a young man and fallen in love with the European way of life.

He knew that if he were set free, he would still have to contend with charges of embezzlement back in Canada. His old friends would obviously still be very upset about the events of 1990. And, he admitted, it was true that he had taken money he shouldn't have.

"Not all of it," he said. "Some of it was lent to me."

After all, he added, he wasn't acting on his own. There was a board of directors connected to his company. He wasn't a solo pilot at the helm of the corporation. There were others, he said. Surely they bore some responsibility.

"One of the members of the board was the senior counsel for Hyundai, the automotive company," he boasted. If only that counsel, David Penhorwood, could hear him now. It was David Penhorwood with whom he had had his most vociferous arguments; Penhorwood who had insisted that Albert Walker, then Chief Executive Officer of Walker Capital Corporation, be sent a list of 15 demands that he comply with for the orderly and responsible operation of the company.

A professional accounting firm had also gone over the books,

Walker continued. What about them? They had audited and approved the financial statements. Albert had a knack for blaming others.

As for the portion that he admitted to stealing, he said he was "sorry." But could he really get a fair trial back in Canada, he asked? He doubted it. There had been "so much publicity" surrounding the circumstances of his flight from Canada, there couldn't be an impartial jury in the land. The courts would likely "have to drop the charges," he said. And in that reasoning shone a ray of hope in Albert Walker's mind—a bright, shining hope that if he could convince an English jury of his innocence on the murder charges, he'd be free to run and roam again.

In the meantime, he was sociable within prisoner circles and had a certain regard for the drug dealers who were incarcerated in Exeter with him.

"I mean, what are they really except businessmen who got caught?" he said.

Albert was especially friendly with one particular guard. At a bail application, the guard actually acted as a character reference for Albert, although bail was denied.

During the day Albert would read Laurie Lee's *Cider With Rosie*, a memoir of a boy becoming a man in the west of England. He thumbed through a bit of *War and Peace*. He read Ben Elton's *Popcorn*, a put-down of the Quentin Tarantino-style of Hollywood culture written by one of Britian's top comic writers.

"He's always lecturing," Walker complained of Elton one afternoon. "Always telling you how everyone has to take responsibility for their actions."

Elton's slam against Tarantino-style culture left Albert's admiration for Tarantino's *Pulp Fiction* undiminished. "A great movie," he said. "A movie full of Christian symbolism. A movie about redemption."

Yes, redemption. Albert dreamt of being delivered from the confines of Exeter s prison walls. That might come. In the meantime, he still professed a love of ballet and opera and the finer things in life. Incarceration hadn't changed that.

"Who can watch *La Bohème* or *Carmen* and not be moved?" he'd say.

The other prisoners regarded him as special.

However, Albert was less than Christian about the Devon and Cornwall police, especially Detective Constable Ian Clenahan and Detective Chief Inspector Sincock. One afternoon he told the story about the day he was arraigned under his own name.

"Oh you should have seen it when they took me up there," he said proudly. "There were seven motorcycles flanking the van; I had seven policemen inside. There were sidecars. You know: Albert Walker, big criminal," he laughed. Then his mood swung suddenly with the memory of it. "It was all probably Clenahan's idea," he sneered. "Clenahan tried to have me re-classified as a Category A prisoner. A number of times. I've even seen the list of calls he's made. He doesn't know that, but I have. Yeah, Clenahan. Of course he was probably just doing Sincock's bidding," he spat.

There seemed to be no end to his griping about Clenahan. Albert recalled that one day when he was being driven to court, packed in a van with a small group of police, one of them turned to him and said, "Oh, by the way, I'm supposed to say hello to you from a friend of yours—Clenahan."

"I said, 'Clenahan, Clenahan . . . let me see,'" Walker said.

"Then another one said to me, 'Yeah. You know. Detective Constable Ian Clenahan?' And then I finally said, 'Oh yeah! Clenahan. Fairly young? Not too bright?'"

When he was set free, Albert threatened, he'd seek compensation for his unjust detention from the European Civil Rights authorities. He'd show them. "There aren't any real civil rights in Britain," he said. "Everybody has to appeal to the European board."

The Canadians, too, came in for criticism. Walker was incensed that the Canadian High Commission hadn't sent anyone out to see him. "No government visitors at all," he said. "You know, there's a Dutch prisoner in here and they have someone come out from their embassy all the time."

One day in prison Albert waded into a discussion about law and ethics. "I would never do anything immoral or illegal,"

Albert said. The words were spoken as though from a pulpit. To hear him tell it, his imprisonment was a mistake, the result of an extraordinary set of coincidences.

Platt's death, he said, "was a problem that I was always going to have to face. I mean, if he died, whenever he died . . . I'd have still been left with all his i.d. I would have had to find another.

"And unfortunately that's exactly what happened. But how he died, whether it was suicide or a boating accident or murder, I don't know. I think it probably was murder. But I didn't do it.

"I'm an innocent man," he said.

In August of 1997, Mr. Justice Neil Butterfield called together defence and prosecution barristers in Courtroom Number 2 in Exeter. It was the first time the Walker case had come before him. Butterfield had been a judge for only a few years, but he was highly respected. Previously he had been one of the finest Queen's Counsels in Devon, and it was not uncommon in those days, in high-profile cases, to find both the defendant and the Crown Prosecution Service rushing for his services. It was said that, as a barrister, he could see the strengths and weaknesses of a case in an instant—and he could argue either side with equal vigour and conviction.

Some said he missed the pitched battles of advocacy. But he wore his robes well.

He looked down over the rims of his glasses and asked the bewigged and gowned barristers when they might be ready to move forward.

"Prosecution?"

"We should be ready for an October or November date M'Lord," said Alun Jenkins, Q.C., who was to lead the case against Walker.

"Mr. Pringle?"

"I would say that we have the situation well in hand, M'Lord, but we have been waiting for a date to be set before settling on a Q.C. to lead the defence. But I should think we would be ready by January 1998."

"Well," Butterfield said, smiling slightly, "I don't seem to have an opening in my calendar until June 1998." The barristers waited. It seemed as though Mr. Justice Butterfield was talking about taking the case himself. He was.

"Shall we say mid-June then? Here in Courtroom Number 2?"

Inside his cell, Albert reviewed his court material, poring over every witness statement as carefully as he could. A mountain of evidence had been compiled by the Devon and Cornwall police. He had never been one for studying, but he was now. For Albert, the trial was life-threatening. If found guilty, he would be sentenced to life, and in Britain, "life" really could mean life—"at Her Majesty's discretion." He might be forced to live out his days behind bars. To prevent that possibility, he would need one of the most outstanding lawyers that the distinguished Inns of Court in London could provide. Andrew Trollope, the eminent barrister and brother of novelist Joanna Trollope, was discussed. One afternoon in a London restaurant, Trollope was heard to say that if Pringle were involved he had "no doubt but that it would be the most fashionable murder trial of the summer." Everyone had had a good laugh.

In the end, Albert Walker chose Richard Ferguson, Q.C., a former Northern Irish MP, whose flinty accent and street-fighting skills in the courtroom had earned him one of the finest legal reputations in the United Kingdom. Everyone ranked him in the top 10, and there were some who said that, in criminal law, he was arguably the best in Britain. He was also accustomed not only to difficult cases but to high-profile cases. In 1995 he defended Rosemary West, wife of the infamous House of Horrors murderer Fred West, a case stunningly similar to the Paul Bernardo and Karla Homolka trials in Canada. Ferguson's defence of West was ultimately unsuccessful, but then, many said, how could it be otherwise, given the evidence?

Ferguson was a man of principle. As a practitioner of law, he said he had an obligation to defend anyone who approached him seeking services in the area in which he specialized. Ferguson was a murder defence specialist.

By February 1998 there was talk in London legal circles that Richard Ferguson had signed on for an interesting case down in Devon.

It was true. Ferguson had accepted Albert Walker's petition. He would defend him and he would take the case on legal aid.

The trial date was set for June 22.

Ripples of rumours immediately went out in the legal community. In a wine bar not far from the Old Bailey in central London, a low-level noon-hour discussion began concerning Ferguson's signing on. The facts of the case were said to be compelling; the larger story surrounding it, intriguing; and the accused apparently was fascinating.

Fine, said another, but could the accused carry himself well under questioning?

A barrister unattached to the case, but obviously familiar with it, said that from what he had heard, the answer was yes. Unequivocally.

"I have never raised animals or raced horses," he smiled ruefully, "but from what I have heard, it should only take the slightest crack of the whip to make the accused perform to the fullest."

There was laughter and a new round of drinks was ordered.

20

"THE SUN, THE SAILING, THE BLUE WATERS, THE WINE—WHAT MORE COULD YOU ASK FOR IN LIFE?"

"M'Lord, the prosecution calls Miss Sheena Walker."

The words had the effect of gunfire in a church.

It was a brilliant strategy. Her selection as witness number one was a surprise to the defence. They had learned she'd be there the first day—but not the first to take the stand. Sheena's testimony could alter everything that came afterward. If strong and convincing, she could put the defence on the run from the outset.

Seated in the prisoner's dock, a grey-haired, bearded Albert Walker turned his head and fixed his eyes on the courtroom door, his eyebrows slightly raised, and in that gesture there was a measure not just of anticipation, but of yearning, of hope. If only he could make her look at him, he knew, he could communicate everything in a single glance. It would be just like their first appearance in Torquay, when they were both up on suspicion of murder, after they had been jailed separately, then reunited in the courtroom where they shared a bonding look of loyalty and defiance. That was November 1996, nearly 20 months ago, the last month he'd actually seen her. Now Albert was poised. He looked and waited, eagerly.

There had been trumpets that sunny morning at the courthouse. Walker's murder trial coincided with the opening of the court's summer session.

A shiny, blue, chauffeur-driven Daimler with a small Union Jack flying from the hood had wheeled Mr. Justice Neil Butterfield up to the courthouse entrance. A footman opened the door and Butterfield emerged wearing his scarlet tunic and robes with an aristocratic, almost regal bearing. He was a man of average height, in his 50s, but fit and youthful. He was met by two small school children who presented him with a posy of flowers. He smiled at the children, nodded to the dignitaries, shook hands, then made his way into court as the trumpets pealed. The commencement of the summer session had always been festive. But the festivities ended at the threshold to Courtroom Number 2.

With its high ceilings and pews, it had an almost church-like atmosphere, helped by a vast allegorical painting at the rear of the court depicting *The Casting Out of Susanna*. Unjustly accused of being unfaithful to her husband, Susanna was about to be put to death when a young man named Daniel came forward, and, with clever questioning, uncovered the lie of her accusers. The painting seemed to point to the principle of reasonable doubt: no one should be too quick to condemn.

All had risen when Butterfield had entered the court and took his seat on the bench. He had looked down and seen several familiar faces. It was a small community. One of the faces was that of Phil Sincock. Butterfield remembered him. Sincock was the investigator who had put Keith Rose away for life, cracking that Devon murder that had lain unsolved for 10 years, by ingeniously finding a way to make Rose's old, acid-soaked gun fire

again. Butterfield had been the prosecutor; Sincock the lead investigator. They were familiar with each other's work.

A jury of eight women and four men had been selected in 14
minutes. The new prosecutor, Charles Barton, a Rumpole of the
Old Bailey figure who had replaced the previous barrister—the
change had come suddenly after hearing of Ferguson's appointment to the defence—delivered a sweeping opening statement. He
reviewed the entire panoply of Albert Walker's splendid guile
and his need to keep Platt's identity for himself—even from the
man to whom it rightly belonged. The prosecution's case was
simple and straightforward, he said: Walker had induced Platt to
move to Canada so that as soon as he did he could steal his identity. Walker was a man on the run wanted by Interpol and had
seen his opportunity to improve his cover. But Platt came back to
haunt him. With his cover, his money and his liberty at risk,
Walker decided to kill him.

When Barton went on to explain that Albert was living with
his daughter as husband and wife, and then uttered "Sheena was
expecting a child," four of the twelve jurors were visibly jolted.
One raised a hand to her open mouth. Barton continued seam-
lessly through the days leading up the murder and focussed on
Ronald Platt's dead body, the anchor fixed to the belt "to make
sure Mr. Platt didn't surface unexpectedly," and the Rolex watch
on Platt's wrist.

"It was an irony that the Rolex was his most prized possession," said Barton. "The person who put him on the seabed left
it with him. We all make mistakes."

Now it was 2:57 p.m. and all eyes were fixed on the courtroom
door waiting for the first witness to appear. It opened. First a
large woman, obviously not Sheena, then, immediately behind, a
slight woman in her 20s, with impeccably cut red-brown hair,
matching lipstick, black slacks and gold jacket, stepped in, head
slightly bowed. It was Sheena.

Albert Walker leaned imperceptibly but intensely forward,
reaching out with his gaze. He did not blink. He did not take his
eyes off her. He watched her move the 10 paces in, directly

toward him, only five metres away, and then, just as she climbed the three small carpeted steps and Albert grew excited, the large woman, a witness support volunteer, placed herself strategically between them, blocking his view. His gaze was thwarted.

Sheena was sworn in and Mr. Justice Butterfield looked down on her over the rim of his glasses and smiled. "You may sit and make yourself comfortable, Miss Walker."

"Thank you."

Barton stood behind his desk.

"Now I want you to look straight ahead," he said. "I want you to look at the jury. Will you do that?"

"Yes," said Sheena, speaking into a microphone.

Her voice was soft, but clear. It seemed to hover over the courtroom. It was steady and promising.

Seated in the prisoner's box, Albert Walker remained transfixed, his gaze unwavering, his mouth open a crack.

Her parents' relationship had seemed "fairly normal, up to a point," Sheena said as the questioning began, "up until I guess I was about 12 years old."

"And what happened then?" Barton asked.

"Things worsened," she said.

By 1990, when she learned that her father intended to take flight, she asked him to take her with him.

"Was it your choice to accompany him?"

"Yes, it was," she said.

Sheena explained that her mother, Barbara, "was after my father for financial support, which he seemed to think was a great deal of money. He wanted to make that difficult for her."

Barton carefully led Sheena through her almost six years abroad with her father. They had first gone to the Ritz Hotel on Picadilly, then to Geneva, then—she skipped the Paris interlude—they came back to London where she and her father moved briefly into a flat in Rosary Gardens, Chelsea, before taking up permanent residence in Moore Park, Fulham. Her father was using the name David Davis then, she said, and she was induced to use the name Noël Davis, for cover. And so began their secret life.

There, she said, in the London borough of Fulham, she eventually met the deceased, Ronald Platt, and Mr. Platt's girlfriend, Elaine Boyes. They had come down from Harrogate. Her father had met Elaine during a trip up there, Sheena explained. Afterward, when she and her father themselves moved to Harrogate, they came to see Ron and Elaine more often. Elaine had become her father's personal secretary.

Ron seemed obsessed with Canada, she said. It was where he had spent his youth. "He always talked about how much he'd like to go back there."

After Ron and Elaine took up her father's offer of free air tickets to Canada, she and her father assumed their identities and moved on to Devon, she said. It was there that she gave birth to her first child, Emily, and where they first began living as husband and wife.

"My father suggested that because there was a small child, that we should present ourselves as husband and wife," she said.

The jury looked on, fascinated.

The identity of Emily's father was not mentioned. The information seemed glaring by its absence.

Sheena had always believed that their undercover lives were aimed solely at preventing her mother's lawyers from catching up with them, she said. She had no idea that her father had stolen money from his former company, or that he was a wanted man.

Later, she, Albert and Emily moved cross-country to Essex where, after a time, she learned that she was expecting her second child, at the same time as they learned by mail that Ronald Platt was coming home. It was March 1995.

Ronald eventually did return, and the very last time she had seen him, she recalled, was at Christmas dinner 1995. Her father then told her "in June" 1996, that Ronald had "gone to France to start a new business."

Consequently, when they had gone down to Dittisham for a holiday on the Dart, in July 1996, first to the Potter's Loft and then to The Old Brewhouse, she had no idea Ronald was only minutes away, staying at the Steam Packet Inn.

"Do you remember Saturday, July 20?"

"Yes, I do."

"And did your father go out sailing that day?"

"Yes, he did."

"At about what time did he leave?"

"I don't recall," Sheena said evenly. "But it was fairly early in the morning. He went out sailing for the day."

"And when did he return?"

"Not until late in the evening. Ten o'clock approximately."

"And did you have a discussion?"

"I asked him how the sailing was. I asked him how the weather was. That sort of thing."

But he was tired, she said. And so was she, so they both went off to bed.

The next day, Sheena explained, her father wanted to go out to the boat, and they all lined up—Albert, Sheena, Emily and Lillian—for Captain Kirk's ferry, just outside their door, when a friend of her father's went by and offered them a lift. Arriving on the *Lady Jane*, they "tidied up" and made sure everything was tied down.

"And how long were you out there, approximately?"

"I'm not sure," Sheena said. "I think it was about three hours."

Albert appeared stunned by Sheena's claim. He leaned over and scribbled a note on his stenographer's pad on the ledge in the prisoner's box. Clearly he had not recalled tidying up on the moored boat for three hours.

"Are you familiar with something called a Global Positioning System?"

"Yes, I am."

"And can you tell us anything about the way your father treated that particular piece of equipment?'

He "always" took it with him whenever he left the boat, she said. He "never" left it on the *Lady Jane* because it was an expensive piece of equipment and it could get damaged.

Barton moved the narrative up a bit, to the call of August 20, 1996, when Sergeant Peter Redman had telephoned to inform her father of the discovery of a body at sea. Was she standing next to her father when he took the call?

"I was in the room."

"And how would you describe your father's reaction?"

"He was shocked," she said. Albert had explained that it probably wasn't Ron. "Maybe he just said that to reassure me, because I was shocked as well . . . it was quite a horrifying thing to have happen . . . and they weren't very clear on the phone either."

It was after that, she said, that her father began talking earnestly about moving house. They went looking around Birmingham and, along the way, they stored some goods in Northampton, including the GPS.

There was a bit of a pause then; Barton seemed to want that fact to sink in.

"Do you remember the events of November the 4th?"

"Yes, I do."

"And can you tell us what happened to you that day?"

"I was arrested on suspicion of murder."

"And were you eventually released and returned to Canada?"

"Yes."

"Did you receive a phone call there on February 2 of the following year?"

"Yes."

"Can you tell us about that phone call?"

"It was from my father. He was phoning from prison."

"And how was he doing that?"

"He said he was using phone cards."

"And do you recall what you discussed during that phone conversation?"

"My father asked me to change my testimony."

The courtroom seemed to shudder. Mr. Justice Butterfield, his index finger stretched across lips, looked disapprovingly down into the courtroom and cocked an eyebrow. Then he took some notes.

"He brought the subject up," Sheena said. "He asked me to say that I knew Ron was down in Devon in July."

"And was there anything else that you were supposed to know?"

"I was supposed to know that Ronald had been on the boat as well. He was supposed to have told me all that."

"And had he?"

"No," Sheena said.

"Did you tell the police?"

"Yes."

"And did you speak to him again?"

"No, I didn't."

Sheena reached for a small glass of water in a little white cup on the edge of the witness box. She had not looked at her father once. She took a long, cool drink. Her testimony, so far, had been devastating. Barton took his seat. Her positioning as witness number one had been a masterstroke. The trial had scarcely begun and already the jury knew Walker to be a supreme manipulator, capable of doing anything to save his own skin—lie, bully, fabricate, tell his own daughter to twist the truth—whatever it took. Maybe even murder.

It was a rare thing to see a daughter testify against her father; rarer still to see her take him down. It was clear from the very outset that the trial could hinge, in the jury's mind, on the daughter-father clash. All the police evidence, naturally, had to be rock-solid, and the forensics had to be firm. But if there was any doubt in the jury's mind, Sheena could be the tiebreaker.

As she was led from the courtroom, Albert continued to fix his stare on her, and she made the mistake of briefly glancing over at him as she moved through a row of seats. She stumbled, regained her footing, and was hustled out of court.

On day two, Richard Ferguson stood tall behind his desk, his glasses propped professorially at the end of his nose, his long pianist's fingers holding a sheaf of paper. He looked across at the witness box over the rim of his glasses and he knew that there lay dynamite. Of a kind. She was at once slight, polished and poised. She had seemed credible in examination-in-chief and sympathetic. The jury liked Sheena and believed her. If he now destroyed her—if she were to break down, her voice cracking into sobs, and perhaps let loose with some potentially explosive outburst—it would do him no good.

But Ferguson had to crack the essential claim that his client had tried to tamper with her story and make her lie.

"Now, Miss Walker," the defence began, his flinty Northern Irish brogue filling the apse of the courtroom, "you say you came to this country with your father in December 1990?"

"Yes."

"And was that at your request?"

"Yes, it was."

"You wanted to come?"

"Yes."

The question seemed designed to carefully introduce a theory of daughterly complicity, but gently, gently of course. Wasn't it true that she knew about the operation of her father's company, Cavendish Corporation? "Your father had explained the setting up of the company, hadn't he?"

"No, he did not."

Sheena shut the door immediately.

"He didn't tell you how the company was set up?"

"No."

"Did he not tell you that Ronald Platt and Miss Elaine Boyes were directors of the company?"

"No, he did not. I don't recall him telling me very much about the company."

There seemed to be a lot more bone structure in Sheena's face on day two. She was square-jawed.

Sheena had met Ronald Platt, yes. But no, she did not know that Ronald Platt was in Devon with her father in July. Her father had definitely told her that Ronald had left for France "in June," she said.

"Do you not recall a telephone conversation on July 9, in which your father told you he had just had the best day's sailing in his life?'

"No," Sheena said.

"I suggest to you that your father telephoned you from the Royal Seven Stars on the evening of the 9th of July and told you that he had just been out on the boat with Ron and had just had the best day of sailing that he had ever had in his life, or words to that effect."

"No," Sheena said. Then, there was a puzzled silence. "Where is the Seven Stars?" she asked.

"In Devon," Ferguson said.

"In Totnes," Mr. Justice Butterfield added helpfully, smiling down from the bench.

When Ferguson pressed a little further about Ron being on the boat, an unexpected piece of information jumped out. "Ron was not partial to water," Sheena said. "He could not swim. He didn't like getting on a boat. Even a large boat."

The jury took note.

Shifting quickly to the phone call of August 20, when Sergeant Redman informed Walker that the Devon and Cornwall police had found a body and thought it was Ronald Platt's, Ferguson asked, "And your father was shocked?"

"Yes," she replied.

"But not worried?"

Sheena chose her words carefully. "He gave me the impression that he was not worried."

It was a signal: time and distance had finally allowed Sheena to come to know her father. The conveyance of impressions was very much what he was about.

As for the phone call of February 2, when Albert Walker is said to have asked her to lie, Ferguson led strongly again. "I suggest to you that what your father told you was, 'You're going to have to change your statement because you *know* that I was down in Devon with Ron moving the boat.'"

"No," Sheena said. She would not be moved. Ferguson was

getting nowhere. Within the confines of the information he had
been given by his client, there was little room to move. Sheena
had stood firm and remained convincing. It was time to let it
drop. The only way Sheena's testimony could be convincingly
refuted would be when Walker himself took the stand. Sheena
stood down. She had won—so far.

The impression that was left was clear: if Albert had murdered
Ronald Platt, he had carefully set out from the beginning to keep
Sheena in the dark. She was a liability. She wasn't supposed to
know Ronald was nearby as they enjoyed their Dittisham holiday, because Albert was plotting to kill him.

As Sheena made her way from the courtroom once again,
Albert glared at her, desperate to catch her eye. Just as it seemed
certain that he would, the large woman moved in between them
once again, like an eclipse. Albert was blocked out. The door
opened. Sheena walked through and was gone.

John Copik explained to the court that it had been a miserable
morning of fishing July 28, nothing but bad luck. In the afternoon, though, they'd pulled up the nets after another trawl and
"we'd got a big bundle of fish and thought we'd cracked it. But
unfortunately we had a body laid on top that had got in. The
body was curled up almost in a fetal position."

Butterfield watched Copik closely. He knew that John was
pretty uncomfortable in that suit, but he also sensed instinctively
that when it came to matters dealing with the sea, he was a
professional. Yes, Copik said, he'd had a discussion with his son
Craig about what to do with the body.

"I told him, if we bring it in, we're going to lose a day's pay."
Regulations require that fishermen dump any catch in which a
body has been trawled up. When John decided to bring the body
in, Craig said, "You've done the right thing, Dad."

There were two things that John seemed to remember that no one else did. One was that the body had earrings on it and the other was that there was "about a fathom of chain" attached to the anchor that had been brought up in the nets. Albert Walker picked up his pen in the witness box and made a note.

Had he ever picked up an anchor before? Yes, John said, he had, but they were admiralty anchors, "and by that I mean what everyone's idea of an anchor is." He had never picked up a plough anchor, though. In fact, it was especially odd that the anchor ended up in his nets anyway.

"And how do you think the anchor could have got there?" Barton asked. It seemed a speculative question that pushed the boundaries of a witness's statement of fact, but in the civil atmosphere that prevailed, it slipped through unchallenged.

"The specialist Rock Hopper gear I was using fished tight to the bottom," Copik said, "and the gear should have passed right over the anchor. The only way it could have got into the net is if something was floating above it, and that would have lifted up the stick of the anchor, where it caught on the lip of the net and flipped in."

It was an interesting theory.

Later in the day, however, the Home Office pathologist, Gyan Fernando, noted that there had been no earrings on Platt. The death was by drowning and Platt had been breathing when he hit the water, he reported.

As the middle days of the trial wore on, witness after witness came forward to testify to the extraordinary fabrications they had been told by Walker. They came tumbling out, lie after magnificent lie, a veritable cascade of Walter Mitty-type stories about Albert Walker's secret life, painstakingly concocted by him and consumed by all. He had portrayed himself as an English literature graduate from the University of Edinburgh, who became a banker in New York, was posted to Geneva and later moved to England where he had retired from banking to become a psychiatrist. It was breathtaking in its scope.

Audrey Mossman, the neighbour in Woodham Walter, remembered that he'd told her how he'd met his young wife: "He said he knew her parents from way back."

Frank Johnson, whose statement was read into the court record, said that Walker's Geneva banking experience had seemed so impressive that Johnson handed Walker £200,000 of his savings to invest. He was still waiting for its return.

Geraldine Thompson remembered him from a conversation in the Steam Packet in which he claimed to be a "psychiatrist."

Elaine Boyes remembered lies by the bushel over the course of two years, as she muled his money across borders. In the end, she had even given him stamps for both her and Ron's signatures before leaving for Canada in February 1993. It was so that he could wind up the company, he'd said.

Isobel Rogers explained how, as part of the requirement for her to qualify as a counsellor, she had had to be counselled herself. Walker gladly did that for her, "on two or three occasions," she said. Most interestingly for the jury, Isobel recalled how she had received a phone call from the man she knew as Ron between 8 and 9 a.m., Sunday, July 21. He was breathing heavily and said he had injured himself "moving heavy objects off the boat."

Albert was emerging as a most despicable character, a loathsome individual who preyed off innocent people, and lied, it seemed, for the pleasure of it. By day five, the jury members could be forgiven if they thought that Albert hadn't uttered a true word in his life.

On day six, Patrick Gill of Sport Nautique spoke of how Walker had bought a 10-pound plough anchor on July 8, 1996. He'd also declined to buy a chain, he said. His colleague, Barry Hall, took the stand to identify the receipt and list the seven items. Among them was the anchor and an expensive sailing jacket, the one Albert had bought for Sheena. Indeed, police found all the items on the *Lady Jane* the day they had seized it—all but one that is: the anchor. That was found beneath Mrs. Johnson's steps.

As the prosecution's case turned the corner toward completion, all of the forensic evidence was entered: the "fibrous" material found on the anchor; the zinc from the anchor found on the belt; the GPS reading stored in the device's computer: 50.29.62 N latitude 03.27.00 W longitude; a fingerprint found on a plastic bag on the *Lady Jane*—the chances were 1 in 3 million that it was not that of Ronald J. Platt. Like the mountain of physical evidence that was allowed to mushroom beside the witness box, the forensic evidence, too, was piling up.

Added to this was a detailed recounting of Walker's arrest on October 31, 1996, and the fact that he had refused to give two intimate samples that had been requested by the police: blood and pubic hair. He later submitted to a head-hair sample being taken, and to a DNA mouth swab.

Finally, the prosecution's case ended with some documentary admissions, agreed to by both sides. Included in that was the fact that Albert Walker, 52, of Paris, Ontario, had left a family behind, fled Canada with an estimated $4 million and had been ranked number four on the Interpol list at the time of his arrest. The effect was like a hammer blow. The jury realized they were seated in front of a big-time accused.

Albert Walker didn't have to go in the witness box, of course. He wasn't bound by law to do so. But he wanted to, desperately. He'd been preparing 20 months for this moment—he wasn't about to turn it down now. He was angry at Sheena, too, and a place in the box would give him an opportunity to try to shame her. He was desperate for that.

For someone who had never laid eyes on Walker—such as a member of the jury—he seemed credible that first day. He solemnly swore on the Bible to tell the truth, then sat down, comfortably crossed his legs, placed his elbow to the left, his left hand in his right, eased back and waited for Ferguson to lead him through. He smiled a lot, had an easy-going manner, loved to tell stories, and seemed genuinely concerned about the well-being of others. He even sounded contrite.

"I know that I'm going to have to go back to Canada," Walker said. "I took money that I shouldn't have. I will deal with that in Canada."

It was a good beginning. He was gaining back ground.

His plausibility established, he led the court through the saga of his incredible six years on the run. There was no shame about it. Quite to the contrary, there seemed to be enormous vocational pride in his telling. Albert was a confidence man who relied on people's trust. He did his job well, he seemed to be saying. Surely, everyone appreciated a job well done? His first landlady in London, Barbara Thomson, "said I must be a secret agent," he recounted proudly. He liked good French wine and French cuisine and literature, he said. What wasn't there to like about a man of taste, he thought?

He had found Elaine Boyes "a lovely girl," and they got along straightaway, he said. When he first met her, he said, "I was thinking, 'Here's the perfect person to use as a front for my corporation. She sounds very trustworthy and she does secretarial work.'" Furthermore, she wouldn't "ask too many questions or delve too deeply into detail." Albert had a knack for putting a nice spin on things. It was never mentioned in court that his "corporation" was essentially a shell company using other people's money, the sole object of which was to launder that money and spend it without being caught. Presumably, he hoped that the jury, too, would not "delve too deeply into detail."

It was as though Albert had shifted all the goal posts of morality, with a kind of sleight-of-hand. His matter-of-factness in his telling seemed to suggest there really wasn't anything so bad about what he was doing, was there?

As for Sheena, the situation as it existed back in 1993 didn't really demand that they live together as husband and wife, he explained. Actually, it was her idea. He just went along with it to make her feel comfortable.

"Because she was pregnant and she was going to have a baby, we were as husband and wife," he said. The jury was keenly interested. "She was somewhat embarrassed that she was a single girl, and wanted to have the appearance that she wasn't single."

"And the child's name?" Ferguson asked, referring to Sheena's first child, born September 22, 1993.

"Emily Jane Platt," Albert enunciated clearly. There was pride in his voice, but why one couldn't say. No one had mentioned a father yet. The jury studied Albert closely.

Sheena had been told on more that one occasion that he and Ron were spending time together out in Devon. She knew that, he said. But "Sheena tends to forget things," he said. As a young mother with two children, she had her hands full.

It was in recounting his reaction to the break-up of Elaine Boyes and Ron Platt that Albert suddenly became emotional. "This saddened me," he said, "because," and his voice began to crack then, "I myself have been through a marital break-up. It's a hard decision." Then he sobbed.

Regaining his composure, he went on to say that he did try to make Sheena change her testimony, with reason.

"What did you say to her?" Ferguson asked.

"I said, 'Listen, you're going to have to change your statement. You know Ron was with me.' She said, 'Okay, fine.' And we went on to speak of other things."

"So far as Ron Platt is concerned, how did you regard him right up until the last time you saw him?"

"He was a friend," Walker said, "someone I felt a responsibility to, to take care of." After all, Platt had freely given him his own driver's licence and birth certificate to help him out, he said.

"Do you have a bad temper?"

"No, I don't."

"Do you have a history of violence?"

"I have never hit anyone in my life. Nor have I ever been hit by anyone in my life. I'm a very passive person. I'm a pacifist actually."

"Did you kill Ron Platt?"

Albert's face became overwrought with emotion.

"No, I didn't," he said, as tears welled up in his eyes. "Ron was a very nice person. I had no reason in the world to kill him or ever harm him." His voice cracked again. The tears began to flow. The court attendant moved forward with tissues.

"I'm sorry. I'm sorry," he sobbed, apologizing for interrupting the court.

Throughout Walker's examination-in-chief, Charles Barton had kept busy, studiously making notes. He was bristling to get his chance at Walker. Shortly after 12 o'clock noon the next day, he got it.

"July 9, 1996," Barton intoned. "The best day's sailing in your life."

"That's correct," Walker said.

Barton had decided he would fix precisely on this day, a day on which Walker had said, during his examination-in-chief, that Ron Platt had actually tried to assist him bringing the boat, the *Lady Jane*, part way to Essex. Walker said he had decided to transfer the boat permanently to Essex. It took less than 20 minutes for Barton to demolish that story. Walker had no proper charts on board, he had no idea how long the trip would take, he had not booked any hotel accommodation, and he had never taken such a journey at the helm of a boat in his life. Oh, Walker was out on the boat that night, Barton said. He had telephoned the Seven Stars from his mobile phone out at sea. They had difficulty getting in, and they needed a room. "That was the first night you tried to kill him," Barton said. Then he paused.

"So you were living a lie?" said Barton.

"Yes."

"You were on the run."

"Yes."

"You were concealing your identity."

"Yes."

"Confidence is what your game's all about, isn't it?"

"Yes," Walker replied.

When Walker had entered into the lives of Ron Platt and Elaine Boyes, it was all about confidence, wasn't it?

"Yes," Walker said, "but I thought Ron would see me as someone who was well-dressed and spoke well and was offering his girlfriend a job."

"Not detecting you for the sham that you were?"

"Yes," Walker said calmly.

"And you fooled him?"

"Yes."

"You fooled him then and you fooled him right up to his death, didn't you?"

"Yes," Walker said.

It was turning out to be a devastating cross-examination. Walker was using Platt's driver's licence, his birth certificate, his bank accounts. Walker seemed to be willing to admit to almost anything, save and except murder.

"I'd said to my daughter that the last thing I wanted was for anything to happen to Ron because then I would be in trouble . . . I'd be in a bit of a fix."

"So everything you've worked for in the last six years is at risk?"

"Yes."

"But if anything were to happen to Ron it couldn't be traceable?"

Walker paused.

"I'd never thought of it that way," he said. "I'd imagined a car accident or something like that. A heart attack."

He had thought about Ron Platt's death. He'd envisaged it.

"Was Ron Platt an honourable man?" Barton asked.

Walker had continually claimed that Platt had willingly given him his driver's licence, birth certificate and bank cards to use. "If you define an honourable man as someone who was prepared to break the law, then yes, he was an honourable man," Walker said.

Besmirching the character of a dead man, a dead man you are accused of killing, did not make a favourable impression on the jury. How low, they must have wondered, would Walker actually go? It had apparently been Walker's own decision to take the witness stand. He was arrogant enough to believe he could con everyone. Now he was doing more damage to himself than anyone could have imagined.

Barton pulled out a collection of letters, which Walker had written to Elaine Boyes over the years. She had kept them all.

They were fantastical in nature, speaking of imaginary sailing trips that Walker was taking to France, other visits to Paris for shopping, and other subjects too, seemingly heartfelt.

"Are you someone who lies just for the sake of lying?" Barton jabbed.

Much to the humiliation of Walker, he read these letters aloud. "We're off to France," Walker wrote on board his imaginary ship. "And I have my own bedroom." He wrote of the cook by first name, who would cook them succulent meals at sea. "The sun, the sailing, the blue waters, the wine—what more could you ask for in life?"

Walker was visibly uncomfortable.

Another, from London: "Noël and I are only here for a few days to pick up our mail and do some shopping before we go over to Paris, where we will spend Christmas with Jillian and her boyfriend." This couldn't have been true, of course. Jill had cut off communication long ago.

And still another: "I want to make it perfectly clear that I do love you . . . and you have been a very dear friend, but not someone I want to marry. . . . I will pray for you. Take care, Love."

Richard Ferguson seemed to sink deeper into his seat.

There was disgust in Barton's tone now. "Why were you insisting on writing her a pack of lies? You just didn't care, did you?"

It would get worse. The following day, using rapid-fire questioning, Barton made Walker stumble into the no-go zone. It seemed unintentional, but suddenly innuendoes of incest were threatening to burst into the courtroom.

"You called Sheena what?" Barton asked.

"Noël," Walker replied.

"And she was calling you what?"

"Daddy."

"But not in front of other people?"

"Yes."

"That must have raised eyebrows."

"Why?" asked Walker, feigning innocence.

"Because you were living as husband and wife."

Walker gratuitously offered, "Emily called me Daddy and Sheena called me Daddy. Occasionally she would call me Ron, but when Ron was there she just called me Daddy, or Dad."

Members of the jury were riveted to their seats. There were lights going on.

With such insights pouring forth in Courtroom Number 2, shortly before noon the jury passed Mr. Justice Butterfield a note and court was adjourned.

When court was reconvened, Butterfield noted that he had three questions from the jury.

"The first I do not propose to answer at all," he said. "Both counsel are agreed that it has no relevance to this case whatsoever . . . so you can forget it."

As for the other questions regarding the declined pubic hair and blood samples, the samples were for identification purposes and had "nothing whatever to do with any sort of sexual connotation in any way."

It was very clear. In the minds of the jury, the paternity of Sheena's two children loomed large. It was a dark cloud that had moved in against the defence case.

Barton moved swiftly back to the real point of the case.

"Do you acknowledge the motive you had for ridding yourself of Ronald Platt—the real Ronald Platt?"

"What motive?" Walker asked.

"I think that answers the question," Barton said. "Did you not regard him as a potential threat for the rest of your life?"

"No."

"Who would jeopardize your money and your liberty?"

"No."

"You took the opportunity on the boat to render him unconscious, didn't you?"

"No, I didn't."

"The planning took longer, but it was the work of a moment to consign him to the deep."

"I did not murder Ron Platt," Walker insisted. "He was a friend of mine."

"The only thing you forgot was the Rolex watch."

"I did not murder Ron Platt."

"The anchor was purchased with an express purpose, wasn't it?"

"To be used on the boat."

No, Barton countered. The anchor that Walker bought was the very anchor that was found with Ronald Platt's body in the nets of Devon fisherman John Copik.

Walker was quick. "Well, what happened to the fathom of chain then?"

Barton was quicker. Barton instantly recalled that Copik—who had been a credible and reliable witness—had not only testified about there having been a fathom of chain, but that the dead man had worn earrings too. The prosecutor moved in for the final rapier thrust. "Did he ever wear earrings, Ron Platt?"

"No," Walker replied firmly.

Barton turned and sat down without so much as looking at Walker. His cross examination was over. He had proven his point: Copik's memory wasn't perfect. He made errors. All witnesses do. But just as there were no earrings on Ronald Platt's ears, so there was no chain in the anchor found in Copik's nets. It was a brilliant finish.

It had been expected to be a four- to six-week trial. But with the alacrity of the English court system, especially under Justice Butterfield, closing arguments were heard on the tenth day. That astonishing speed was helped by the fact that the defence had only a few paltry witnesses: under Walker's arrogant direction of the defence, he alone was to be the star. It was a strategy gone wrong. Barton's strength was cross-examination, in fact in Bristol, it was legendary. Over three days in Devon he had torn Walker to shreds.

It finally came down to this: two be-wigged barristers coolly arguing over the guilt or innocence of Albert Walker before judge and jury. There were no great theatrics; there was no prancing about the courtroom; no finger-waving, no shouting, no gavel-thumping. Indeed, it is a measure of the civility of the English courtroom that judges have no gavels. There is no need. It was left simply to reason and persuasion.

"That man is a murderer," Barton said flatly. "That's our case." Barton said that Walker had "executed Platt, with a degree of planning that I would call chilling." That word "chilling" instantly put all of Walker's easy charm into a sinister context. He was evil—with intent. In the jury's mind, all of that would be folded in with other facts: Walker could not account for the whereabouts of the anchor he'd purchased on July 8; he could not explain why the GPS reading from the *Lady Jane* showed the date and time it did; and his story-telling concerning his whereabouts on the 20th at the approximate time of the murder was unbelievable to say the least: motoring up the River Dart backwards because of a gear problem. It was all too far-fetched.

Rarely had Barton seen such despicable social behaviour in a single individual. "He was determined, unscrupulous, with a veneer of pious concern for others," Barton said.

For Sheena Walker, he had high praise.

"What a job for a daughter," he said. "She came over to nail the fundamental lie: you knew where Ronald Platt was at all material times. You knew where he was down on the Dart. Just imagine," Barton said, "the scope of the story that he *could* have constructed had she not come."

"Now it's up to you to find your way through the web of deceit."

Richard Ferguson rose. In every case, he said, the prosecution as well as the defence has a low point. For the defence, Wednesday afternoon was theirs.

The jury scarcely needed reminding: that was the afternoon Barton had savaged Walker, leading him through the muck of his disingenuous and fantastical letters to Elaine Boyes. It left a bad taste still.

"I am not seeking to justify his behaviour in this country. I assumed you were not impressed Wednesday by Mr. Walker. To try to persuade you otherwise would be impossible and insulting to your intelligence.

"But let's get to the real point of the case. We're not here to determine what you may think of Albert Walker as a man, or how he's behaved toward other people. We're here to decide what conclusions you can safely reach based on the Crown's evidence. That is what this case is about. That's all it's about.

As for Mr. Walker's lies, said Ferguson, well, he was living a lie. That was an essential ingredient of the defendant's case. He had reason to lie.

"Indeed, he programmed himself to lie."

But lying wasn't what this case was about either. The charge was murder.

"It's the Crown that makes these allegations, and it's the Crown that has to prove them, and to a very high standard. Mr. Walker doesn't have to prove anything."

Ferguson came as advertised. He was utterly rational, highly organized and persuasive. The Crown didn't have a confession, he said, and it didn't have an eye witness. What it did have was a good deal of circumstantial evidence and a theory.

"But how does the Crown's evidence stand up against its theory? The Crown's case has many fatal flaws. Where is the burden of proof?" he asked.

There was ample room for reasonable doubt, he said. The Crown had not proved its case.

On the morning of Monday, July 6, 1998, after Ferguson had finished up, Mr. Justice Butterfield began to instruct the jury. There was no break. He reviewed the law, he reviewed the evidence, and he appeared to bend over backwards to the defence, careful, it seemed, not to give any grounds for appeal. In the end, he said, above all, "Please take with you your common sense and your knowledge of the world."

The jury went out at 1 p.m.

At 3 p.m. they returned, as did the defendant.

Albert Walker was asked to stand up and face the jury.

"Has the jury reached a verdict?"

"Yes, we have M'Lord. We find the defendant guilty."

Albert Walker stood rigid and blinked, not once, but twice, as though he wished to adjust his vision. But he had heard right: he was going down for life. He was told to sit down.

Mr. Justice Butterfield read from a few prepared notes.

"This was a callous, premeditated killing designed to eliminate a man you had used for your own selfish ends. He became not only expendable but a danger to you, and he had to die.

"The killing was carefully planned and cunningly executed with chilling efficiency. You covered your tracks so effectively only the merest chance led to your coming under suspicion."

"You are a plausible, intelligent and ruthless man who poses a serious threat to anyone who stands in your way, and I shall have regard to that when making recommendations to the Home Secretary for the length of your sentence."

Butterfield then commended the detectives "for police work of the highest order." The investigation had been "painstaking in its meticulous attention to detail," he said, "and all concerned demonstrated true professionalism and are to be congratulated."

Then Butterfield looked into the prisoner's box. Everyone had expected him to gruffly say, "Take him down," as many English judges do. Instead, Butterfield gently said, "You may go down." It was entirely deferential and probably the last gesture of kindness Albert Walker would experience for a very long time.

As he turned to be led to the holding cells, his face contorted a bit and it looked as though he were about to cry. He had the face of a little boy. Caught. And wounded at being caught. It was the look of fear.